Teaching English Literature 16–

'This new book represents a major step forward in the teaching of English literature at 16–19. Principled, persuasive, and packed with great teaching ideas … it's an essential handbook for anyone teaching the subject in the sixth form today'.

Sean McEvoy, Head of English at Varndean College, Brighton, UK

'Written by a "dream team" of people involved in the 16–19 curriculum, from a clear, well-informed and sensible view point, this book is an outstanding resource for teachers of English literature and English language. It will also assist with the "stretch and challenge" agenda, help students develop independent learning and bridge the gap between secondary education and university study'.

Robert Eaglestone, Professor of Contemporary Literature and Thought at Royal Holloway, University of London, UK

Teaching English Literature 16–19 is an essential new resource that is suitable for use both as an introductory guide for those new to teaching literature and also as an aid to reflection and renewal for more experienced teachers. Using the central philosophy that students will learn best when actively engaged in discussion and encouraged to apply what they have learnt independently, this highly practical new text contains:

- discussion of the principles behind the teaching of literature at this level
- guidelines on course planning, pedagogy, content and subject knowledge
- advice on teaching literature taking into account a range of broader contexts, such as literary criticism, literary theory, performance, publishing, creative writing and journalism
- examples of practical activities, worksheets and suggestions for texts
- guides to available resources.

Aimed at English teachers, teacher trainees, teacher trainers and advisors, this resource is packed full of new and workable ideas for teaching all English literature courses.

Carol Atherton teaches at Bourne Grammar School, Lincolnshire, UK.

Andrew Green is Senior Lecturer in Education at Brunel University, UK.

Gary Snapper is editor of *Teaching English* and teaches at the Cheney School, Oxford, UK.

NATE

The National Association for the Teaching of English (NATE), founded in 1963, is the professional body for all teachers of English from primary to post-16. Through its regions, committees and conferences, the association draws on the work of classroom practitioners, advisors, consultants, teacher trainers, academics and researchers to promote dynamic and progressive approaches to the subject by means of debate, training and publications. NATE is a charity reliant on membership subscriptions. If you teach English in any capacity, please visit **www.nate.org.uk** and consider joining NATE, so the association can continue its work and give teachers of English and the subject a strong voice nationally.

This series of books co-published with NATE reflects the organisation's dedication to promoting standards of excellence in the teaching of English, from early years through to university level. Titles in this series promote innovative and original ideas that have practical classroom outcomes and support teachers' own professional development.

Books in the NATE series include both pupil and classroom resources and academic research aimed at English teachers, students on PGCE/ITT courses and NQTs.

Titles in this series include:

International Perspectives on Teaching English in a Globalised World
Andrew Goodwyn, Louann Reid and Cal Durrant

Teaching English Language 16–19
Martin Illingworth and Nick Hall

Unlocking Poetry (CD-ROM)
Trevor Millum and Chris Warren

Teaching English Literature 16–19
Carol Atherton, Andrew Green and Gary Snapper

Teaching English Literature 16–19

An essential guide

Carol Atherton, Andrew Green and Gary Snapper

 Routledge
Taylor & Francis Group

LONDON AND NEW YORK

 NATE

First published 2013
by Routledge
2 Park Square, Milton Park, Abingdon, Oxon OX14 4RN

Simultaneously published in the USA and Canada
by Routledge
711 Third Avenue, New York, NY 10017

Routledge is an imprint of the Taylor & Francis Group, an informa business

British Library Cataloguing in Publication Data
A catalogue record for this book is available from the British Library

Library of Congress Cataloging in Publication Data
A catalog record for this book has been requested

ISBN: 978-0-415-52822-1 (hbk)
ISBN: 978-0-415-52823-8 (pbk)
ISBN: 978-0-203-11855-9 (ebk)

Typeset in Galliard
by Saxon Graphics Ltd, Derby

Contents

List of panels

About the authors

Carol Atherton teaches English at Bourne Grammar School in Lincolnshire, where she is also Director of Professional Development. She is the author of *Defining Literary Criticism: Scholarship, Authority and the Possession of Literary Knowledge, 1880–2002* (Palgrave 2005), based on her doctoral research at the University of Nottingham on the history of English as an academic discipline. She has written on a range of issues relating to the teaching of English in the 16–19 phase and the transition from school to university. Her work includes articles and teaching resources on tragic drama, literary theory, pastoral poetry, the graphic novel and the work of Philip Larkin: she contributed to *A Practical Guide to Teaching English in the Secondary School* (Green 2012) and publishes regularly in the English and Media Centre's *e magazine*. She has worked with a number of organisations, including NATE, the British Library, the Poetry Archive and the British Council, and was made a Fellow of the English Association in 2009.

Andrew Green has taught English within a range of 11–18 schools. He now teaches professional English at postgraduate level. He has published on a range of A Level texts from Shakespeare to Pat Barker and is particularly interested in 16–19 English teaching. He has published teaching resources on Gothic literature, the poetry of William Blake and Philip Larkin, as well as books on *Frankenstein, Wuthering Heights, High Windows, The Whitsun Weddings* and William Blake's *Songs of Innocence and of Experience*. He is also the author of the following Higher Education Academy publications: *Four Perspectives on Transition: English Literature from Sixth Form to University, Teaching the Teachers: Higher Education and Teachers' Continuing Professional Development* and *Working with Secondary Schools: A Guide for Higher Education*. His latest books are *Starting an English Literature Degree* (Palgrave Macmillan 2009), *Transition and Acculturation* (Lambert 2010), *Becoming a Reflective English Teacher* (Open University Press 2011) and *A Practical Guide to Teaching English in the Secondary School* (Routledge 2012). He is the author of one novel, *The Dickens House* (Createspace Books 2012).

Gary Snapper is a teacher of A Level and IB English, the editor of NATE's professional journals *English Drama Media* and *Teaching English*, and a Research Associate at Brunel University. He taught English in 11–19 comprehensive schools in Cambridge for fourteen years, including six years as Head of English at Impington Village College, Cambridge, and currently teaches at the Cheney School, Oxford (A Level) and for Oxford Study Courses (IB). His doctoral research at the Institute of Education, London, explored the relationship between English as a school and as a university subject, and he continues to focus on issues in 16–19 English. He has contributed chapters on 16–19 English to

Becoming a Reflective English Teacher (Green 2011), *Poetry Matters* (Dymoke *et al.* 2013), *English in a Globalised World: International Perspectives on the Teaching of English* (IFTE 2013) and *Teaching Literature* (Knights 2013). He is a member of the NATE Post-16 Committee and provides workshops on 16–19 literature teaching for trainee teachers, practising teachers and university lecturers.

Acknowledgements

Many colleagues and friends have inspired and supported the development of these ideas over the years. We have benefited enormously from working, at different stages of our careers, with teachers, friends and colleagues who have made us think about literature and education in ways that we might not have done otherwise. We'd particularly like to thank the following:

Lucy Newlyn, Josephine Guy, Philip Smallwood, Tony Burgess, Ben Knights, Rob Pope, Robert Eaglestone, Barbara Bleiman, Sean McEvoy, Julie Blake, Gabrielle Cliff Hodges, Sue Dymoke, John Hodgson, James Durran, Nadia Valman, David Ripley, Liz Stephan, Ruth Smith, Charlotte Wright; the NATE Post-16 Committee and many other friends from NATE; the English 14–19 Reform Group; colleagues, past and present, at Bourne Grammar School, especially Richard Cave, John Lee, Natasha Marie, Peter Cozens, Wendi Matthews and Linda Hill; colleagues, past and present, from the English departments at Netherhall School, Impington Village College and Cheney School, especially Carol Kelsall, Sandra Morton and Fiona Swanson; colleagues past and present from the English Departments at Carshalton High School for Girls, Ewell Castle School and Brunel University, especially Tony Mann and Elizabeth Ridout.

We'd also like to thank our own inspirational English teachers at school and university. In particular, Janet Nevin, Jane Moody, Tim Nightingale, Robert Hampson and William Ruff made enormous differences to our lives by encouraging us to study English at university, supporting us as A-Level and undergraduate students, and offering us new, life-changing perspectives. Jane Moody's death, in 2011, was an immense loss to the study of the humanities in general, but also to the students who benefited from her warmth and generosity.

We all benefited from the support of our partners and families. Pietro Roversi, Nikki Green and Matthew Hartley were unstintingly generous with their support while this book was being written, and Levi Hartley and the Green children provided their own inimitable brand of distraction.

We would like to thank Philip Allan for kind permission to reproduce materials first published in *Wuthering Heights* (2010: 85–8) and *Frankenstein* (2010: 85–7).

We would like to thank Rhiannon Findlay of Routledge and Anne Fairhall of NATE who have provided timely and invaluable assistance in preparing this manuscript throughout its composition and publication.

Finally, we would like to thank our students – high-spirited, cake-eating and thought-provoking – who help every day to make teaching English such a rewarding job.

Foreword

This book attempts to provide a comprehensive vision for the teaching of advanced English literature in schools and colleges. By this, we do not mean a utopian vision, but one firmly grounded in the actual context of early twenty-first-century classrooms and syllabuses around the English-speaking world. The last book on this topic in the UK was Brown and Gifford's *Teaching A Level English Literature: A Student-Centred Approach,* published in 1989 – twenty-four years ago. Since then there have been many changes in curriculum and theory both in the UK and internationally. Meanwhile, we have often heard the plea 'Does anyone know a good, up-to-date guide to teaching literature?' This book, we hope, is the answer to that plea.

This is not to say that Brown and Gifford's excellent book (now out of print and outdated in its references to specific UK A Level syllabuses of the time) no longer has a great deal to offer. Many longstanding teachers have been strongly influenced by the book, which offered a progressive, modern version of advanced literature teaching at a time when schools and the discipline of English were undergoing significant changes. Brown and Gifford both *reflected* trends in the teaching of literature and *created* new orthodoxies, which have helped to shape contemporary notions of curriculum and pedagogy in advanced English literature courses.

Brown and Gifford's philosophy is as relevant now as it was then: the study of literature, they argued, must involve and engage students at a meaningful level, using teaching methods that take into account the ways students learn effectively, their existing knowledge bases, and their varied cultural starting points and experiences. Contemporary reports (for instance, HMI 1986; Barnes and Barnes 1984) and extensive anecdotal evidence suggested that much literature teaching was at that time characterised by transmission pedagogy and relentless exam preparation (passive students, teacher dictation of notes, denial of alternative interpretations, lack of discussion, a narrowly canonical approach, inhibitingly reverent attitudes to texts and authors, mechanical approaches to preparation for exam essays). Brown and Gifford set out a manifesto based on active approaches to pedagogy (drama, discussion, textual engagement and intervention, student research, negotiated tasks and topics and so on), a broadening of the canon and of approaches to interpretation, and the central role of coursework in developing intellectual commitment to and independent skills in both reading and writing.

All this is without question still vital. Nevertheless, things continue to move rapidly in a discipline which is barely more than a hundred years old. Since 1989, literature courses have undergone considerable change – in many respects embedding the principles that informed Brown and Gifford – as have the social, cultural and institutional contexts within which they are taught. One might argue that the following features of the contemporary scene have in particular exerted significant pressures on literature teaching, and forced us (teachers and syllabus-makers) to develop and rethink aspects of courses and the way we teach them:

- the development of new ways of approaching language and culture in the 16–19 curriculum through the introduction of courses in English language, media studies and creative writing, and through internationalist approaches such as those promoted by the International Baccalaureate (IB);
- a growing awareness of the ways in which student-centred approaches to literature teaching can be framed so that students gain access to wider cultural discourses and knowledge frameworks;
- the development of widening participation in post-compulsory education, and increased recognition of the implications of the diverse cultural backgrounds and experiences of 16–19 students;
- the development of centralised and often government-controlled approaches to and reforms of curriculum, pedagogy and assessment;
- the development of university English in the aftermath of the 'theory wars' of the 1980s, and consequent pressures on 16–19 English to reflect modern elements of the discipline;
- technological advances over the last twenty years – in particular the proliferation of the internet and broadcast media – and their effects on cultural habits and attitudes and pedagogic strategies.

In the light of all these developments, this book discusses the issues teachers of advanced literature need to consider in planning and organising courses, preparing and teaching lessons, and setting and assessing students' work. It guides teachers through the demands of teaching literature at this level, addressing issues of subject knowledge and pedagogy, outlining the knowledge and skills that students are likely to need, and suggesting activities and resources that teachers might find valuable. In particular, it addresses issues about the relationships between texts, contexts and interpretations, and illustrates ways of placing the study of set texts and topics in the broader context of knowledge about literature.

The underpinning philosophy of the book may be summarised as follows:

- students' responses to texts and to aspects of culture should form the starting point for study at this level, but students need to be introduced to and assimilate clear conceptual frameworks for literary study;
- students will learn best in the literature classroom when actively engaged in discussing and working with texts with other students, and when encouraged to apply what they have learnt independently;
- literature courses for 16–19 should embed detailed study of set texts in broader contexts and with concepts drawn from literature, literary criticism and literary theory, as well as performance, publishing, creative writing, journalism etc;
- the cultural values often enshrined in literary study are open to contest, and students should be engaged in questions about the values, purposes and attitudes behind literary texts and behind literary study;
- although English literature is often formulated as a separate subject at this level, it is nevertheless closely connected with other manifestations of the subject such as English language, media studies and theatre studies, and should draw on and make connections with these subjects.

The book is informed throughout by our work in teaching, teacher training and research, as well as our recent involvement in debating and formulating the shape of the A Level English Literature curriculum in the UK. We have all worked for many years as teachers of English in 11–19 schools in the UK state system (and two of us still do so); we all regularly provide INSET for practising and trainee teachers of literature; and we have all undertaken doctoral research into aspects of the teaching of literature at 16–19 and in Higher Education (HE). The advice we offer on strategies and resources for teaching is all taken from our own teaching practices with 16–19 classes (A Level and IB).

We must stress, however, that we do *not* suggest that it is possible to cover *all* the issues and activities we discuss with any one class. Restraints of time, energy, syllabus and other institutional factors inevitably mean that teachers have to be selective – and many of the issues we discuss might be covered in passing rather than as the primary focus of lessons. Nor do we suggest that all the issues and activities we discuss will be appropriate for every class or context. Instead, we hope to have outlined a broad vision for literature teaching, providing a range of stimuli and resources which teachers will be able to draw on in formulating subject philosophies, course outlines, lesson plans and pedagogical strategies.

Although we are British authors working within a British context, we take a generic approach to issues in the teaching of literature. Thus the book is intended to be valuable for courses at this level both in the UK and in other English-speaking countries. Whilst we do not reference or provide detailed guidance for specific courses or syllabuses, we have tried to take into account the variety of approaches adopted not only around the UK, where there are eight substantially different syllabuses taught (if one includes the various literature options in A Levels, Scottish Highers and the IB) but also around the world – in the US, Canada, Australia and New Zealand, for instance.

It may be helpful to say a few words about the authorship of the book. We agreed from the beginning that we wanted to write together, perhaps mainly to ensure that the vision of literature teaching we present is not entirely idiosyncratic, but rather represents shared practices and understandings of what it means to teach literature at this level. By writing together, we also wanted to learn from each other, given how little exchange of ideas about practice at this level there has been over the years.

Although we knew from previous conversations that we would share many ideas and practices, we have nevertheless been surprised by the extent to which this has proved to be true. In writing together, however, we have had to find ways to make the book into a coherent whole whilst to some extent preserving individual voices and approaches. Sections or chapters of the book were distributed between us, and we each took primary responsibility for our allotted portions. However, we have all contributed sections, ideas and refinements to each other's chapters.

The organisation of the book probably speaks for itself. An introductory chapter outlines the broad approach we take to issues of curriculum and pedagogy. In Chapters 2, 3 and 4, we show how this general approach translates into specific ideas for the teaching of poetry, the novel and drama. Chapters 5 and 6 address broader issues in teaching literature – teaching about theory and criticism, and context and interpretation. Whilst the previous chapters are largely concerned with issues about reading, Chapter 7 looks at the teaching of writing, and the relationships between thinking, talking, reading and writing, as well as between creative and critical writing.

There is surprisingly little written about the teaching of literature at this level. We hope, therefore, that this book provides a focus for professional conversations about the advanced teaching of literature not only amongst training and beginning teachers, but also amongst their more experienced colleagues in schools, colleges and teacher training institutions. We hope not only to have provided a focus for teaching practice, but also to have opened a debate about what we do as teachers of literature.

Chapter 1

Developing literary response 16–19

Introduction: Imagining literature in the classroom

English literature in the advanced stages of high school has, over the last century, gathered to itself a popular image perhaps unrivalled by any other subject. It is often perceived as the liberal subject *par excellence*, strongly associated with the realisation of the individual through enjoyment, self-expression and self-discovery; the broadening of the mind through confrontation with social, cultural and political ideas; and the opportunity to access the riches of culture, past and present. English literature teachers are frequently cited in later life as a particularly strong influence – perhaps because of their personal charisma, their kindness or humaneness, or their status as eccentric or wise outsiders – or a combination of all of these. Literary and media texts in the last thirty years, in particular, have seemed to encapsulate this Romantic stereotype of literature teaching in the twentieth century: the charismatic individualist John Keating in *Dead Poets Society*, the humane liberal outsiders Frank Bryant in *Educating Rita* and Douglas Hector in *The History Boys*, for instance, all attest to this.

There is no doubt that this popular image captures, in essence, the experience of many students and teachers across the generations. English as a subject has always had a special connection with the ideals of Romanticism, as noted by several writers – perhaps most significantly Ian Reid (2004) in his book *Wordsworth and the Formation of English Studies*. And there is no doubt whatsoever that many people's lives have, directly or indirectly, been touched or transformed over the last century by their exposure to literary education, and by the influence of charismatic teachers of English literature.

Nevertheless, the image is idealised and selective; the reality is more complex, more problematic, more varied – as indeed *Dead Poets Society, Educating Rita* and *The History Boys* all to some extent acknowledge. We might relish aspects of the stereotype of the English teacher in these dramas, especially the idea espoused by all of them that appreciation of literary texts can directly change lives or inspire great moral or cultural insight (and there's no doubt that it *can* do that); but closer inspection of all three characters – Keating, Bryant, Hector – shows that they all have complex and in many respects problematic relationships with themselves, their students, the institutions in which they teach, and the systems and social structures within which they operate; and all three narratives, to a greater or lesser extent, pose difficult questions about the values which the teaching of literature seeks to promote and the methods through which it is achieved.

Equally problematic is the political impetus that tends to invest English literature with a range of responsibilities, not only for upholding academic rigour but also for maintaining the canon and defending the national literary heritage. Neither of these polarised positions is particularly helpful in trying to establish a meaningful domain for the subject and a durable pedagogy for it.

Real literature teaching is subject to a complex set of variables – for instance, the variety of cultural backgrounds and attitudes, educational experiences and motivations which characterise English students and teachers; the political and institutional pressures, policies and ideologies which form the backdrop to the work of English teaching; and the tension between the ideas and ideals which inform English teaching and the practicalities of curriculum and pedagogy which 'actualise' it in the classroom (Kress 2005). Further, these 'ideas and ideals' are themselves varied and contested, from one teacher to another, from one classroom to another, from one school to another, from one country to another, and from one generation to another.

Our challenge in this book, then, is to represent a nuanced version of advanced literature teaching in the early twenty-first century, one which acknowledges and reflects the debates about the nature of literature teaching that have taken place over the last century, and which is sufficiently flexible to take into account the multiplicities described above; and one which also coherently enshrines the realities of contemporary classroom experience and contemporary disciplinary thinking.

In seeking to develop our position, we acknowledge the important division of literary response between affective, aesthetic and analytical-critical domains. We recognise the central importance of students voicing personal affective responses, but believe that in order to develop as more nuanced and reflective readers it is essential, in the tradition of critical literacy, to bring critical and analytical understandings increasingly to bear, in order to make sense of the political, aesthetic and theoretical principles that underlie and enhance such personal responses (Freire 1970).

We start by outlining some of the issues, debates and principles that inform notions of curriculum and pedagogy in 16–19 English literature.

Debating the literature curriculum

Models for a literature curriculum

In starting to think about the fundamental principles which inform the advanced literature curriculum, we might look to a number of models of English teaching that have been suggested in recent decades, many of which have attempted to reconcile diverse approaches. One of the most well known of these models, for instance, is that proposed by Cox (1989), who suggested that good English teaching must take into account a number of different paradigms for learning in the subject. Three of his five paradigms are particularly relevant here – making learning contribute to the 'personal growth' of students, helping them to acquire a sense of 'cultural heritage', and contextualising the knowledge they acquire through 'cultural analysis'. (The other two, 'cross-curricular learning' and 'adult needs', are also of interest, and relevant to the discussion of transition from 16–19 English towards the end of this chapter.)

The distinction that Cox suggests between 'personal growth', 'cultural heritage' and 'cultural analysis' in particular characterises three quite distinct arguments about the literature curriculum. The idea of 'personal growth' evokes the Romantic idealism of literature teaching, nurturing the spirit and creativity of the individual through the power of the imagination, building an appreciation of the moral and aesthetic qualities of literature as art and story, encouraging a love of reading and storytelling, and providing a springboard for the articulation of our personal responses to the world. It also perhaps suggests the humane project of developing powers of empathy and social understanding through encountering representations of self and other in literary narratives. The idea of 'cultural heritage' is often encountered as a more conservative and objective approach in which acquisition of knowledge about, appreciation of and reverence for the history of literature, and in particular certain canonical texts and authors, is central; it also, however, suggests the acquisition of a potentially empowering knowledge of the sweep of history, and of the texts and ideas that have been significant in shaping the present. The idea of 'cultural analysis', meanwhile, takes us into a more socio-cultural and linguistic study of the ways in which literature operates and in which its representations are produced, consumed, valued and achieve meaning. This approach has the potential of developing understanding of the cultural, political and historical significances of literature as a form, further contextualising the insights offered by 'personal growth' and 'cultural heritage'.

Debates about the literature curriculum

Whilst it is probably true that most contemporary literature classrooms embrace all three of these ideas to some extent, there are considerable tensions between them, and contemporary debates about literature teaching reflect those tensions. In most parts of the English-speaking world, there has, over the last century, been a gradual move away from a literature curriculum dominated by formal appreciation of the 'cultural heritage' to one more concerned with 'personal growth' and 'cultural analysis', focusing on diverse responses, interpretations and evaluations of texts of all periods, with an increasingly strong element of the study of modern literature and a more catholic interpretation of what constitutes 'text', to include film and a plurality of other texts. More recently, there have been moves to strengthen the 'cultural analysis' element, emphasising the theoretical frameworks of the subject. These changes in the landscape of 16–19 English have reflected changes in the broader educational and cultural landscape, responding both to discipline-specific change and to more general changes in education, both at school level and at university level.

In schools, increasing democratisation of education during the twentieth century ran in parallel with a powerful growth in student-centred approaches to study and a growing awareness of the problems posed by a fixed literary canon. These forces eventually resulted in current versions of 16–19 English literature which, to a greater or lesser extent:

- recognise the value of students' active engagement with discovering meaning in literary texts, and with extended personal and critical response in discussion and writing;
- focus on texts, considered relatively accessible and interesting in one way or another to students from a range of social and cultural backgrounds, both from the literary canon (such as Shakespeare, the Romantics and the Victorians) and in modern and contemporary literature.

In universities, meanwhile, the revolutions of linguistics, cultural studies and literary theory further challenged notions of canon, and developed ideas both about the complex relationships between reader, writer, text, culture and ideology, and about the relationship between language and learning. A further challenge came from the rise of university courses in creative writing. These developments led not only to the introduction of 16–19 courses in English language and media studies, but also, more recently, to debates about further modernisation of paradigms for literary study.

In these debates, notions of both personal growth and cultural heritage are challenged further. Dominant approaches to literary study, it is argued, are under-theorised, placing too much emphasis on 'personal response' without helping students to locate their subjective responses critically in contemporary socio-cultural contexts (McCormick 1994; Atherton 2003, 2004; Snapper 2007; Jacobs 2010). At the same time, and ironically, personal response is circumscribed by being validated only in relation to a canon (albeit a broader canon than previously) of texts which are recognised as 'worthy of literary study' and only within the paradigm of literary 'appreciation' (a phenomenon which Mitchell [1994] calls 'collective subjectivity') – in contradistinction to the more open approaches to textual criticism which characterise linguistics, cultural/media studies and creative writing.

In the light of these debates, strong arguments have been made, on the one hand for a more theorised version of English literature which seeks to broaden notions of the literary and empower students to approach the canon less reverently and more critically, and on the other hand, for a radical reshaping of English as an integrated study of culture, language and textuality in which literature is treated more equally as one of a number of significant cultural discourses (Scott 1989; NATE 2005). Strong arguments have also been made for creative writing as an alternative, more open approach to literary study (for instance, Knights 2008).

Interestingly, these models describe what to some extent already happens in many *pre-16* English classrooms, where the study of literature, language and media texts tends to be relatively integrated, and students are encouraged to see themselves as capable of a variety of forms of literary production. Such approaches, however, have only to a limited extent penetrated 16–19 English literature classrooms and courses over the last thirty years. They have been particularly influential in parts of the US and Australia (see for instance, Beavis 1995; Appleman 2000), and have informed the development of 'English language and literature' A Level in the UK; they have, too, just begun to feature in some A Level English literature courses in the UK. However, there is a long way to go before dominant approaches to 16–19 literary study fully embrace these discourses and practices. Meanwhile, students making the transition to advanced literature studies are presented with a particular set of challenges as they have, in a sense, to disarticulate learning that was encouraged in their pre-16 studies.

A cultural analysis approach

Bearing in mind both the ways in which 16–19 literature courses tend currently to be constituted and the debates we describe above, we seek in this book to suggest ways in which contemporary classrooms can embrace aspects of the emphasis on 'cultural analysis' which has become a central part of the discipline in the last thirty years, whilst retaining the strengths of the 'personal growth' and 'cultural heritage' models which are vital to what happens in literature courses.

We see the literature curriculum as crucially *framed* by questions of *cultural analysis*. Whilst the detailed reading and discussion of literary texts remains central to advanced literary study, we advocate helping our students not only to develop the fine reading, writing and thinking skills necessary to respond to individual texts, but also to place their experience of these texts in the context of broader ideas about the history, meaning and function of literature in society, the values associated with it, and the roles it plays in their own lives and the lives of others. In order for them to do this effectively, they must be taught in a way which enables them to build on both their *subjective* experiences of and responses to life and literature (*personal growth*) and their more *objective* developing knowledge of the *cultural heritage* of literature. Such holistic perceptions of literary study and of learning in general are also key in preparing students for their continuing education and for the world of work.

Defining the literature curriculum

It's relatively easy to generalise about the kind of principles that should inform a curriculum; it's often more difficult to pin down what that curriculum should actually look like. It's also necessary to be clear about the distinction between *curriculum* and *syllabus* – the two main forces that determine what is actually taught in the classroom. The immediate focus of most advanced literature classes is a *syllabus,* usually provided by the organisation which will at the end of the course provide assessment and certification of students' achievement, and often focused on a list of set texts to be studied; but it's important to recognise that a syllabus does not necessarily constitute the whole *curriculum* of a literature course.

The question of set texts

Historically, 16–19 English literature syllabuses have, as suggested above, *tended* to consist of little more than a list of set texts rather than, as in most other subjects, a *synopsis* of what is actually to be *learnt about the subject.* (Indeed, this kind of broad learning is often referred to as *synoptic* learning.) Even where syllabuses do not already specify set texts, the practicalities of the classroom mean that broader notions of literary learning are often reduced into a list of specific texts, the study of which will constitute the actual business of the class. A further reductive tendency operates in relation to assessment. Historically, again, literature examinations have tended to focus on questions about specific set texts rather than more synoptic questions about the broader literary concepts that might have been learnt (Daw 1986).

There are, of course, good reasons why this has been the case. Learning needs to be concentrated in manageable units that offer the opportunity for close study of certain phenomena; set texts offer convenient literary units of that kind. Furthermore, the Romantic in the English teacher has tended to aspire to the idea that learning about literature should emerge in some sense *organically* from reading, discussing and appreciating 'good books'. From this perspective, spelling out *what is to be learnt* from reading those books might seem to be reductive and technocratic. From a cultural analysis perspective, however, the central focus on set texts might be seen to be reductive in other ways, curtailing discourses about the nature of learning through literature, and conflating the activity of 'reading literature' with the idea of 'studying literature', in potentially unhelpful, and unrealistic, ways.

We are not suggesting that specific whole literary texts should *not* retain a central place in the literature curriculum and in assessment practices; there are clearly sound practical and intellectual reasons why they should. Rather, we are suggesting that it is crucial to remember that *texts* are exemplars of the broader idea of *literature*, and need to be seen as much as a means of teaching *about literature* as entities for teaching in and of themselves. We also note that, sometimes, literature students study *only* their set texts and nothing else – whereas we would argue that set texts are taught most effectively when students are introduced additionally to a range of related texts and ideas which help them to place the set text in a variety of contexts.

There have been some bold experiments in the last few decades with alternative ways of constructing syllabuses which emphasise such approaches, for instance the 'Pacesetter' course designed by Robert Scholes, Professor of English at Brown University in the US, working with local high schools (Scholes 1998), and some of the 'alternative syllabuses' in the UK in the 1980s (Greenwell 1988). Some current syllabuses and examinations, too, successfully promote a strong sense of a broad literary course, organised around concepts such as genre, narrative and period, or around topics for wider and comparative reading, whilst still focusing study on specific set or chosen texts – for instance, the IB English course Snapper (2008), and some of the revised 2008 A-Level English literature courses in the UK (Atherton 2011). But even if a syllabus does not specify such methods, the principle is still applicable to learning about literature more broadly.

A common objection to such an approach is that it places too many intellectual demands on students at this level, especially the less able, taking them too far away from the 'words on the page' (as Leavis [1932] put it) of their set texts. We would argue, however, that this approach, when supported by appropriate pedagogy and resources, has the potential to improve the accessibility of literary study for a wide range of students by contextualising it more fully, helping to clarify notions of 'appreciation' and 'response', to distinguish more clearly between 'reading' and 'literary study', to open up discussions about literary and cultural value, and to make explicit the purposes, frameworks and parameters of the subject (Marland 2003). By approaching set texts in such ways, we would suggest, students can develop strong personal paradigms of subject and are enabled to place their learning about texts within increasingly sophisticated conceptualisations of literature and its social, political and cultural functions (McCormick 1994). This kind of knowledge development well places students to face the demands of HE, employment and citizenship in a culturally and politically complex world.

A broader curriculum

Just as set texts do not constitute the whole of what is to be learnt through a literature syllabus, so the syllabus does not necessarily constitute the whole of a literature curriculum. Even where syllabuses *do* consist of more than a list of set texts, they do not always identify clearly what learning in the subject should consist of, or how it might be conceptualised beyond the structures of the syllabus. It is therefore crucial for teachers and departments to have considered how the syllabus might relate to a wider vision of learning about literature. What follows is an attempt to define, in outline, a literature curriculum in just such a way.

This curriculum outline is intended to complement rather than replace or conflict with existing literature courses, and to help teachers to think about the shape of the subject rather than to specify exactly what should be taught. We recognise – not least from our own experiences as teachers in schools – that teachers are constrained by the structures of syllabuses and assessment regimes, by institutional approaches to course construction, by limited time, energy and resources, and by the sometimes awkward realities of classroom dynamics. It would be hopelessly idealistic to think that every aspect of what follows could be dealt with effectively in any 16–19 literature course. We nevertheless hope that it suggests a vision of the subject that might shape and inform practice in valuable ways. It also provides a general background to the more specific discussion of the elements of literary study, which forms the remaining chapters of this book.

---

1. The history and development of literature

Students should develop an understanding of aspects of the history and development of language and literature in English from the origins of English to the present day; and of the history and development of narrative, poetic and dramatic forms in culture.

Key concepts include: history of English, history of literature, literary forms, narrative, genre, mode, poetry, drama, the novel, oral and print culture, the relation of these to broader social and cultural movements.

Historical frameworks for the study of literature – that is, the study of texts in a comprehensive chronological framework, taking in the broad sweep of the literary canon across history – are unfashionable both at school and university level in the English-speaking world. They are, however, common in European language cultures other than English, where students often study literature (both native and foreign) by learning about famous authors and their key texts throughout history, and studying short extracts from those texts. Thus, an Italian seventeen-year-old is far more likely to know about and have read Chaucer, say, or Milton, or even Dickens, than an English seventeen-year-old.

It's probably true that there was a time not so many decades ago when a greater proportion of 16–19 literature students knew more about the cultural heritage than they do now, and it can certainly be dispiriting when English-speaking students engaged in the specialist study of English literature at the 16–19 phase have not even heard of some of the most important literary figures. But it's important to remember that such a situation is partly a product of social change rather than some kind of moral failing – and that the idea of a golden age when everyone had read Dickens by the age of sixteen is in any case vastly over-stated. It also signifies the powerful way in which further education has opened to a broad social and cultural range of students, many of whom are not pre-programmed with the 'cultural capital' required to impress with a sometimes superficial knowledge of 'the great writers'.

More importantly, we must remember that the historical approaches referred to above are unfashionable *for good reason*. In many other countries in continental Europe, in the dominant 'knowledge-centred' learning system (sometimes described as 'encyclopedic' [Peterson 1972]), students learn almost exclusively by memorising received facts and opinions about writers, their texts and contexts from hefty textbooks containing hundreds of extracts in chronological order. Critically framed personal responses (of the kind generally fostered by the more 'student-centred' learning systems dominant in the English-speaking world) are generally not required, merely regurgitation of learned facts and ideas (Leahy-Dios 1996). Italian seventeen-year-olds, then, know more about the canon of literature but are often far less motivated by their literary study than English seventeen-year-olds, and far less critical in their approaches.

This is not to say that students in our system should not learn about the history of literature; arguably, indeed, they *should* learn more than many of them currently do. Contemporary syllabuses are unlikely to feature much in the way of pre-nineteenth century literature (apart from Shakespeare), but, as we have suggested above, syllabuses need not constitute the whole curriculum – and it is quite possible to introduce ideas about the history and development of literature into courses in ways that will ultimately inform students' prescribed learning, and make them more knowledgeable about literature, whilst retaining a critical focus on personal response and engagement. Subsequent chapters examine in more detail how this might be done; for the moment we outline the general principle.

More important, we believe, than 'coverage' of canonical authors is a general overview of the shape of the development of literature and what constitutes literary study. This might mean discussion of the origins of literature in the oral and manuscript cultures of pre-industrial (and perhaps even pre-historic) societies, and of the origins and changing significances of the three main literary forms – poetry, drama and prose fiction. Such a discussion is likely, for instance, to be relevant to an understanding of the nature of poetic and dramatic form and language, the functions of epic verse storytelling, the writing and performance conditions in ancient Greek theatres and in Shakespeare's theatre, the decline of poetry and rise of the novel (and subsequently film) in modern culture, and debates about literary values, the canon and popular culture, and so on.

There is much to be said, then, for planning exposure (beyond *set* texts and whole books) to a range of canonical (and other) texts to *support* study of set texts and topics (Daw 1996). For instance, in helping students to understand Shakespeare's language as 'modern' English, it can be illuminating – and entertaining – to introduce them to short extracts from 'old' and 'middle' English texts. More conventionally, in helping students to understand the radicalism of modernist poetry, one could introduce them to a number of short pre-modernist texts; or, in working with students on aspects of narrative in a modern novel, one could introduce them to illustrative extracts from a range of 'classic' novels.

---

2. The craft of the writer

Students should develop an understanding of the work and craft of literary writers – in particular, the ways writers use language, form and structure, working within and around genres and conventions, and responding to contemporary cultural and social contexts, to represent aspects of society and culture.

Key concepts include: creativity and creative writing (including reader/student as writer), contexts of production, narrative, genre, convention, language, form, structure, changing modes of textual production and perception.

Barthes (1977) proclaimed 'the death of the author', a crucial concept for considering the nature of literary study, and one which is easily grasped by students:

> Classic criticism has never paid any attention to the reader; for it, the writer is the only person in literature. We are now beginning to let ourselves be fooled no longer by the arrogant antiphrastical recriminations of good society in favour of the very thing it sets aside, ignores, smothers, or destroys; we know that to give writing its future, it is necessary to overthrow the myth: the birth of the reader must be at the cost of the death of the author.
>
> (Barthes 1977: 148)

However, whilst this movement towards privileging the reader and the process of interpretation has been extremely influential and remains highly significant, consideration of the author is still in some senses vital (though Barthes perhaps might not agree). This is not because through such consideration we can, as Barthes suggests we might, aspire to 'know' the author's intentions so that 'the text [can be] explained', producing 'victory to the critic'. Rather it is because to begin to understand something of the writer's craft and motivations is to begin to understand how literature functions: what writers do, how their texts come into being, and how they are influenced by literary traditions and conventions, and by social, cultural and historical forces of which they might not even be conscious. It is also to begin to feel what it might be like to be a writer, and to mould language in particular ways.

Many 16–19 literature students have little understanding of literary convention, and how writers work with and around it, when they start advanced literary study (Noel-Tod 2005). Until this point, and quite rightly, they are likely to have been mostly preoccupied with discussion of meaning rather than analysis of form. But it has been a mantra of advanced literature teachers and examiners for many decades that many 16–19 students continue only to want to talk about the 'trinity' of 'plot, character and theme', and seem unable to engage with the ways in which the alternative 'trinity' of 'language, form and structure' operates to convey those things (see, for instance, OCR 2012). Where students attempt to engage with language, form and structure, examiners say, it is often at the level of 'device-spotting' without critical comment ('this is a metaphor'; 'this is an example of alliteration' etc.); and it is often restricted to a limited range of textual features (metaphor and alliteration in poetry, but not form or tone, for instance).

One of the keys to overcoming this problem, we suggest, is to teach elements of language, form and structure, and features of genre and narrative, explicitly and systematically, rather than simply hoping that the bigger picture will emerge from and be assimilated through the reading of set texts. Too often students are expected to 'appreciate' what the writer has done without actually understanding what it *is* that the writer has done: demystification here is crucial. The Leavisite notion of 'appreciation' as some kind of objective, reliable process within which the text rather than the interpretation of the text has primacy still tends to dominate the discourse of 16–19 classrooms. Hence our emphasis in this book on the importance of helping students to locate their knowledge firmly within the bigger picture of literature, textuality and literary study.

As we hope to show in the central chapters of the book, this does not have to be a dry or passive process. Students need to know 'the facts' of, say, poetic form and narrative structure, but those facts can be deduced, explored and applied through a variety of dynamic problem-solving and discussion-based exercises, based both on work with set texts and with additional texts. What is essential is that the acquisition of this knowledge is a planned part of textual study, and that aspects of language, form and structure are not tackled as an afterthought to the main business of meaning. We would also argue that such work should go beyond the set text in question: students who are studying, say, the verse of Dylan Thomas, are likely to understand the modernism of his language and form more clearly when they compare it, for instance, with the language and form of Thomas Hardy. The generic features of revenge tragedy, and what Shakespeare did with them in *Hamlet*, will be far more clearly understood if students have some exposure to other revenge tragedies, even if only in the form of extracts and plot summaries – as provided, for instance, in the resource *Reading Hamlet* (Mellor 1989).

Equally important here is that students should experience directly what it is to be creative writers themselves, an issue we explore further in Chapter 7 (Teaching writing). The fact that creative writing might not be on the syllabus is beside the point: carefully placed creative and re-creative writing exercises provide substantial insights into the composition of literary texts, and the relationship between reader, writer and text.

---

3. The response of the reader

Students should develop an understanding of the ways in which readers respond to, interpret and value texts, balancing personal views, interests and tastes, and contemporary social and cultural attitudes and preferences, with understanding of the specific contexts of a text's production and reception.

Key concepts include: reading, appreciation, contexts of reception, consumption, interpretation, representation, response, evaluation, attitudes, reviewing, alternative interpretations, literary theory.

'The death of the author' is, as we have seen, the price we pay for 'the birth of the reader' – and this rousing validation of the interpretive process has influenced literary study profoundly, both at school and at university. The idea of the active reader as 'someone who holds together in a single field all the traces by which the written text is constituted' (as Barthes puts it) has complemented the move to more student-centred approaches in literature teaching, and reflects the recognition in the broader field of reader-response theory that reading is as much a process of meaning-making as writing.

Just as ideas about the craft of the writer need to be taught so do ideas about the response of the reader – and the role of teachers and critics in guiding that response. Central to the modern discipline is the idea that readers are free to interpret texts legitimately in ways that their writers did not consciously intend – for instance by association with contexts of reception such as the readers' own personal experience, or historical events that happened, or theories that were developed after the publication of the text. Yet, in the context of advanced literary study, rather than in the context of independent reading for pleasure, the reader is not entirely free. Certain interpretations might simply be based on misunderstandings or misreadings; others might be so personal as to be inappropriate for the discourse of formal literary study. Interpretations must be argued for, supported and evaluated, and these processes must be modelled for students by teachers and critics. At the same time, students need to understand the nature of teachers' and critics' authority, recognising that they act as knowledgeable guides: they cannot magically open up a direct line into the author's mind or 'know' the meaning of texts, but their status and experience allows them to make judgements on the validity of interpretations.

Whilst discussion of alternative interpretations of texts does not need to be overtly theoretical, the idea that texts might be examined through various theoretical lenses is now fundamental to the discipline. Literary theory at quite a demanding level is often covered during the first year of an English degree at university, and students who go on to study other arts or humanities subjects are equally likely to encounter such theoretical positions in their chosen disciplines. Thus we would argue that introducing students to some basic aspects of literary theory *at a foundational level* is desirable, even if it is not prescribed in the syllabus. We would go so far as to say that, for reasons of citizenship as much as literary knowledge, no student should leave a contemporary literature classroom without at least understanding the fundamental arguments about class, race and gender that underpin Marxism, post-colonialism and feminism, and some of the ways in which they might be relevant to literature – for instance through challenging the ways in which writers represent social relationships or examining the social and cultural contexts in which texts are produced and consumed. Again, as we hope to show later in the book, this can be a dynamic and rewarding classroom experience if pitched appropriately. To argue that such content is too demanding for literature students does not convince; students following 16–19 courses in film studies, media studies, politics, history, sociology, economics and so on routinely engage with such theory (Eaglestone 2001; Atherton 2003, 2004).

Finally, we come to the related question of literary criticism. Many English teachers are, for a variety of reasons, reluctant to bring the work of critics into the classroom. However, just as we believe that students may find that producing their own literary writing provides insights into the craft of the writer, so they may find that reading other readers' responses provides them with insights into the processes of literary interpretation and judgement. Exposure to carefully chosen literary criticism can provide a useful focus for textual discussion whilst broadening students' understanding of what a critic is and what a critic does (Daw 1996; Atherton 2004). Equally, exposure to literary journalism such as newspaper book reviews and discussions of literary events or ideas, can show students that the functions of criticism extend beyond the academy and into 'real life'. Students' writing will benefit greatly from engaging regularly with good writing about literature.

---

4. The idea of literature

Students should develop an understanding of the ways in which the idea of literature operates in society – through publishing, the media and education, for instance – and of the ways in which the idea of literature is defined, valued, challenged and debated.

Key concepts include: the definition of literature, the purpose of literature, literary values, literary reading, literary education, the canon, literary language, national literatures, world literature, media, cultural values, political values.

Far from being convinced devotees of the idea of a literary canon or of the distinct nature of literariness, in our experience most teenagers lead complex cultural lives which span a variety of related literary and media forms at various different levels of cultural production – as do most adults. Many will see no difficulty about separating 'literature' from other forms of cultural production, because they feel that what is generally described as literature is in some senses better than, more challenging than, or at least different from other types of reading material. This could be a sign that they consider themselves 'literary' readers, and indeed many 16–19 literature students are passionate readers; often, however, it means that 'literature' is not the kind of thing that they would read themselves if it were not set for study in school. For some, especially (but not only) in education systems where 16–19 study of literature is compulsory, extended reading of any kind is off the agenda; in our media-rich world, various kinds of non-literary consumption are more immediate and pressing, whether they be film, music, computer gaming or the internet.

Whatever the mode and extents of students' cultural consumption, the question of what literature actually *is* is likely to be more complex than they initially allow, or than they have had an opportunity to explore in depth. Unquestioning acceptance of the value judgements of syllabuses and other establishment apparatus is not a good starting point for a critical approach, and so we owe it to our students to remind them that the definition of literature is difficult and controversial, and that they should engage with the issues that it raises as they proceed through their course. (Try debating whether crime or science fiction should be on a syllabus, for instance.) The simple question 'what is literature?' can raise enough theoretical issues to inform an entire literature course. Terry Eagleton's seminal text *Literary Theory: An Introduction* (1983) sets out to argue that a bus ticket might be read as literature: show this to students and wait for the outrage. Whether they agree with this view or not, this discussion – and many others like it – will take students' engagement with the idea of literature and the project of studying it to a new level, opening up a range of significant questions and issues, many of which might lead to a sharpening of their approach to the central content of their literature course.

The question of what literature *is* is also a question for teachers, syllabus-makers and course-writers. Might there be as much to gain in terms of cultural understanding from the study of the types of literature that do *not* generally find their way onto 16–19 literature syllabuses as there is from more *conventionally* literary kinds, even if it only helps to demonstrate the 'literary' qualities of 'good' literature by setting them in relief? This is not an idea supported by the convention that texts on literature courses should be 'worthy of literary study', as the A Level criteria put it; but the very fact that we assign different value categories to different types of literature suggests it is important for both teachers and students to consider what *is* worthy of literary study and to question why that is. Should literary study merely confirm dominant literary values by restricting itself to 'good' literature, or should it investigate the challenge posed by literary values that deviate from those norms? (It's worthwhile reflecting that academic critics in universities do not restrict themselves to conventionally literary texts but, seeing English as part of the project of cultural studies, study the whole range of literary production.)

The world outside the classroom offers innumerable opportunities for students to test such propositions, and to learn about the different ways in which literature operates. They might, for instance, consider how bookshops and publishers deal with different definitions of the literary; they might consider how the idea of literature is constructed in literature syllabuses and through governmental edict; they might read literary journalism that seeks to challenge or confirm literary values. The ongoing proliferation of media and multi-modal texts complicates things further. Is our definition of 'the literary' constrained by notions of the book? If our goal is critical analysis and cultural understanding, why should we not consider the broader world of cultural representation? In what senses are film, theatre and television drama not literary? And what about graphic novels, computer games and wordless picture books (e.g. a book like Shaun Tan's *The Arrival*), contemporary forms of storytelling which (as Burn 2004 points out) can have highly complex and sophisticated narrative structures, and highly poetic use of language and imagery?

Reflecting on the idea of literature also raises linguistic questions. Is there such a thing as 'literary language', and what are its characteristics? Again, this question raises complex and fascinating issues about the nature of creativity and the extent to which what we define as literary depends on context (Carter 2004).

In many other subjects, fundamental questions such as these are a formal part of the syllabus; in 16–19 literature they are only just emerging as facets of what it means to study the subject. Clearly, teachers and students need to work within the parameters of their syllabuses. But if this means that students study literature for two years without ever discussing some of these questions, which are almost always of great interest to them, and which help them to see their set texts and their literary study in new and broader ways, then we would argue that their experience of literature is inappropriately circumscribed.

---

5. The nature of literary study

Students should develop an understanding of the role of literary study, literary criticism and literary theory in producing knowledge about literature and critical thinking about the nature of language, culture and society. They should also develop the ability to think about, discuss and write about literature in an informed and critical way, understanding the mechanisms of critical writing, independent authorship, referencing and so on.

Key concepts include: literary study, literary criticism, literary theory, critical response, personal response, wide reading, the essay, attributing and assimilating ideas, referencing, plagiarism.

Famously, English literature as a discipline was dismissed in its early days as nothing but 'chatter about Shelley' (Professor E. A. Freeman, quoted in Kernan 1990). The value of literary study is nowadays more generally accepted, although questions about *why* it might be valuable and what its purposes might be are far from straightforward, and are likely to provoke heated discussion in almost any social context, and not least in the political domain. Unsurprisingly then, 16–19 literature students do not always have a clear view about why they are studying literature and why (and for whom) it might be valuable. These issues have an important place in 16–19 literature classrooms.

Discussions about the nature of *literature,* as described above, will generally encompass questions about the nature of *literary study,* and often revolve around the differences between what students read themselves and what they read for study in class. The difference between reading for pleasure and reading for study is a profitable one to pursue with students, as is that of the difference between 'reading' and 'studying' as different activities with different purposes and methods. That is not to say that there is no overlap between the two, of course: there is often a great deal. However, helping students to think through these differences and similarities, and to position themselves as increasingly autonomous learners and readers, can help them to adjust to the demands of 16–19 literary study and to make choices about their continuing education.

One crucial issue here is the extent to which students perceive the individual and societal value of a literary education – or indeed any kind of education. Although this question might be applied to any subject, students are perhaps less inclined to see the social value of English than of many other subjects – certainly the sciences, but perhaps other humanities subjects, too. What benefits does the study of literature bring to society? Why should the state subsidise students to learn about literature? Do we become better citizens through studying literature? Do literature students develop certain skills and knowledge that society values? To what extent does the *study* of literature strengthen literature as an art form? The question of whether English is a humanities subject, an arts subject or a social studies subject might usefully be explored here, too, as a means of helping students to understand the parameters of the subject. Furthermore, this issue relates strongly to the perceived connections between the different branches of English – language, literature, creative writing etc. – which might also usefully be explored at various points of the course.

Finally, students need to begin to learn the methods of academic scholarship. We have already discussed the need for exposure to literary criticism and literary theory at a foundational level, and therefore to begin to learn about the functions of the critic. They also need to start to develop their own critical voices in discussion and in writing, achieving a fuller understanding of the form of the critical essay and other types of critical and creative response. Understanding how to evaluate, assimilate, attribute and reference others' words and ideas is essential, especially in the new internet-led world of the twenty-first century.

The 16–19 curriculum: a bridge between secondary and higher English

The curriculum outlined above is not, we emphasise, a syllabus or a course outline. Rather it is an attempt to envision a framework for the kinds of things that students might explore in advanced literature study regardless of what syllabus or course is followed, regardless of what texts are set. Implicit is a notion of a specialised 16–19 literature curriculum that goes well beyond the study of literature which generally characterises pre-16 English. Pre-16 students are likely to encounter a narrower range of texts, and teaching is likely to emphasise development of personal response to specific texts, informed by a number of fundamental concepts such as the ways in which writers respond to the cultural contexts of their time and use literary devices. The 16–19 curriculum described above is a considerable development from that.

Indeed, we argue broadly that 16–19 English study should provide a foundational overview of the subject as it is constituted at university. Whilst providing a broad base of abilities as readers and producers of text, literature courses at this level should encourage students to be critical 'readers' of culture who are well prepared to meet the demands of HE and/or employment. University English is conceptually complex, demanding breadth and depth of knowledge and theoretical engagement. In the 16–19 phase, it would not be appropriate to do more than *introduce* students to the range of ideas they might encounter in HE, and to give them a taste of some of the areas of debate and knowledge (Gibbons 2010). But no student should arrive at university to read English – as many have done in recent decades – unprepared for the scope and nature of the subject in HE; and those who are going to read *other subjects* at university will, we believe, benefit equally from the broad, critical approach described. Furthermore, beyond the requirements of HE, intelligent and humane citizenship in a complex world is similarly demanding; again, *all* students, whether going on to university or not, are likely to benefit from a broad, critical approach at this level.

However, this approach is not all about *difficulty* and *challenge*. It's also about *access* and *enlightenment*. We often hear of very able students who feel that literary analysis 'destroys' texts for them, and of less able students who find themselves unable to 'appreciate' the texts they encounter. A 'cultural analysis' approach has the potential to demystify literary study and place it in a context which opens up understandings of how culture and language function in society, making literary study more *meaningful* for a range of students, and ensuring that it is not just a set of hurdles on the way to an examination in which they regurgitate half-understood appreciative gestures (Marland 2003; Atherton 2007).

Clearly, in these circumstances, teachers will need to consider how to give their students access to the repertoires they need. This needs to be done sensitively. As McCormick (1994) points out, students can be overwhelmed when teachers simply hand over large amounts of 'background information' or theoretical material without helping them to make sense of it – a technique that can lead students to believe 'that they themselves are incapable of reading, understanding and certainly analysing such texts, which appear to contain secret and specialized knowledge' (1994: 59). Yet equally, teachers need to avoid resorting to a naive student-centred approach that relies on unconstrained subjectivity: students must not be 'coddled into believing that their readings [are] valuable just because they are their own' (1994: 62).

This means on one level that teachers might have to carry out quite radical alterations to the ways in which they approach particular texts. Yet it also has much more serious implications: namely, that teachers might find themselves having to adjust to theoretical approaches that differ significantly from the ways in which they themselves were taught. In effect, they might find themselves having to learn these approaches from scratch – in other words, to relearn their subject – with very little in the way of in-service training, or even remitted time, to help them to do this.

We recognise both the cognitive and metacognitive challenges this is likely to present to students of different backgrounds and abilities moving up from the secondary school, and the challenges for their teachers. We do not, however, believe this is unattainable. Appropriately pitched literature courses *can* take into account principles such as those described above and, as the next section of the chapter argues and the remainder of the book demonstrates, pedagogical strategies exist to make them function effectively.

Actualising the literature curriculum

The nature of 16–19 study

So far, this chapter has highlighted the complex forces that have shaped the study of literature in the 16–19 phase and how these might, in their turn, shape broad notions of what we wish students to encounter through the study of literature. It will now turn to the ways in which the subject is enacted in the classroom – in other words, how it is 'actualised' by those who teach it and the decisions they make. This process has been described by Englund as one of making choices from the range of possibilities offered by the subject one teaches, which can be 'concretised in different ways in different classrooms' (1997: 277), and by Jones *et al.* as consisting of 'the various ways in which teachers draw from the academic discipline which informs their teaching ... how they position their teaching in relation to the various paradigms of the subject that exist in educational practice' (2005: 253). As the first two parts of this chapter have shown, courses and syllabuses for 16–19 English literature already embody a wide range of choices (some highly controversial) about the nature of the curriculum. Nevertheless, there are still decisions to be made, from the obvious (such as the selection of set texts) to the more subtle (such as when and how to introduce particular critical concepts or teaching methods, or how much emphasis to place on the demands of external assessment). All of these will affect students' experience of English literature in the 16–19 phase as it is inflected by a range of different philosophies and approaches.

The 16–19 phase has been at the mercy of all manner of unexamined assumptions regarding how English is best tackled. Jacobs refers, for instance, to the common conviction that 16–19 teaching is 'a more "natural" kind of teaching than at 11–16' (2010: 2), as though English teachers know instinctively how to handle 16-19 classes. The idea that there can ever be a kind of English teaching that is more 'natural' than another, whether in the 16–19 phase or elsewhere, is, of course, extremely contentious in itself. As Grossman and Shulman (1994), drawing on Elbow (1990) and Scholes (1985), point out, 'any act of teaching is implicitly theoretical': no syllabus, no lesson in fact, is ever theoretically 'innocent' (1994: 5). Nevertheless, the notion that English teachers can 'simply walk into the … classroom armed with only their favourite book and deliver the utopian goods' (Jacobs 2010: 2) is still remarkably widespread. At one extreme, this belief manifests itself as the 'charismatic pedagogy' (Beavis 1997) represented by the fictional English teachers alluded to at the beginning of this chapter, whose approaches to teaching literature embody a heady, counter-cultural experience that, in its worst incarnation, shirks its responsibilities to students and the courses they are following. Similar to this is the adherence to the primacy of unfettered subjectivity that treats all responses to literature as equally valid: a belief that evades 'questions of what makes an interpretation good, better or really excellent by emphasizing and valuing instead individuality and confidence or passion as the characterizing elements for critique' (Holt-Reynolds 2000: 27). At the other extreme is an overly didactic methodology that treats 16–19 students as embryonic undergraduates, best taught through what essentially amounts to a series of lectures. Gibbons describes this approach as involving '[the] heavily directed annotation of texts, large quantities of background notes, a standard whole class 'seminar' style lesson structure, a reliance on students' note-taking skills, heightened expectation of independent reading and research' (2010: 3). In such a model, essential skills go untaught as it is assumed that students possess them already: the fact that these students have only recently emerged from a very different kind of learning experience is forgotten.

Pedagogical thinking

What both of these models lack, crucially, is what Feiman-Nemser and Buchman have termed 'pedagogical thinking': 'thinking about how to build bridges between one's own understanding and that of one's students' (1985: 6). Ball *et al.* elaborate further:

> Teachers need to sequence particular content for instruction, deciding which examples to start with and which examples to use to take students deeper into the content. They need to evaluate the instructional advantages and disadvantages of representations used to teach a specific area. During a classroom discussion, they have to decide when to ask for more clarification, when to use a student's remark to make a … point, and when to ask a new question or pose a new task to further students' learning. Each of these requires an interaction between specific [subject-based] understanding and an under-standing of pedagogical issues that affect students' learning.
>
> (Ball *et al.* 2008: 9)

This constructivist methodology is central to all good literature teaching, and underpins the approaches we advocate in this book. It has at its heart a collaborative and recursive process of exploration in which the teacher acts as a guiding and refining influence. It therefore places considerable demands on the teacher. Perhaps its most important requirement is the attitude known in the field of clinical psychology as 'mindfulness', described by Bishop *et al.* as involving the adoption of 'a particular orientation toward one's experiences in the present moment, an orientation that is characterized by curiosity, openness, and acceptance' (2004: 9). This is absolutely vital if teachers are to be alert to the possibilities of literature in the 16–19 classroom – to the directions that can be taken by texts and students and to the need to respond, refine and change tack as appropriate. It is not, of course, exclusive to the teaching of English, but it is particularly important *in* English, where learning outcomes may differ radically (and justifiably) from one's intentions and where no two groups ever interpret a text in exactly the same way. It is, in effect, the opposite of the sense conveyed by the expression 'lesson delivery', with its overtones of packaging and transmission. English teachers who are fully conscious of the messiness of learning but who, nevertheless, retain control over this messiness are those who do most justice to their subject. And while this state of alertness to the possibilities of one's subject is vital for all English teachers, it becomes even more important in the 16–19 phase when the teacher is not only an educator but an experienced reader, able to act as a role model for students who are still relatively new to the world of literature for adults. Many older teenagers confess to feeling lost when they leave behind the familiar realms of children's books and young adult fiction: one of our students confessed that there were just so many books that she didn't know where to begin. An English teacher who can recognise where students 'are' in terms of their relationship with literature, make connections with other areas of experience, point students in the direction of particular authors and introduce them to the wider culture that surrounds the act of reading (and the sharing of this act) will be an invaluable guide through this new and initially bewildering environment, providing the 'scaffolding' that students need in order to access their zone of proximal development.

Performing this Vygotskian function is important enough in itself, but it is rendered more complex (and therefore more problematic) in English literature by the fact that it is not confined to a purely cognitive domain. One of the biggest hurdles that teachers of literature have to confront is the conflict between the preconceptions, experiences and expectations that students bring to the study of English and the learning environment in which they find themselves. This conflict is worked out in a space that Bourdieu has termed the 'habitus', 'the site of the internalisation of externality and the externalisation of internality' (1990: 205). The degree of congruence between the individual habitus – the means by which the student relates to his or her learning environment – and the educational institution itself plays an important part in how successfully students adapt to 16–19 study, and therefore poses certain challenges for the teacher. Knights uses the concept of the 'implied student' of the discipline to describe the kind of identity that the subject expects its learners to occupy (2005: 38). Most 16–19 teachers would have no problem in identifying students who are able to assume this role; but what about those for whom this identity is less natural? How do teachers cope, for instance, with students who are resistant to certain kinds of books and certain ways of thinking about them, or who – for any number of reasons – feel excluded from particular cultural debates and the networks in which they take place? What about students whose social and familial backgrounds make them reluctant to challenge authority and question received opinion? How about those students – and many teachers would claim that there are more than ever before – who simply want to be told what they need to know in order to achieve a particular grade? Green argues that teachers of English need to draw a 'map' of the subject for their students, 'forg[ing] a workable model of English ... [which is] profoundly important and powerful in shaping students' experiences and consequently their expectations of English studies' (2007: 13). This mapping – an initiation not just into the body of knowledge that the subject encompasses, but into its unwritten codes and ways of thinking – is a complicated process, but it is nevertheless essential if students are not to feel alienated by practices that can sometimes seem bewildering.

Learning in class: some basic principles

What does good 16–19 teaching actually look like? One important point to make is that it contains many of the same features as good pre-16 teaching. A clear sense of one's learning intentions; starters that capture students' attention and get them thinking; activities that enable all students to participate and make progress; opportunities for students to share their thinking and test out their ideas; high-quality resources tailored to the learning needs of the group; the opportunity to be creative and show divergent approaches; attention to the full ability range; plenaries that allow students (and their teacher) to assess learning and reflect on what they have achieved: all of these have their place in the 16–19 classroom, too. As Gibbons points out, these techniques should be present right from the start of 16–19 programmes of study: 'if as a teacher you don't build these approaches into [16–19] teaching early in a course, it becomes increasingly difficult as a different teaching and learning discourse roots itself in the classroom' (2010: 8). As many a teacher has discovered, there is nothing worse than a 16–19 group made up of students who expect to be told what to think.

Embedding these principles, then, should be a priority in every English department's course planning at advanced level. Whatever course students are following, a focal point of the first few weeks should be to create the kind of learning environment in which learners are comfortable sharing ideas, testing out interpretations and respecting and building on the contributions of others. Some programmes of study allow for an introductory period in which teachers can establish key methods and approaches through the exploration of a range of texts and extracts. Others, more rigidly hemmed in by the demands of external assessment, will be less fortunate, but it is still worth devoting some time to laying the foundations for effective 16–19 study before embarking on the first set text, bearing in mind that students might be new to each other (and their teacher) as well as to their course of study. Panel 1.1 below outlines some suggested activities for the first few weeks of the 16–19 course.

Panel 1.1   Introductory activities

'The rights of the reader'

This activity draws on the French author Daniel Pennac's book *The Rights of the Reader* (2006). Pennac sets out a manifesto consisting of ten points that he thinks all teachers of reading should adhere to. Students, in groups, could be given a copy of the manifesto and asked which of Pennac's 'rights' they think is most important. Can they explain their decision? Is there anything that Pennac has omitted? This activity is useful for getting students to talk about their experiences of reading, and for exploring their choices and behaviours. Do they find it easy, for instance, to give up on a book once they have started it? How often do they re-read books? It could also form the basis of a short piece of written work in which they reflect on the journey they have made since they learned to read.

Equally interesting is to use Pennac's ten 'rights' to consider what rights the study of literature takes away from students. Do they have the right not to finish a set text? Do they have the right to finish a text if it is only presented to them in extract form? What about the right to silence to read in the classroom?

The ten 'Rights of the Reader' are available in pdf form, illustrated by Quentin Blake, at www.walker.co.uk

Beliefs about reading

As a variation on the previous activity, you could get students to explore a number of different views about reading and the study of literature. Give them a number of statements, printed on slips of paper, and ask them to work in groups to sort them into a continuum, from 'Agree strongly' to 'Disagree strongly'. Some possible statements are listed below: it's useful if they're as provocative as possible!

1   Everyone should have the opportunity to study Shakespeare at school.
2   Analysing books in too much detail spoils them.
3   *EastEnders* is more relevant to today's young people than Jane Austen and Charles Dickens.
4   It makes no sense to say that one book is 'better' than another.
5   Poetry is much harder to understand than prose.
6   Literature is about universal values and experiences that everyone can relate to.
7   You can make a poem mean whatever you want it to mean.
8   Reading makes you a better person.

Once they've made their decisions, students should report back on a statement they felt particularly strongly about. Like the exercise above, this will enable you to explore different views and perhaps encourage students to question each other.

Exploring sonnets

This is an effective exercise for getting students working with and talking about texts, allowing you to make some initial observations about their analytical skills. It focuses on the sonnet, since sonnets are short enough to explore within a lesson, yet allow you to make connections with concepts such as genre, intertextuality and the literary tradition. This particular exercise involves Shakespeare's Sonnet 130 ('My mistress' eyes are nothing like the sun') and Simon Armitage's sonnet, 'I am very bothered'.

First, get the students to pool their knowledge of the sonnet form. How many lines does a sonnet have? What are sonnets typically about? Why were they written? (You could do this as a sorting activity: put a number of true/false statements about sonnets onto cards, and get students to categorise them.) Next, introduce the poems. In what ways do they exemplify the characteristics of the sonnet form? In what ways do they subvert them? Students could do this activity in pairs or small groups, with each group working on one of the poems and then sharing their observations with another group before reporting back as a whole class. As a follow-up activity, you could get them to produce an annotated version of their allocated poem, enlarged onto A3 paper, for a wall display.

Note that what these three activities have in common is their focus on student talk: on getting them discussing, reporting back, challenging each others' ideas and responding to follow-up questions. They therefore help to establish the 16–19 classroom as a space characterised by the shared construction of knowledge rather than the transmission of established ideas from teacher to student. Placing the emphasis very firmly on active engagement is vital if teachers are going to cultivate the enquiring minds that students will need to succeed in the 16–19 phase and beyond.

An active learning classroom: the importance of questions and active reading

A crucial aspect of good 16–19 teaching is the questions that teachers ask. These questions are fundamental to the building of knowledge about literary texts – from helping students to orientate themselves in the basics of plot and character to exploring increasingly more sophisticated issues of context and interpretation. Some, particularly in the early stages of study, will be closed questions, but many will be the kind of probing, open-ended questions that encourage speculative thinking and further debate. Some of these questions will arise during the course of a discussion: others might be planned in advance, with careful attention to the development of higher order thinking. Students should also be encouraged to ask these open-ended questions themselves: of their teacher, the text and each other. Of course, not all of these questions need to be answered there and then. It is often valuable to leave particularly complex questions hanging, and to return to them a week or a month later – or even at the end of a particular unit of work – to see how students' thinking has developed and changed. It is also interesting to look for creative alternatives to questions in order to generate discussion. Panel 1.2 outlines Fisher's (2011) suggestions.

Panel 1.2   Strategies for encouraging response

Withhold judgement	Respond in a non-evaluative fashion; ask others to respond.
Invite students to elaborate	'Say more about...'
Cue alternative responses	'There is no one right answer. What are the alternatives? Who's got a different point of view?'
Challenge students to provide reasons	Give reasons why.
Make a challenging statement	'Supposing someone said...'
Contribute your own thoughts/experience	'I think that/remember when...'
Use 'think-pair-share'	Allow thinking time: discuss with partner, then group.
Allow 'rehearsal' of response	Try out the answer: in your head and to partner.
Invite student questions	'Anyone like to ask Pat a question about that?'
Use 'think-alouds'	Model rhetorical questions: 'I don't quite understand...'
Student to invite response	'Ali, will you ask someone else what they think?'
Don't ask for show of hands	Expect everyone to respond.

An excellent example of how this kind of questioning might work in the context of 16–19 English literature is provided by Campbell's account of a lesson at an English sixth-form college (2006). Campbell focuses on the way that carefully sequenced activities, structured around key points for discussion, help to build a sense of learning as a collective enterprise, based on the belief that 'knowledge is tentative, contestable and revisable' (2006: 13). 'The discourse is characterised by a gradual and collective accumulation of ideas, incorporating a readiness to challenge and be challenged [...] Through this iterative process ideas are shared and constructively built upon' (2006: 10). Campbell goes on to describe how the teacher intervenes at crucial moments 'to trigger clearer articulation of the examples and the argument' (2006: 10). What is clear is the level of engagement achieved by this approach: 'There is whole class sharing of these ideas, again characterised by high order questioning by the students of each other and by students contributing to the ideas of their peers' (2006: 10). Crucially, this kind of teaching does not have to involve the kind of surface features that are often held to be an indicator of 'effective teaching and learning', such as the use of ICT, the explicit flagging-up of learning objectives or the attempt to cater to all learning styles. As Campbell remarks:

> This is not 'instruction' nor is it the 'whole class interactive teaching' promoted under the national literacy and numeracy initiatives, since the knowledge, skills, understandings and values being collectively generated are constructed tentatively; the objectives for the session are not cognitive outcomes specified in advance, so much as pedagogical processes to be adhered to.
>
> (Campbell 2006: 13)

At the heart of this kind of lesson is, then, something that should be at the heart of the subject of English literature itself: a belief that meaning is not fixed and immutable but something that can be generated anew by every reading and every discussion of a text.

The importance of this discursive, exploratory approach to the study of literature in the 16–19 phase cannot be overstated. Former students often look back on this stage of their education as the time when they had to begin to think for themselves, rather than simply being told what to think; and for Richard Jacobs, the development of this autonomy should be something that 16–19 teachers plan for right from the start of the course: '"Now do it without me" is the goal, in which "it" is the empowered reading of texts of all kinds because of the work shared on the particular literary text' (2010: 7). To bear this in mind is to remember that in spite of the short-term goals that are often emphasised by our assessment-driven culture, teachers in the 16–19 phase also have a responsibility to prepare their students for whatever might come next: building their capacity for independent study is a crucial part of this. Furthermore, it marks an important step in the direction of Robert Scholes' model of textual study, in which what is taught is not a particular canon of texts, but a method of approaching texts, cultivating 'a judicious attitude: scrupulous to understand, alert to probe for blind spots and hidden agendas, and, finally, critical, questioning, skeptical' (1985: 16).

The collaborative, exploratory building of meaning that stems from this kind of teaching can, however, only be fostered in the kind of classroom where students are used to engaging actively with the process of learning, to being active makers of meaning rather than passive receivers. On a practical level, it helps to build up a repertoire of techniques that can be used to elicit responses and ensure that all students are taking part. Panel 1.3 contains some useful suggestions.

Panel 1.3 Encouraging active engagement

1   Group annotation: write a key word, phrase or quotation on the board, and get students to annotate it using whiteboard markers. This is particularly useful if you give markers to just two students and get them to pass the pens on once they have recorded their ideas. Everyone in the group has to contribute and you end up with a shared spider diagram that can be photographed for future reference.

2   Use 'wait time': pose a question and give students a minute to think before asking for answers. If we, as teachers, want considered and thoughtful responses (and if our questions are worth considering) students need time to formulate their ideas before committing to a response.

3   As above, but give students the opportunity to write their answer down so that they can formulate it more precisely. To extend this, they could write their answer on a sticky note and stick it to the board: the teacher can then get them to examine and categorise these responses.

4   Read out a series of statements on a topic – students have to go to one side of the room if they agree, the other if they disagree. Ask individuals to explain their views, challenge those with different opinions and use evidence to justify their points.

5   Give each student a short extract from a text, or a critical statement. They have to formulate a response to this text and then share it with another student.

6   Mount longer extracts on large sheets of sugar paper so that there is space for students to annotate. Stick these around the room. In small groups, students have a limited amount of time to discuss and annotate each extract, then move on to another text, where they must read the points made by the previous group and add new ideas of their own.

Active engagement with literary text is a crucial element here, too. Students often find it hard to fully and imaginatively enter into the spirit of a text, thinking themselves into its impact as a work of art and the motivations of its writer and readers beyond the classroom. In this book, we advocate a range of approaches for working actively with text. As well as traditional approaches to close reading, based on class and group discussion, we refer to 'Directed Activities Related to Texts' – DARTS (Lunzer and Gardner 1979) – often used in pre-16 English, but, if used carefully, valuable in 16–19 English, too. We also refer frequently to activities which draw on elements of creative writing and performance, designed to focus students on the ways in which texts have a life beyond the page of the book and beyond the classroom – in the imagination of the writer, in private leisure reading, in social contexts such as theatre and poetry readings, in media and publishing, and so on – and on their multimodality, often encompassing sounds, images and physical action.

The success of such techniques, however, depends at least in part on the kind of learning culture that prevails in the institution as a whole. It is difficult to engender close, enthusiastic debate with high levels of student participation, or dynamic engagement with active reading exercises, in English literature if students are accustomed to passivity and spoon-feeding elsewhere in the curriculum. In some schools and colleges, there might be scope for conversation between departments (and perhaps within the institution as a whole) about how to bring about the kind of changes that are needed in order to develop this shared sense of learning. Hymer *et al.*'s GRACE model (2008), which draws on Carol Dweck's notion of the 'growth' mindset, offers a useful tool for thinking about how a spirit of flexibility, openness and risk-taking can be encouraged (see Panel 1.4). GRACE, an acronym that stands for Grow, Relate, Act, Challenge, Exert, invites all members of an educational community to examine their current practice and explore possible alternatives, moving the focus away from a narrow concept of academic achievement rooted only in league tables and exam results.

Panel 1.4   The GRACE model of providing challenge (from Hymer et al., *Gifts, Talents and Education: A Living Theory Approach*, 2008)

G	Grow	• Use emotional maturity as a tool for learning. • Allow space for divergent thinking, risk-taking and constructive failure. • Allow students to work co-operatively. • Encourage respect for alternative experiences and points of view. • Help students to identify the skills they need to pursue their goals. • Help students to develop the attitudes, learning strategies and work habits they need.
R	Relate	• Encourage staff to be open about the fact that they are learning as well as the students. • Foster open-ended understanding, openness, sharing, engaging others. • Encourage staff and students to share their passion for learning. • Support all learners in expressing their ideas. • Promote thinking, discussion and open dialogue. • Encourage collaborative learning and shared responsibility.
A	Act	• Emphasise the process of learning as well as its products. • Make links, question, evaluate, challenge. • Encourage students to set their own challenges and identify lines of enquiry. • Focus on how questions are framed so that they can explore issues that are critical to students' understanding. • Encourage students to recognise that learning depends on the readiness to express and discuss, not just spot correct answers.
C	Challenge	• Encourage Socratic questioning. • Emphasise thinking and reflection: use thinking time. • Plan open-ended activities. • Encourage students to think of the questions they still need answers to. • Have a model of learning that is fuzzy and messy – not all tied up neatly. • Don't always provide the answers!
E	Exert	• Foster a 'community of learning'. • Show your students that you are willing to go beyond your comfort zone. • Be learning-centred, rather than performance-driven. • Encourage staff to engage in small-scale action research projects. • Encourage collaboration between departments and with other schools.

Work-related learning

We argued earlier that the kind of curriculum we envisage for 16–19 literature is as much for citizenship and employment as it is for HE; the same applies to pedagogy. While it is undoubtedly true that the vast majority of 16–19 students will not seek employment in fields where there is a daily need to analyse iambic pentameter or show a detailed understanding of seventeenth-century stagecraft, their study of literature will, nevertheless, enable them to develop personal qualities and attributes that will prepare them for the world of work: not only important skills of literacy and oral communication, but also the ability to weigh evidence, formulate a line of argument, respect alternative viewpoints, read with sensitivity, manage a complex workload, meet deadlines and work with others. With careful planning, the 16–19 teacher will be able not just to allow students to build on these skills, but also to recognise and reflect on their development.

One broad definition of work-related learning, from the work of Knight and Yorke, states that it includes activities 'that are intended to contribute to a student's fitness for employment' (2004: 103). A useful starting point for a consideration of these skills is the CETH Employability Framework, developed by the Centre for Excellence in Teaching and Learning Employability, based at the University of Central Lancashire. This framework is a checklist that enables departments to audit the ways in which their courses contribute to the development of particular skills, including personal development, research skills, problem-solving, social and cultural awareness, communication skills, team working, innovation and creativity, and project planning and evaluation (Day 2010: 7). While the Framework was developed for use at degree level, it also has an obvious relevance for the 16–19 classroom. Much of what students do in this phase will contribute to the skills that will help to make them employable in the future.

Different schools and colleges, and the qualifications their students pursue, will place differing amounts of emphasis on work-related learning. Nevertheless, it is worth considering some of the specific contributions that English literature could make to this agenda. The following are some suggestions for activities, both within and outside the curriculum, that will help students to develop particular skills:

- prepare a presentation or lead a seminar on a particular topic, either solo or in a group;
- organise a reading group for their peers or for younger students;
- organise an author visit or theatre trip;
- create resources for the school or college's website or virtual learning environment (VLE);
- speak to prospective students at an open day;
- edit or contribute to a literary magazine, e-zine or blog;
- review a novel, poetry collection, film or play for the school or college website;
- organise a workshop or mini-conference for students from other schools;
- take part in a poetry reading or drama workshop for younger students;
- create an electronic anthology of students' favourite poems, with photographs, illustrations and links to further reading.

Often, the best activities are those that stem from students' own strengths and enthusiasms. Many students will be prolific bloggers, contributors to discussion forums and authors of fan fiction: they will be highly skilled in crafting posts, handling disagreement and dissent, and offering constructive feedback. Others will excel at sharing their enthusiasm face to face, in reading groups or talks to prospective students. Nevertheless, students should also be given opportunities to work outside their comfort zone. Some students will find it difficult to take responsibility for organising an event, liaising with others or working in a group. It is, of course, vital that such students are supported in broadening the range of their experiences, and that the progress they have made in doing so is acknowledged.

The benefits of enabling students to take part in work-related learning projects are enormous. In 2006, the English and Media Centre carried out a project to explore the contribution made to work-related learning by several 16–19 settings in the UK (EMC 2006). One of the present authors carried out a small-scale, school-based project with a group of three Year 12 students. This project required the Year 12 students to plan, prepare and teach a lesson to a Year 7 class. Their evaluation of this project, and of their role in it, was subtle, wide-ranging and incisive. This particular project would have addressed many of the strands of the CETH Employability Framework, and showed what can be accomplished within the familiar environment of the school.

There is a school of thought that the study of literature should not need to justify itself in vocational terms; that it should remain aloof from the demands of employers. Nevertheless, as Gweno Williams states:

> the best future employment opportunities ... particularly in changing and unpredictable times, are most likely to be provided by a combination of the lifelong intellectual resources generated by the breadth and depth of English studies, together with flexible employment oriented skills and attitudes.
>
> (Day 2010: 2)

The depth of thought, communication skills, self-reliance and open-mindedness fostered by English literature will provide students with an excellent basis for future employment. If these qualities can be developed further, both through the curriculum and beyond it, then students' experience of English, as well as their prospects for the future, will be enriched.

Further reading

Teaching literature

Brown and Gifford's *Teaching A Level English Literature* (1989) and Protherough's *Teaching Literature for Examinations* (1986) remain valuable discussions of 16–19 literature teaching. More recent discussions of issues in 16–19 literature teaching by Gibbons (2010) and Jacobs (2010) may be found at the English ITE website www.ite. org.uk and in *World and Time: Teaching Literature in Context* (Barlow 2009). Special 16–19 editions of NATE's journals *English Drama Media* (June 2006, October 2008, November 2011) and *English in Education* (Spring 2013) also contain a range of articles, whilst the English and Media Centre's resources are invaluable.

Teaching Literature to Adolescents (Beach *et al.* 2010), *Teaching English Texts 11–18* (Dymoke 2009) and *Creativity and Learning in Secondary English* (McCallum 2012) are valuable introductions to a range of issues related to teaching literature from 11 to 19. Dixon's *Growth Through English* (1967) remains a seminal text in thinking about responses to literature in school English.

A number of texts discuss issues concerning the relationship between 16–19 and HE English, the transition between the two, and the underlying philosophies which inform both: *The Culture of Reading and the Teaching of English* (McCormick 1994), *The Rise and Fall of English* (Scholes 1999) and *Defining Literary Criticism* (Atherton 2005). A series of reports written for NATE, The English Association and the English Subject Centre also cover a range of these issues: *Text: Message – The Future of A Level English* (NATE 2005), *Second Reading* (Barlow 2005), *Four Perspectives on Transition* (Green 2005), *The Experience of Studying English in UK Higher Education* (Hodgson 2010). Finally, *Teaching Literature* (Showalter 2003) and *Teaching and Learning English Literature* (Chambers and Gregory 2006) reflect on a number of practical and theoretical issues for teaching English in universities.

Critical introductions to studying literature

Some recent texts written for students address issues about the transition between school and university English, and are also valuable material for 16–19 teachers: *Doing English* (3rd edition, Eaglestone 2009), *Thinking about Texts* (Hopkins 2001), *Starting an English Literature Degree* (Green 2009a). Other useful undergraduate introductions to the study of literature include *The English Studies Book* (Pope 2002), *The Essential Guide to English Studies* (Childs 2008), *Studying English Literature* (Young 2008), *Studying Literature* (Goring *et al.* 2010) and *The English Literature Companion* (Wolfreys 2010).

Texts more concerned with the definition, significance and value of literature than with the business of studying it include, for instance, *Literature* (Widdowson 1999) and *Literature: A Very Short Introduction* (Bate 2010), both fascinating discussions. Further books on literary theory and contexts are dealt with in Chapters 5 and 6.

Chapter 2

Teaching poetry

Introduction: Poetry in the 16–19 classroom

In his poem 'Introduction to Poetry' (1988), the American poet Billy Collins writes about his frustration regarding what is done to poetry in the classroom in the name of education. He 'ask[s] them to take a poem / and hold it up to the light', but instead he finds that 'all they want to do / is tie the poem to a chair with rope / and torture a confession out of it.'

The situation that Collins captures so beautifully here is one which will in essence be familiar to most English teachers, especially at the higher levels of school and college, and represents one element of a complex network of very particular issues which the teaching of poetry presents to the 16–19 English teacher. We do not intend to suggest that the scenario that Collins describes is common to *every* classroom where the analysis of poetry is taught; nor do we suggest that it *sums up* the experience of poetry in *any* classroom. However, we would argue that it embodies a tension that lies at the heart of poetry teaching: how to examine something (often) small and beautiful in a critical way without losing sight of its aesthetic purpose and pleasures.

Apart from a specialised genre of poems about the teaching of poetry (a genre of which there are few examples and of which Collins' poem is one of the most interesting), there are few familiar literary representations of poetry teaching. Another, however, is offered by the film *Dead Poets Society*, in which American English teacher John Keating enlists a group of disturbingly impressionable students on a dangerously transformative moral-aesthetic odyssey with hero-worship of the Romantic poets at its heart.

How can such reductive approaches to poetry be avoided? Is there an alternative to the dichotomy that Collins presents, or are we doomed to 'destroy' poetry when we teach it? Even if it were possible to manipulate our students in the way that Keating does in *Dead Poets Society*, is reverence for the poet as genius, for poetry as unheard oracle, or for the canon as the soul of poetry a model we want to inculcate? Whilst we do not pretend that all such issues *can* be fully resolved, this chapter attempts to address these and similar questions by examining the contexts of poetry teaching, identifying a broad agenda for poetry in the 16–19 classroom, and suggesting approaches and activities designed to establish a sympathetic framework through which students can develop knowledge and understanding of the form as well as of the specific poems they will encounter.

The cultural context: the experience of poetry in society

We live, more than at any other time in history, in an age of prose narrative. Whether in the form of drama or in the form of the novel, prose dominates our experience of fictional representations. The rise and rise of the novel and short story – thanks to the development of mass literacy, of print and electronic technology, and of privacy and individualism, amongst other things – continues unabated. Similar influences on playwriting (such as the mass availability of the printed script, the development of the proscenium arch theatre and technologies of sound and lighting) as well as the influence of the rise of the novel, also made prose the dominant mode of drama from the nineteenth century onwards and, through film and television, the realist mode of prose dialogue in drama has now achieved supreme valency. Conversely, verse as a means of literary communication has declined, barely used in drama or storytelling let alone in history or philosophy as it once was – a situation explored by Gioia (2002) in his discussion of poetic culture, *Can Poetry Matter?* Verse is now used – in a literary context – almost exclusively in poetry; and most poetry is now in the lyric rather than the epic or dramatic mode.

Such sentiments may be truisms for us as English teachers, but the extensive historical past of verse as the dominant mode of literary communication is something of which many of our students are likely to be relatively unaware. The only extensive exposure to verse as a dominant narrative mode that our students are likely to have had when they reach 16–19 study is through Shakespeare's plays; and, even here, their awareness of Shakespeare's dramatic writing *as verse*, rather than simply as dramatic narrative, is often sketchy (as well as their awareness of the *theatrical context* of the verse – these issues are covered further in Chapter 4). Students need to be made aware that the novel and prose drama are newcomers in the literary scene, and of some of the implications of this for understanding the development of literary forms and language.

If verse as a literary mode has declined, what of *poetry?* Of course, there has never been a golden age when the reading of poetry was commonplace for the general population – although perhaps more households once held copies of Palgrave's *Golden Treasury* and similar – and this is as true now as ever. It is vital to recognise that the vast majority of our students (and their families) do not read poetry outside the classroom, even those who profess to love literature (by which they often mean novels and plays). If we are being entirely honest, we must recognise, too, that poetry is frequently low on the list of cultural preferences of English teachers; indeed, copious anecdotal evidence (and some research evidence, for instance Cremin 2011) suggests that many English teachers rarely or never read or hear poetry except when they are preparing to teach it. (At the same time, we must also recognise that some students and many teachers are passionate and extremely knowledgeable about poetry.)

If all this seems to drive us towards the conclusion that poetry is in many senses a relatively alien form in our culture, and that for many of our students English lessons are the only place where they will encounter it, we must, however, remember the following: not only do we live more than ever in an age of prose narrative, we also live more than ever in an age of song. Almost all our students consume poetry (in the form of song lyrics) daily, and have done since early childhood, and this can offer us a considerable base on which to build, and a means to make profitable links between the relatively obscure world of literary poetry and the popular and oral culture which predominates outside the classroom. (It's also worth remembering that many children's stories are written/told in verse.)

Purists might baulk at embracing the song lyric in the advanced literature classroom, and certainly it's unlikely that song lyrics will become set texts in the near future; but if Cambridge University can do it, why not us? The Cambridge English tripos exam in 2008 became notorious (in the outraged popular press) for asking students to compare 'poems' by Shakespeare, Milton, Wordsworth and Raleigh with 'lyrics' by Amy Winehouse, Billie Holiday and Bob Dylan; and the revered Keats critic and Cambridge Professor of English Christopher Ricks rarely gave a lecture without referring to the lyrics of Dylan (who won the Pulitzer Prize in 2008). Seamus Heaney once singled out the rap artist Eminem for praise because of the 'verbal energy' in his work which 'has sent a voltage round a generation' (*Guardian*, 1 July 2003). What better way could there be of helping our students to consider the similarities and differences between literary and popular cultures, to appreciate the ways in which poetic form unites both, and to become engaged in important questions about literary value and culture? The end result of such an exercise might well be to decrease their feeling of alienation from the form and increase their knowledge of the way it operates.

The educational context: experiences of poetry in the classroom

Students' misgivings about poetry, if they exist, often seem to exist despite, or perhaps in many cases *because of*, their experiences of poetry in the pre-16 classroom. It is perhaps worth reflecting on why this might be. There is likely to be considerable variation in students' classroom experience of poetry, both in the way it is taught and what is taught; but in general terms, the primary and lower secondary years are likely to focus on creative approaches to poetry, which might include poetry writing, performance, storyboarding and so on, as well as informal explorations of response through discussion, and some introduction to features such as metaphor and alliteration. Rhyme and heavily patterned verse often dominates at these stages. Study tends to be relatively informal, with teachers – and sometimes students – free to choose whatever poems they wish, and no pressure to 'cram' for exam essays. Typically, such creative and informal approaches are replaced as students approach the senior years of school with more formal critical approaches, often associated with formal assessment such as high-stakes coursework or exam papers, and the nature of the verse studied often becomes less 'fun' and more 'serious' (Andrews 1991; Dymoke 2003).

In recent years, in England, curriculum strictures have also meant that students have had to prepare a large number of poems from exam-board-supplied anthologies for examination answers in GCSE papers (at age sixteen). Whilst many of the poems have been very interesting, and the centrality of poetry in the specifications has led to the burgeoning of poetry readings for students such as the well-known *Poetry Live!* series, there is a great deal of evidence that many students are 'put off' poetry at this stage because of the sometimes gruelling and mechanical process of preparing so many poems for formal exam response – even where teachers have tried their hardest to engage students using a variety of pedagogical methods (Dymoke 2002; Hennessy and McNamara 2011).

This has clear implications for 16–19 teaching. For many students, the experience of responding creatively to poetry will have been forgotten, replaced by the routines of exam preparation. The challenge for 16–19 teaching must be to re-establish the idea that responding to poetry is both creative and critical in meaningful and enjoyable ways (Snapper 2013).

Addressing the creative is in some ways the more problematic of the two. The demands of 16–19 literary study mean that creative responses such as poetry writing and performance are not highly valued in themselves in relation to assessment, and, with limited time available, this means that it can be difficult to incorporate such activities: difficult, but not impossible – and it should be remembered that investment in such activity can in the end pay dividends in improved critical response. However, there are two other ways in which creativity can be addressed. First, as reader response theory shows us, critical activity is in many ways creative – and students can be encouraged to enjoy the creativity of poetry response and interpretation that is often evident in the open group and class discussions which are such a powerful part of 16–19 literature study (Dias and Hayhoe 1988). Second, through critical activity students can also learn to understand the *nature* of creativity more fully, in this case the creativity of the poet and of poetry.

Understanding the creativity of the poet and the poem, whether achieved through critical or creative activity (preferably a mixture of the two), is perhaps the key 'breakthrough' we have to make. Like Billy Collins' students, ours are often inclined to see poems as classroom captives, without being able to imagine them having a complex, fully fledged existence beyond the classroom walls. Try making this point explicitly, early in the course, pointing out provocatively that the most important thing students need to know about poetry is that *it is not intended to be studied in a classroom*, and that, to understand poetry, they need to understand that first. This, of course, opens up further valuable discussion: '*Why* is it studied in the classroom if that's not what it's intended for? What *is* it intended for? *Who* is it intended for? Who becomes a poet? *How* do you become a poet? What do poets feel about their poetry being studied in classrooms? What is the point of studying poetry if we don't like it?', and so on. It should also prompt discussion about students' own life experiences of poetry. Some will speak of their love of poetry. Many will, for the first time, have a formal classroom opportunity to express their doubts about poetry, in some cases their resentment of it – and it's important that such expressions are taken seriously if those students are to be 'brought on board'. 'It's OK to find poetry problematic' is the message; 'now let's think about why that is'.

Such explicit airing of these issues – through which we seek to break down the unspoken barriers that might impede students' full commitment to poetry study, and to invite 'full disclosure' of their feelings about poetry – can be significant. We cannot expect all our students automatically to understand what makes a poet tick (or, even more, *made* them tick in previous centuries), or how poets set about doing what they do, or why poetry might be considered valuable; nor can we expect them automatically to understand why – or *if* – studying poetry in a classroom might be a good idea. We must explicitly guide them towards these ideas (Snapper 2009); and once these issues have been aired, the contexts of poetry and of the study of poetry are likely to be clearer for many.

Moving on from this point involves helping students to understand the contract between writer and reader that is poetic form, and the way in which poets work within, around or against traditions that originated in song and storytelling – in oral culture – with rhythm and sound at their heart, and, crucially, the pleasure of an audience in view (Stibbs 2000; Gordon 2004). (Again, this can be a rich area for discussion: 'What *kinds* of pleasure can we get from poetry? Why is it often/for many pleasurable?') Here again, the traditions of popular culture can be immensely valuable: you only need to mention hip-hop for students to become instantly more alert to the possibilities of alliteration, rhyme and rhythm in poetry. For this reason, getting students to perform poetry in class – or to watch poets or actors performing it – can be a particularly rewarding activity. We also need to help students to see that *studying* poetry and *reading, writing and performing* poetry are in many crucial senses quite different activities and to distinguish – and perhaps challenge – the values and purposes of each.

A related issue with implications for 16–19 teaching is the extent to which students have been taught 'poems' rather than taught 'about poetry'. It's natural that the emphasis before advanced study should be on responding to what individual poems *say*; the extent to which students will also have discussed the *idea* of poetry, or learnt the rudiments of poetic form and other frameworks such as the historical development of poetry, will inevitably vary considerably. It would be all too easy to continue an atomistic approach to poems in 16–19 study, especially given the centrality of set texts in syllabuses; but we should ideally recognise that, in advanced study, wide reading and understanding of broader contexts in 'poetry' can help students to engage with and understand 'poems' more effectively. To this end, the next two sections of this chapter are called 'Teaching poetry' and 'Teaching poems'.

Teaching poetry

Teaching the history and development of poetry

Clearly a comprehensive overview of the history and development of poetry is not something that is required by post-16 study until university level is reached; and, given the demands of set texts and examinations, there is not always much time in an advanced literature course for even an overview. But if the time and will allows, there is much to be gained from attempting the latter. As suggested above, students need to be aware of the role of verse in pre-print culture and its dominance until the rise of the novel; at the very least, this can help them to understand the use of verse in Shakespearean drama, but it can also raise a number of other issues about language, literature and culture. A quick, selective romp through the history of English poetry – and the English language – up to the seventeenth century can also be enjoyable and broaden students' literary and linguistic awareness.

Panel 2.1 sets out a sequence of three or four lessons that can be taught as part of an introduction to Shakespeare (although it can be adapted for various purposes). This sequence involves reading and discussing one Old English and two Middle English texts in the original and in translation – an Anglo-Saxon riddle, one stanza of *Sir Gawain and the Green Knight*, and a short extract from the Prologue to *The Canterbury Tales* – followed by a couple of Shakespeare speeches.

Panel 2.1 From Old English to Shakespeare's English

Starter

- Ask the students whether Shakespeare wrote in Old English, Middle English or Modern English. Take a vote. Reveal the correct answer – Modern English. Most students, unless they are exceptionally well informed, are likely to have said 'Old' or 'Middle', and will be surprised.

Old English

- Show students a passage of Old English, for instance a couple of riddles from the Exeter Book (texts and translations easily available online). Get them to try and read it (without looking at the translation). Play a recording of someone reading Old English (there are several YouTube clips and one or two sound files on other sites), or have a go yourself. It is NOT necessary for you to have studied Old English to do this.
- Ask them if they can see any possible similarities with Modern English, or any other languages.
- Show students the translation of the passage. Get them to look again at the original and find similarities between the Modern English and the original Old English. Take suggestions.
- Ask if they notice anything about the sound or layout of the original. Try to draw out:
  — the use of metre (four beats per line, with a caesura halfway through each line). Introduce the idea of metre. What is the purpose of metre? Introduce the idea of the oral tradition – with metre as a mnemonic, rhythmic device before the printed word.
  — the use of alliteration (Anglo-Saxons used alliterative metre, with beats often marked out by alliteration – the origin of alliteration as a device: again, a mnemonic, rhythmic device).
  — that there are fewer words in the old than the new English (Anglo-Saxon was an inflected language, like Modern German – fewer words, more compound words; Modern English is an uninflected language).

Diversion: Origins of poetry and language

Ask students about the origins of poetry or verse. How long has it been around? How did it come about? What was it used for? (Try to draw out ritual, song, dance, storytelling). Emphasise the idea that the novel is a very modern form. Telling stories through verse is more ancient.

This activity can also be extended to a discussion of the origins of language, the spread of people and language around the world, the development of language families, and so on. A PowerPoint slide with a map of the world is helpful here.

Diversion: Origins of Old English

- Ask students where Old English came from, which people brought it to England (Denmark/Germany – Angles, Saxons, Jutes arrived in Britain after the Romans left, c. AD 500. Old English = Anglo-Saxon).
- Ask them which people lived in Britain **before** the Anglo-Saxons invaded, and what languages they spoke (Celts; Celtic languages such as Gaelic, Welsh, Cornish, Manx, Breton [all still spoken]). Use PowerPoint maps of Britain and Europe to illustrate how the Anglo-Saxons (and later Vikings) pushed the Celts out to the west (Scottish islands, Ireland, Wales, Cornwall).

- Students may mention the Romans, so it will be necessary to explain that the Romans came and went during the Celtic period. Although the Romans spoke Latin, the Celts continued to speak Celtic during and after the Roman occupation.

Middle English

- Ask students who the next people to invade England were (Normans, 1066 – though note that there were also Danes and Vikings before 1066, but they were closely related to the Anglo-Saxons and spoke similar languages).
- Ask them what language the Normans spoke (French, derived from Latin). Explain that their language gradually merged with Old English to form Modern English. The intervening 400 years (1066–c.1500) were known as Middle English.
- Show students one stanza from *Sir Gawain and the Green Knight* (the one in which Gawain chops off the Green Knight's head always works well). Get them to try to read it. Ask them how it compares with the Old English. Note its greater similarity with Modern English but its continuing use of features of Old English such as alliterative verse.
- Get them to spot possible meanings/similarities with Modern English, and even attempt to say what happens in the stanza. Read a translation and ask students to look closely at the links between Middle and Modern English.
- Discuss the form of the poem.
- Show students a passage from *The Canterbury Tales* (the description of the Miller in the General Prologue works well). Students will immediately see that this is closer to Modern English. Get them to translate the passage. (You can also get them to *draw* the Miller from his description.)
- Ask them what they notice about the form of *The Canterbury Tales* (iambic pentameter, rhyming couplets – no more Anglo-Saxon alliterative verse).

Diversion: The iambic pentameter

- Explain the significance of the influence of classical metres such as iambic pentameter – based on the ancient Greek and Roman metrical systems. The Greeks and Romans used long metrical lines similar to the iambic pentameter to tell epic stories such as Homer's *Odyssey*, Virgil's *Aeneid* etc. From Chaucer's time, English literature was influenced strongly by classical culture, and since then the iambic pentameter has been at the heart of English verse, replacing Old English alliterative verse as a way of telling stories. (Reintroduce the idea of the oral tradition, metre and rhyme.)
- Explain that the iambic pentameter is the metre closest to ordinary English speech rhythms. Ask students to speculate why poets might have wanted to use a metre close to ordinary speech rhythms to tell long stories.

Modern English

- Look at a passage of simple pentameter in Shakespeare (the Prologue from *Romeo and Juliet* works well). Get students to write their own simple pentameters of ten syllables.
- Ask students to compare Shakespeare's English with Chaucer's. Emphasise that Shakespeare writes in Modern English.

The objectives of this sequence are various, as follows:

a   *To show students what Old English (Anglo-Saxon), Middle English and Early Modern English look like and give them some experience of engaging with such texts.* Although some institutions still teach the few Middle English options which are offered in 16–19 literature courses (e.g. Chaucer, mystery plays), the majority of students no longer study any texts older than Shakespeare; our students should nevertheless have some engagement with these texts, however brief. (Again, it is not necessary for the teacher to know or have studied Old English in order to do this.)

b   *To help them to understand the development of the English language,* such that they understand what it means to call Shakespeare 'Modern English', as many will consider Shakespeare some form of 'Old(e) English(e)'. This can have the added benefit of encouraging them to feel more confident about Shakespeare's language.

c   *To help them to understand the origins of poetry, and poetic form and devices, in oral culture, and its development in literary culture.* The alternative form of metre (alliterative metre) in Anglo-Saxon verse (still being used in some Middle English verse, such as *Sir Gawain and the Green Knight*) is a good starting point for a discussion of the origins of alliteration, rhyme and metre as sound effects and mnemonic and performance devices in oral culture – linking with ideas such as the nature of handwritten scripts and the conditions of outdoor performance in Shakespeare's theatre.

d   *To help them to understand why Shakespeare wrote largely in verse* by illustrating the long oral tradition of public song and storytelling which preceded Shakespeare; perhaps also to open up discussion about why he did not *always* write in verse.

e   *To (re)introduce them to the iambic pentameter and make links between the epic metres of oral culture (e.g. Homer) and Shakespeare.* This also allows them to see the way in which classical traditions of metre replaced Germanic (Anglo-Saxon) traditions in late medieval texts, as exemplified in Chaucer.

f   *To broaden their contextual awareness* by increasing textual experience and making links between literature and general knowledge in history, language and culture.

g   *To engage them in a quick-fire set of textual activities,* which involves close reading and comparison between texts, which contrasts in many ways with set text study, and which gives them a sense of the scope of the subject.

This sequence is clearly particularly related to reading pre-twentieth century literature. Whatever the set poetry text though, it's a good idea to encourage wider reading in the poetry of the period, either by means of independent reading or a short sequence of lessons in class designed to illuminate contemporary trends or concerns in poetry. Such an activity might be placed either as an introductory, pre-reading exercise designed to illuminate the eventual reading of the set text, or as a synoptic, post-reading exercise designed to place the set text in a broader context.

For instance, when teaching poems by W. H. Auden, it is effective to precede the detailed study of the set selection of poems with informal study of a small selection of influential modernist poems from T. S. Eliot to Dylan Thomas, in order to draw out some of the features of modernism, followed by informal study of a group of Auden's poems which are not part of the set selection. By the time they start formal set-text study, students have already discovered a number of contexts in which they can understand the set poems and a number of texts with which they can make comparisons. In addition, when teaching any modernist poetry, one might teach a brief sequence which takes modernist art as a starting point for an exploration of the complexity of ambiguity in modern poetry (discussed in detail in the section below).

Teaching about reading poetry: the pleasures and interpretive processes of poetry

> I know that some of the poetry to which I am most devoted is poetry which I did not understand at first reading; some is poetry which I am not sure I understand yet.
>
> (Eliot 1933: 144)

> The ordinary reader, when warned against the obscurity of a poem, is apt to be thrown into a state of consternation very unfavourable to poetic receptivity.
>
> (Eliot 1933: 150)

Above, we spoke of the need for students to understand the life of poetry outside the classroom, and to develop a growing awareness of the interaction between reader and writer. Billy Collins' image of poetry being tied down and tortured to extract meaning from it is particularly resonant here as it identifies the way in which students often instantly reduce the reading of a poem to a search for its meaning, forgetting that a poem is a great deal *more than* its meaning. Once meaning is identified, or even possibly before that, the 'technique-spotting' (of which so many examiners complain) begins, often with little sense of why these techniques might be effective in the context of the whole poem. Again, this might perhaps be partly a result of routines learnt in pre-16 English; in the UK, at this level, the structure and conditions of the course, leading to essays (written at speed under exam conditions) on several poems from a large anthology of previously learnt set poems, might sometimes seem to reward this kind of reductive approach, especially given the sort of pressurised cramming that this encourages.

However, we should remember, too, that it is in many ways quite natural for students with little experience of poetry outside the English classroom to need to be *taught* about the significance of language, form and structure, and about the aesthetic appeal and functions of poetry. More importantly, they need to be given the opportunity to experience these for themselves away from the pressure of responding to the high-stakes set texts.

When beginning to work on poetry with students, it is helpful to introduce them to the idea of the aesthetic 'impact' of a poem, and teach them that an awareness of this impact – the impact of the text as a whole work of art – is likely to be crucial to their response. An effective way to make this idea come alive is through art, and it's an exercise that also raises important issues about the nature of interpretation and its role in aesthetic pleasure. Panel 2.2 sets out a sequence of two or three lessons along these lines. This sequence involves inviting students to discuss freely their responses to a number of modernist paintings, all of which offer resistance to straightforward interpretation, and then to make comparisons with a similarly resistant poem.

Panel 2.2   Interpreting art and poetry

Stage 1: Responses to art

Give students (working in groups) sheets with photocopies of modernist art works. A selection that works well is Kandinsky's 'Sketch for Composition IV'; Dali's 'Apparition of Face and Fruit-dish on a Beach'; Pollock's 'Number 14', Mondrian's 'Composition with Yellow, Red and Blue', and Munch's 'The Scream' – though many pictures by these painters and others will do as well. The selection is designed to represent a set of different modes of expressionism, from the sinister surrealism of the Dali, to the faux-childhood naivety of the Kandinsky, from the ordered geometry of the Mondrian to the haphazard splatters of the Pollock. (The Munch is there because students are likely to know it and because of its connection with the poem they will look at later.)

Ask students to discuss their responses to and feelings about the paintings in groups. In class discussion afterwards, ask students to talk about their responses and feelings and/or explain what their groups talked about. It usually works to start by asking which paintings students like and which they do not, and attempt to draw out reasons. It should be easy to draw out the following issues as discussion progresses:

- Responses will be a mixture of the *sensual* – responding to the image, colour, texture, geometry etc. – and the *intellectual* – responding to possible meanings or ideas about the nature of the art.
- On the whole, viewers of visual art are likely to be less concerned with establishing 'a meaning', and more with the *aesthetic impact* of a work. They are also more likely to value the sensual, enjoying *ambiguity* in meaning and seeing it as part of the aesthetic impact.
- Unless they are art critics or advanced art students, the *primary* aesthetic impact of a painting is likely to be the most significant, or only, encounter with the work.
- Although viewers may speculate about possible meanings, it is usually impossible to establish a specific meaning for a painting; the *intention* of the painter remains largely undeterminable, especially in modernism.

Having discussed the paintings, ask students to assign titles to them. Then reveal the actual titles and discuss the implications of the students' titles and the actual titles for responding to the paintings.

Stage 2: Responses to poetry

Now give students a poem to discuss. 'Lineage' by Ted Hughes from *Crow* works well because of its deliberate ambiguity. Ask students to discuss their responses to the poem. Discussion will almost certainly focus on the meaning of the poem, but again – in class discussion afterwards – start by asking whether students liked the poem or not, and attempt to draw out reasons. (Students often find it harder to express a like or dislike for the poem than they did for the paintings, preferring to focus on analysis.)

Discussion of the meaning will almost certainly focus on trying to establish a logic for the list in the first half of the poem. Students may identify a religious or philosophical stance in the poem, perhaps suggesting that it is atheist, but there is likely to be considerable disagreement and uncertainty. Draw students' attention to the title of the poem and its role in interpretation.

Try to draw students away from discussion of meaning to consideration of the poem as a work of art. What is its aesthetic impact? What did they feel about it on first reading? Is the process of analysis necessary for an enjoyment or appreciation of the poem? Is it necessary to 'understand' the poem in order to enjoy it? Is it necessary to enjoy it in order to study it? What is the purpose of poetry? Who might be the intended audience for the poem, apart from students in an English lesson? In any case, is it possible to establish a meaning for the poem? Who has the authority to say what the poem means? It's crucial to stress that, although the teacher might be able to suggest, with some authority, a meaning for the poem, the work does not and cannot wholly depend on the identification of meaning for its effect; nor can the teacher 'know' the 'meaning' of the poem.

Stage 3: Comparisons and conclusions

Now ask students to compare the poem with the paintings. Are there any elements of the paintings that are similar to the poem in terms of form, style or meaning? Have their discussions of the paintings and the poem suggested any similarities between art and poetry? Has their view of poetry changed at all? The paintings and the poem have been chosen in order to highlight issues about aesthetic impact and ambiguity, so students should easily be able to draw out elements of each. Finally, ask students to discuss what they have learnt about aesthetic impact and ambiguity through these activities, and/or to discuss the following statements:

1   The sensual impact of poetry is as important as its meaning.
2   Poetry is not intended to be studied in the classroom.
3   There are good reasons for studying poetry in the classroom.
4   Ambiguity in art is pleasurable.
5   We can never know the meaning of a work of art.

6   Just because we can never know the meaning of a work of art does not mean that any meaning will do.
7   The job of the English teacher is to tell us the meaning of the poem.

Again, the objectives of this sequence are various:

a   *To open up a relatively free space for discussion of aesthetic tastes and responses.* This exercise can be a great icebreaker. Students are likely in some ways to feel less inhibited in discussing art than poetry, partly since most will not have been expected to study art in school in the way they have studied poetry. More importantly, the non-verbal nature of art allows students to focus more on their *feelings* about the work, rather than on the search for meaning – and one of the key purposes of this sequence is to encourage students to respond in more broadly aesthetic (rather than purely intellectual) ways to poetry.

b   *To raise issues about the nature of ambiguity.* The key point here is that all of these paintings – and the poem – use ambiguity deliberately as part of the aesthetic project of the works. Many students feel very suspicious of ambiguity in poetry, seeing it as a test, a puzzle they have to solve; in art, they are more likely to find pleasure in this ambiguity, or at least to accept that not being able to find a 'solution' does not negate the aesthetic impact of the work or the value of the process of trying to find meaning.

c   *To highlight the significance of titles.* The titles of these five pictures – and to some extent the poem – deliberately refuse any substantial help with establishing a concrete interpretation, but rather force the reader to accept the deliberate ambiguity, and place the onus on the reader to interpret. Students should be able to see the significance of titles in guiding interpretation.

d   *To raise issues about the role of the reader in interpretation.* Building on the previous point, this exercise asks students to think about whether the authority for meaning lies with the artist/writer, or with the reader. In relation to the art, students should be able clearly to see that, even were the artist to be available to answer questions about the meaning of the work, establishing a single meaning might be difficult if not impossible, and that – in 'real-world' conditions of artistic consumption, rather than in the classroom – the onus is on the reader to interpret.

e   *To raise issues about the authority of the English teacher.* Again, following on from the previous point, this can lead to a valuable discussion about where students might go if they wanted to understand more about the meaning of a work, and how such understandings are established. A key point here is whether the English teacher is the final authority in the classroom (Dias and Hayhoe 1988: 7). Does the teacher 'know the meaning' and spoon-feed it to the students? Or is the teacher's job rather to guide students through the process of interpretation? What additional knowledge, skill or experience might teachers have which makes them an authority?

f   *To raise issues about the motivation and craft of the writer.* In addition to the issues discussed above, students are likely to want to discuss the unconventional approaches to expression adopted by these artists, and whether there is value to them. Some students might be outraged: 'I could have done that'; 'a three-year-old could have done that' etc.

This can lead to a consideration of why artists/writers choose to use certain styles and modes of expression.

g   *To steer students towards an understanding of the importance of the sensual impact of poetry* – sound, colour, shape, pattern etc. – as well as its intellectual impact ('meaning'). Many students will talk about what they like or dislike in the way the paintings look, or about how the paintings make them feel; elements of colour, shape, texture and pattern are likely to emerge as features of the aesthetic appeal of the paintings, and a sense should emerge of how each painting might have a sensual and possibly emotional impact on certain viewers. Students can begin to see how this might also apply in some ways to the poem.

This sequence of lessons has the potential to transform the way students approach poetry in the classroom, especially if the ideas are revisited once formal study of poetry is undertaken. Further, it provides an introduction to certain more general ideas about interpretation, which can be developed further in relation to work on all kinds of texts and when beginning to discuss critical positions and perspectives in literary theory.

Teaching about the definition and purpose of poetry

The questions 'What is poetry?' and 'Why poetry?' are also very useful ways to get students to consider the nature of the form and to develop a more profound understanding of what poems do, as well as of the differences and similarities between poetry and other forms and uses of language (Andrews 1991).

Panel 2.3 sets out a sequence of activities that offers a variety of ways of defining poetry – both on its own terms and by defining it against the concepts 'prose', 'rhetoric', 'verse' and 'lyrics', using examples of all those forms and testing them against poems. There's also a very simple exercise that asks students to think about the function(s) of poetry by getting them to ask what a poem does beyond delivering a message or narrative.

Panel 2.3   Defining poetry and poetic language

Starter

Ask students to work in pairs to come up with a definition of poetry; it is in fact almost impossible to do so. Most offered descriptions – about self-expression, description etc. – will be applicable to prose too; and many – about rhyme and metre, for instance – will not be applicable to all poetry. In fact, the only really workable definition of poetry is 'writing in verse', although, of course, even that might be disputed. The following exercises are designed to examine these issues further. Each exercise could be given to a different group in the class, or all the exercises to all groups.

1. Poetry v. prose

Ask students to discuss the differences between poetry and prose. Then, introduce the idea of poetic language, and ask them to define or give examples of it. Show them examples of 'found' poems (see Abbs 1990 for instance) and/or William Carlos Williams' poem, 'This is Just to Say' – all of which play with the distinction between prose and poetry – to focus them on the nature of poetic and non-poetic language, and the differences between prose and poetry. Finally, prepare examples of poetry transformed into prose, i.e. laid out on the page as prose, and ask students to compare the original poem with the prose version. What difference does the different layout make? Is it possible to define the language as prosaic or poetic? Prose poetry (e.g. Heaney's collection *Stations*) is useful here, too.

2. Poetry v. rhetoric

Show students the following text and a copy of Martin Luther King's 'I have a dream' speech and ask them to discuss whether or not they are poetry:

> *Born to reveal*
> *the woman you've become.*
> *Not just a perfume*
> *A rite of passage.*
> *Valentino.*

3. Poetry v. song

Show students the lyrics of a number of pop songs. Paul McCartney's lyrics have been published as part of Faber's poetry imprint so one of his songs would be a good choice. As suggested in the introduction to this chapter, Amy Winehouse, Bob Dylan and Eminem are also effective choices. Ask students to discuss whether these are poetry, and why they think the definition might be disputed. Are there any examples of lyrics that students think are definitely NOT poetry?

You may want to show students the notorious Cambridge Tripos question which asked students to compare 'As you came from the holy land', a lyric poem by Sir Walter Raleigh, with lyrics by Amy Winehouse ('Love is a Losing Game'), Billie Holiday ('Fine and Mellow') and Bob Dylan ('Boots of Spanish Leather'). An internet search for 'Winehouse' and 'Raleigh' brings up some interesting commentary on the issue, which could be shared with students.

4. Poetry v. verse

a   Show students a section of verse dialogue and a soliloquy from a Shakespeare play. Are these poetry? Are they poems? And/or are they verse?

b   Show students a selection of verses from greetings cards. Are they poetry? And/or verse?

Finally: Why poetry?

Ask students to discuss the question 'Why poetry?': What is it for? Why is it valued? What useful functions might it fulfil? Show them the following texts, and ask them to discuss the difference in function and effect between the two sets of words:

a   The words *'War is bad'* and the complete text of Wilfred Owen's 'Anthem for Doomed Youth'.
b   The words *'The six hundred soldiers rode on bravely with gunshot all around them despite the danger that faced them'* and the complete text of Tennyson's 'The Charge of the Light Brigade'.
c   The words 'Happy Birthday' and the verse:

> *I'm wishing you this birthday*
> *All the joy in the world*
> *Surprises, fun and laughter*
> *As another year's unfurled*
> *I wish you all the very best,*
> *As I have in other years.*
> *Sharing with your happiness*
> *Love and joyous tears.*

The objectives here are:

a   *To challenge conventional and simplistic ideas about the nature of poetry.*
b   *To highlight the fact that 'poetic' language may be found in many types of writing, not just in 'poetry'.*
c   *To highlight the fact that the layout of words on the page affects the way they are read.*
d   *To clarify the formal distinctions and aesthetic values that underlie distinctions between poetry, verse and prose.*
e   *To highlight the links between poetry, music and art, and to increase awareness of the role of pleasure in poetry.*

Other wider reading and thinking activities

In addition to such structured activity, designed to raise issues about the reading of poetry and help students to become more critical readers, there are many less formal, less directed approaches which can be adopted to encourage students to become more experienced and confident readers and interpreters of poetry, and perhaps also to locate what they – and others – personally find enjoyable in poetry. Of course, time is always against such informal activities, which tend to be only indirectly related to the business of covering set texts; but, again, they can pay dividends later.

Chief amongst these is the informal selection of poems by students – perhaps for reading and/or performance to the class, perhaps for publication in a personal or class anthology

– which can do a great deal to build students' image of themselves as independent readers of poetry. Poetry book boxes can be tremendously useful here, and the process of preparing readings of favourite poems can be valuable, too. It would be wise to ensure that students have clear guidelines and are encouraged to be adventurous in their choices.

Other potentially valuable activities include:

- shadowing poetry competitions (for instance by taking part in the T. S. Eliot Prize Shadowing Scheme, run by the English and Media Centre for 16–19 students in conjunction with the Poetry Book Society);
- getting students to interview parents, grandparents, friends etc. about their own feelings about and experiences of poetry, and/or their favourite poems;
- gathering reviews of recent poetry books from the review pages of newspapers and asking students to discuss what the reviewers seem to enjoy or find valuable in poetry;
- attending local poetry readings or performances and, most valuable of all, getting poets to visit school and work with students; alternatively, use available media resources such as *The Poetry Archive* and *The Poetry Channel* (both online) to bring performance into the classroom;
- displaying poetry posters in the classroom; particularly attractive are *Poems on the Underground*, which can be bought on subscription.

Teaching about writing poetry: the craft of poetry and the elements of poetic form

Above, we have suggested approaches that are designed to widen students' experience of poetry and their broad understanding of its various forms and functions, and to boost their confidence in reading poetry. It's also, however, vital that they should understand something of the nitty-gritty of poetic form and other elements of the craft of the poet.

In working with 16–19 students, undergraduates, teacher trainees and practising teachers in a variety of contexts outside school, we have often found that they have studied many poems but never been taught or achieved a coherent overview of the elements of poetic form or the agency of the poet; alternatively, they may have understood the elements of poetic form but never quite *connected* this with the agency of the poet. There's a sense in which, for many, poetic form remains a mystery, a shadowy force lurking behind the surface of poems. Perhaps we harbour a fear that if we *demystify* poetic form, we will somehow become less susceptible to the *power* of poetry? Rather, however, we find that when we equip students with such knowledge they become more confident readers, more alert to the dynamics of poetry.

Understanding form

With all 16–19 groups, it is helpful to teach the rudiments of poetic form before beginning detailed study of set texts. Panel 2.4 sets out the basic elements of form that students at this level need to know. One might talk through these elements with students and ensure that they have the document for future reference.

Panel 2.4   Understanding poetic form

The form of a poem is the way it is constructed in terms of stanzas, shape, layout, rhyme and metre. Much modern poetry tends to play down or ignore elements such as stanza, rhyme and metre, using 'free verse', and so often gives the appearance of being spontaneous and free-flowing. This is partly why poetry has gained a reputation for being about personal, emotional, spontaneous self-expression. But it is vital to understand that poets in fact usually write very carefully and deliberately, crafting their work, and often writing many drafts before they reach a final version, whether or not they use rhyme and metre. The poem may still be a powerful form of self-expression originating in spontaneous imaginative impulses, but the form of a poem is usually carefully chosen and structured, as is the combination of words contained within the form.

Different types of poetic form: regularity v. irregularity

The form of any poem can be described by identifying or describing the number and length of stanzas, the line lengths, and the use of rhyme and metre (although, of course, not all poems use rhyme or metre).

- A poem may have a *regular* form, in which each stanza has the same number of lines, the same rhyme and metre etc. There are also some traditional 'set' forms such as limericks, sonnets, haikus and so on, which have a set number of lines with specific rhythms, rhyme schemes or lengths.
- On the other hand, poems may have a wholly or partially *irregular* form, in which there is little or no regularity in rhyme, metre or layout.
- Until the twentieth century, almost all poetry was written in *regular* forms. Many modern poets, however, have enjoyed the freedom of *irregularity*, although many others have continued to use regular forms, either in a traditional way or in a new or experimental way.
- In *regular* forms, the rhyme and metre can dominate, especially where lines and stanzas are short. The longer the lines and stanzas, the less dominant the rhyme and metre are likely to be. Poetry that is regular in line length, metre and/or stanza length, but which has *no rhyme*, is called **blank verse.** Poets may use blank verse if they want to have a regular structure but don't want rhyme to dominate the poem, often in longer, more serious or reflective poetry.
- Modern poets often use *irregular* forms to make rhyme, metre, line length or stanza length even less dominant or noticeable, and to give the impression of freedom or spontaneity. Completely irregular poetry – with no regularity of stanza length, line length, etc. – is called **free verse.** However, poets will sometimes continue to use rhyme, metre and so on, but will attempt to draw attention away from the regularity of form by hiding, disguising or subverting the metre or rhyme scheme.

Lines of poetry: end-stopping, enjambement and caesura

Sometimes the grammatical sentences in a poem fit exactly onto the lines and stanzas. Where the end of a sentence coincides with the end of a line, this is known as **end-stopping**. Sometimes, however, the sentences run onto a new line, or even a new stanza. This is known as **enjambement.** By contrast, a sentence may finish in the *middle* of a line, creating a pause – or a pause may be necessitated in some other way. This is known as a **caesura**. Both enjambement and caesura can create a tension between the artificial constraint of the form and the natural length of the sentences, drawing attention away from the regularity of the form.

Rhyme and other sound effects

There are different kinds of rhyme. 'Full' rhymes are the traditional kind – for instance, where 'boat' rhymes with 'goat'. However, many modern poets use 'half rhymes' of various kinds, often again to draw attention away from the regularity of the poem's form:

Full rhyme	boat	rhymes with	goat	
Half rhyme	boat	rhymes with	got	
Vowel rhyme	boat	rhymes with	toad	*(assonance)*
Consonant rhyme	boat	rhymes with	boot	*(consonance)*
Visual rhyme	come	rhymes with	home	

Sometimes there are rhymes or sound effects within a line rather than at the end of a line:

Assonance	vowel rhyme, e.g. 'ground down'
Consonance	consonant rhyme, e.g. 'creak and croak'
Alliteration	a form of consonance using consonant rhyme at the *beginnings* of words, e.g. 'gravelly ground'
Onomatopoeia	words or phrases that sound like the thing they describe, e.g. 'rattle' and 'crackle'. Onomatopoeia is often created or reinforced by assonance and/or consonance
Euphony	pleasing sounds – usually long vowels, soft consonants, e.g. 'soothing and mellifluous music'
Cacophony	harsh sounds – usually short vowels, hard consonants, e.g. 'they clashed on the bare black cliff'

The number of syllables that rhyme can also have an effect:

Single syllable rhyme	thorn, scorn
Double syllable rhyme	water, daughter
Triple syllable rhyme	prettily, wittily

Single rhymes are heavier; double rhymes are lighter; triple rhymes are usually humorous.

Metre

Most metre in Western culture derives from ancient Greek and Roman poetry. In English verse, it is usually measured *rhythmically*, in which case the important element is the number of *beats* or *stresses* in a line. The number of beats and stresses is also strongly connected with the number of syllables.

There are various types of metre, but the most commonly used is the iambic pentameter.

- 'Iambic' refers to the basic unit or 'measure' of the metre, the iamb, an unstressed syllable followed by a stressed one: 'di-**dum**'. Different metres are composed mainly of different units, e.g. iambs (di-**dum**), trochees (**dum**-di), dactyls (**dum**-di-di), spondees (**dum-dum**).
- Each unit of a metre in a line of verse is known as a 'foot'. 'Pentameter' refers to the number of feet in the line. In a pentameter, there are five feet. So an iambic pentameter has five iambic feet. Other line lengths include tetrameters (four feet), trimeters (three feet) and dimeters (two feet).

Metre is a very complex subject and at this point it is not necessary for you to know much about it, though it is useful to be able to recognise an Iambic Pentameter. It's also important to be aware that the *metre* of a line of verse is not necessarily the same as the *rhythm* of the poem: skilled poets often use *natural speech rhythms* and *sentence structures* to *override* the artificial constraints of the metre or draw attention away from it.

At this point, of course, the knowledge remains abstract; for students to benefit from it, they must immediately see it in action. A good poem to reinforce and allow students to practise applying the ideas is Ted Hughes' 'Wind'. Doubtless many other poems would be just as good, but this particular poem is a veritable *compendium* of poetic form, the elements used in a powerful way, which can be linked explicitly with the meanings of the poem. The poem introduces students to the idea that poets consciously manipulate rhyme, metre, stanza and line in sometimes powerful and unexpected ways for particular effects, which might be integral to the meanings of the poem.

After a whole-class discussion of the overall meaning and effect of the poem, divide the class into groups to talk about the elements of form in the poem, using the reference sheet as a guide, and in whole-class discussion afterwards attempt to draw out from them the ways in which Hughes has shaped the poem through the elements of form. This discussion never fails to be revelatory, and it's always particularly interesting to see students' reaction (usually sceptical at first) to the idea that the poem – which at first sight seems not to rhyme at all – in fact rhymes throughout, though almost entirely in half-rhymes. Discussion of the use of rhyme, metre and enjambement usually leads to the students identifying the possible link between Hughes' deliberately 'chaotic' use of elements of form with the overarching theme of the poem, the power of strong winds to threaten and deform the landscape – though it might be necessary explicitly to ask the question, 'How might these things be connected with the meaning of the poem?', in order to finally draw this out. It's useful to end this discussion by asking students if their attitude to or understanding of the significance of poetic form has changed, and how.

An activity such as that described above is useful in providing a starting point for a greater awareness of form. The lessons from this can then be reinforced and developed through other poems as encountered; or other poems can be chosen particularly for the insight into form they might afford. For instance, Thom Gunn's poems 'Considering the Snail' and 'The Human Condition' are useful for illustrating further ways in which form and meaning might be explicitly linked.

The isolated block stanzas of 'The Human Condition' powerfully reflect the message of the poem that 'each of us is condemned to be an individual', whilst the arrangement of lines in 'Considering the Snail' – each line doggedly sticking to seven syllables regardless of the grammatical structure of the sentences contained within them – suggests the 'slow passion' behind the 'deliberate progress' of the snail. A great exercise to do with 'Considering the Snail', and one that can be done with many other poems, is to present the poem in three or four different forms and ask students to discuss which they think is the authentic one, and why. It's perhaps particularly effective with this poem because of Gunn's unorthodox decision to measure the lines syllabically, but regardless of the poem used this activity always raises students' awareness of the way in which the arrangement of lines in poetry affects the way we read it.

Understanding tone

Again, the idea of tone (relevant, of course, to all kinds of text, not just poetry) can be taught through any number of poems, but it's valuable to plan to raise students' awareness of tone through poems in which tone is of particular interest. A poem that lends itself particularly well is Sylvia Plath's 'The Bee Meeting'. Tone is arguably one of the most interesting aspects of all Plath's poetry, and it's not that the tone of *this* poem is more interesting than in many of Plath's other poems. What's particularly interesting about 'The Bee Meeting' is that an analogue text is available to read in parallel with the poem – a short extract from Plath's diary (published in her book *Johnny Panic and the Bible of Dreams*, 1979) which recounts the same events as recounted in the poem, but in an entirely different form and in a very different tone. The following pairs of corresponding extracts from the poem and the diary demonstrate the transformation which Plath effects in writing the poem using her diary notes as a starting point. Asking students to compare the diary entry with the poem is a valuable exercise, which can lead to some quite powerful revelations about the nature of tone and how poets deliberately combine words in particular ways to create tone.

Diary entry – extract 1
Everybody was holding a bee-hat, some with netting of nylon, most with box screening, some with khaki round hats. I felt barer and barer. People became concerned. Have you no hat? Have you no coat? Then a dry little woman came up, Mrs B, the secretary of the society. She went to her car and came back with a small silk button-down smock, the sort pharmacist's assistants use. I put it on and buttoned it and felt more protected...

(Plath 1979: 241)

Poem – extract 1
I am nude as a chicken neck, does nobody love me?
Yes, here is the secretary of bees with her white shop smock,
Buttoning the cuffs at my wrists and the slit from my neck to my knees.
Now I am milkweed silk, the bees will not notice.
They will not smell my fear, my fear, my fear.

(Plath 1965)

Diary entry – extract 2
We threaded our way through neatly weeded allotment gardens, one with bits of
tinfoil and a fan of black and white feathers on a string, very decorative, to scare the
birds, and twiggy lean-tos over the plants. Black-eyed sweetpea-like blooms: broad-
beans, somebody said...

(Plath 1979: 241)

Poem – extract 2
Strips of tinfoil winking like people,
Feather dusters fanning their hands in a sea of bean flowers,
Creamy bean flowers with black eyes and leaves like bored hearts.
Is it blood clots the tendrils are dragging up that string?
No, no, it is scarlet flowers that will one day be edible.

(Plath 1965)

A similar exercise – though focused less on tone and more on the general idea of the agency
of the poet – can be undertaken by comparing the various drafts of Wilfred Owen's 'Anthem
for Doomed Youth', which are available online at www.oucs.ox.ac.uk/ww1lit, the website
of the Oxford First World War Poetry Digital Archive. Sue Dymoke's book *Drafting and
Assessing Poetry: A Guide for Teachers* (2002) also contains many valuable examples of poets'
drafting processes (and is an invaluable introduction to issues in the teaching of poetry).

Understanding imagery

Often, students have little difficulty in seeing individual images in poetry, but need help
(a) to spell out the metaphorical significances of the images, and (b) to see that the images
in a poem might be connected, drawing on the same metaphorical field. Ted Hughes'
'Wind', discussed above, is an excellent example of a poem where most of the images
metaphorically reinforce one idea – in this instance, the instability of otherwise stable
objects in the face of an exceptional force. Understanding what connects the images leads
to a fuller understanding of the poem. Isolating the imagery in a poem and asking students
to discuss what the images have in common can therefore be an effective method to use to
reveal the poet at work.

A similar approach might be to examine the images before reading the poem – an approach
that can be demonstrated effectively with Seamus Heaney's poem 'Blackberry Picking'. The
following is a list of selected images from the poem:

clot, flesh, thickened, blood, stains, tongue, lust, inked, hunger, scratched, bleached,
burned, eyes, sticky, fur, fungus, glutting, stinking, sour, rot.

Put these on the board, and ask students to discuss what kind of poem this might be. Even better, ask students to *write* a poem, or a passage of prose, using all these words. The results are likely to verge on the obscene! Then reveal that the poem is, after all, 'only' about blackberry-picking; this will set up a lively discussion of why such images might nevertheless be appropriate and effective in such a surprising context.

Active reading, creative writing

In the exercises above, we are aiming to help students to see beyond the surface of the poem, to reconstruct the acts of poetic imagination that have taken place in the creation of a poem, and thus to understand better the interaction that takes place between reader and writer. These exercises are effective, but perhaps there is no more powerful method than actually getting students to engage in creative writing themselves – see Chapter 7 for further discussion.

Mention creative writing, and English teachers are liable to quake, imagining, perhaps, lengthy and complex workshops, nightmares of differential abilities and attitudes, and the exposure of the teacher as a charlatan with no creative faculty. But the truth is that creative writing used for particular ends in poetry teaching can be simple, directed and accessible to all – and is often most effective when carefully structured. A few short activities can be enough to teach specific aspects of poetry and to give students a feel for what it is like to write poetry. Simple writing exercises can be dropped into lessons, or used as very effective 'starters'.

For instance, some of the exercises described above based on specific texts can be easily transformed into active reading/creative writing exercises – as in the examination of imagery in Heaney's 'Blackberry Picking' discussed above. The exercise on tone in relation to Plath's poem 'The Bee Meeting', also described above, could likewise be adapted, with students actually being asked to rewrite the events of the poem in a different tone. The exercise on form in relation to Gunn's 'Considering the Snail' could lead to students experimenting with other ways of laying the text out on the page.

Quick and simple creative writing exercises do not have to be anchored to a specific text, however. Tightly controlled writing exercises designed simply to give students an insight into what might be going on in the mind of a poet can be very effective. The possibilities are endless. For instance, at a recent seminar, the poet Mandy Coe asked those present to suggest words and phrases they might associate with, or use to describe, snow. A long list duly appeared on the board. She then asked everyone to write a poem about snow *without* using ANY of those words: a superb lesson in how a poet might summon original and striking imagery by avoiding the obvious and embracing the metaphorical.

Such exercises can be used to make students more familiar with formal aspects of poetry, too. For instance, Stephen Fry's book *The Ode Less Travelled* (2005) – a valuable resource – is full of amusing exercises involving writing iambic pentameters, ballad stanzas and so on, many of which can be tackled easily by students at this level. It's even worth having a go yourself at more difficult tasks such as writing a sonnet: even if the students (and you?) fail, it provides a valuable insight into the mechanics of the form.

Performance

So far, the approaches to teaching poetry we have discussed have focused on poetry on the page. The kind of poetry that tends to inhabit advanced literature syllabuses is generally experienced, 'in real life', through private, silent, page-limited reading, and perhaps particularly so now that reading poetry aloud together is no longer the fashionable social activity it might have been in certain circles in previous centuries. Nevertheless, there are very good reasons for thinking beyond this position when we plan what to do in the classroom.

Hearing or seeing poetry read and performed are still popular and social ways of experiencing poetry; indeed, there are probably more poetry readings by poets than at any previous time in history – in reading groups, bookshops, poetry societies and festivals. Recordings of poetry readings, whether on CD or through the radio and the internet, are at least as popular as (and certainly more accessible than) they have ever been, perhaps particularly archive recordings of poets reading their own work. We should also note that there exists today a dynamic tradition of poetry performance, which in some respects inhabits the middle space between 'literary' and 'popular' verse. Somewhere between the world of rap and the world of 'poetry', there is, on the one hand, the balladry of the singer-songwriter, and, on the other, the showmanship of 'slam' poets and performance poets.

What all these performances have in common is a concern with poetry as sound, as communication and as a social and physical experience. Thus, despite the silent and private nature of most poetry reading, it's clear that there are many advantages to hearing it read and seeing it performed, both for the general reader and for the student and teacher of poetry.

First, and most obviously, hearing and seeing poetry read and performed can bring the rhythms and sound patterns of verse to life in ways that can be difficult to recreate in the classroom, however well the teacher reads. Crucially, this can help students to learn to 'hear' poetry when they read it, and to understand an aspect of the aesthetic – the musical – appeal of poetry that might otherwise be difficult to access. It might also create a stronger link in students' minds between the poetry they study in school and the oral culture and folk song of the past and present. (As suggested earlier, this can also be powerfully achieved by introducing song lyrics into the poetry classroom.)

Second, the experience of poetry as live communication and as a physical, multimodal phenomenon that exists in the social realm can be a powerful motivator and teacher, both in its more literary and its more popular manifestations. The late lamented Simon Powell, founder of *Poetry Live!*, was proud of the fact that his poetry readings had brought thousands of students into contact with real-life poets, an opportunity he had never had when at school (Powell 2009). The work of performance and slam poets, meanwhile, has captured the imagination of many young people outside formal education, creating a bridge between poetry and pop culture, opening up a space where poetry can be relatively accessible, open and utterly contemporary.

How can we capitalise on all this in the classroom? First, by bringing audio recordings into the classroom, whether on CD or from the internet. A particularly rich resource is *The Poetry Archive* (www.poetryarchive.org), which contains a wealth of readings by poets of their own work and even includes historical recordings such as Tennyson reading 'The Charge of the Light Brigade'. YouTube and other more dedicated sites (such as the English and Media Centre's *Poetry Station* at www.englishandmedia.co.uk) can also bring film recordings into the classroom. One word of caution: not all poets reading their own work are inspiring – though many are. Whether inspiring or not, hearing them read can nevertheless sometimes (though not always!) illuminate their work in interesting ways.

Second, by engaging students in performance themselves. Group readings/performances of poems can motivate students, but they can also be a way for students to demonstrate their understanding of and response to poems: ask students to ensure that their performances reflect the tone, structure and/or sound patterns of the poem – for instance, through the way they divide the lines between speakers, position themselves on stage or adapt the poem to create particular emphases. These performances can also provide a good focus for class discussion.

Third, by getting students to reflect on how visual and textual renderings of poems could illuminate their meanings. One approach here is to get students to plan and perhaps 'storyboard' a film or stage version of a poem, suggesting both the images and sounds that will make up the scenes. There are good examples of such filmic renderings available online, for instance, on YouTube. Students' choices about how to represent the characters, settings, voices, themes, sounds, structures and language of the poem are likely to prompt lively discussion, and at advanced level have considerable scope for revealing symbolic meaning. An alternative, used with undergraduates by one university lecturer in the UK, is to get students to use a computer program to animate the text of a poem using different fonts, patterns and soundtrack.

Teaching poems

Exactly how one chooses to teach poetry at this level is likely to depend to a great extent on what the desired outcome is in relation to examination or coursework assessment. Our argument in the previous sections has been that, regardless of such final outcomes, all students need to be taught about 'poetry', not just about a series of selected poems, and to read more widely in poetry than just those selected poems. However, time is usually limited and the specific demands of assessment usually pressing, and at some point teachers and students will need to shift to a more specific focus, whether that is the study of a set text, or whether it is preparation for response to unseen poetry.

Unseen poetry or set text?

If response to *unseen poetry* is the final outcome, then the kind of activities described above will need to form a substantial part of the study, since what is being primarily assessed is the ability of the student to apply what s/he knows about *poetry* to a specific unseen poem. As well as covering the topics indicated above, it's important to ensure that students read a range of different types of poem so that they are prepared for the possible range of types that might be set in the exam. Thus, one might plan to ensure that they look at examples of different forms of verse, including free verse (both of the relatively unstructured and of the relatively structured sort), blank verse, verse using traditional stanza forms, metre and rhyme, verse using modernist variations on traditional metre and rhyme, set forms such as sonnets and villanelles; different periods of verse; verse reflecting a range of different themes and tones; and verse reflecting a range of different modes – from, for instance, the highly metaphorical to the rather more literal.

Another important part of teaching towards unseen response is to equip students with a routine for reading and responding to a previously unseen poem. There is no one absolute method; nor is it sensible to dictate a single method to students, when many will feel more comfortable doing it in their own way. Nevertheless, a set of guidelines, such as laid out in Panel 2.5, is a valuable starting point. The crucial factor, as suggested above, is for students to try to remember when reading the poem that it is an artwork crafted by a poet, intended to have a sensual and intellectual impact on an audience, and open to exploration and challenge by a critical reader, rather than merely a puzzle to be solved in an exam.

Panel 2.5   Routine for poetry analysis:
IMPACT – CONTENT – FORM

1   The most important thing about a poem is its **IMPACT** – its *aesthetic* effect on the reader, both *sensual and intellectual*. After first reading, think about your own response to the SOUNDS, PATTERNS, IMAGES, RHYTHMS, SHAPES and COLOURS of the poem, as well as its MEANING, THEME and NARRATIVE. Read again slowly.

- Try to *hear* the poem in your head. Imagine the poem is a painting in an art gallery and try to *visualise* it like that.
- Think about whether the poem has an overarching *message or theme*.
- Try to notice the *form and structure* of the poem, and how it *develops* from beginning to end.
- Look at *the title* of the poem to see how it relates to the poem as a whole.

2   Ask the following questions about the **CONTENT** and meaning of the poem:

- **What is the poem about?** It could be (a) a description of, or reflection on, a place, person or event; (b) something more serious and philosophical about life or relationships or the nature of the world; or (c) something more light-hearted and playful, perhaps playing with language or humour. There may be other options. It could be a mixture of all three. Any clues about *where and when* the poem is set/ written?
- **What is happening in the poem?** A poem almost always *develops* in some way. It may tell a story or portray a dramatic situation, which leads to a final event where something has changed in a way that might produce an emotional reaction. Or it may follow a series of thoughts to end up with a new idea that allows you to understand something differently. It may ask a question or pose a problem that it then gradually answers. It may describe a relationship or a person or place about which you eventually understand something new. Does it have a particular *mood?*
- **Whose voices do you hear in the poem?** It's important to establish this. Can you distinguish between the voice of the poet, the voice of a narrator and the voice of a character or characters? Any of these voices might be 'the speaker' of the poem – or different voices might be speaking different parts of the poem. Additionally, there might be dialogue *within* the poem spoken by different characters' voices. Why have these voices been chosen? What are the voices like? What is their *tone?*
- **Does the poem seem to have a message or meaning?** Not all poems have an exact meaning that can be summed up briefly, but many do. Some poems tell stories that may not have very clear meanings, but the story is usually told for a reason. Think about why the author may have wanted to write the poem. This may give you a *rationale* for the poem, and hence a kind of meaning.

3   Now look at the structure and **FORM** of the poem. How is the poem organised? What patterns and shapes do you notice?

- *Structure:* Is it in stanzas or in continuous verse? What kind of stanzas? How many? What logic is used to divide the poem into stanzas? Does each stanza develop the poem in some way?
- *Form:* Is it a complex form like a sonnet? Or is it a simple form like rhyming couplets? Is it blank verse (regular but no rhyme) or free verse (irregular)? Is there a regular metre or rhythm? What do you think is the effect of the choice of form? Does the form seem to complement the meaning significantly? (It may or may not.)
- *Patterns:* Do you notice any other repeating patterns in the poem – rhythms, repetitions, sound effects, grammatical patterns etc.? What effects do these have on the meaning?

4   Now that you have established the basics, you can **read the poem in detail**, looking for the following, but always remembering the overall form and content of the poem:

- Diction/word choice/lexical fields; imagery; tone; style; syntax/sentence structure; sounds.
- More detailed and precise meanings of various parts of the poem.

If response to a *set text* is the final outcome, then, clearly, detailed study not only of the individual poems in the text but also of the connections between them will be of central importance; knowledge of the specific content and contexts of the poems will be a major part of what is being assessed, in addition to more general knowledge about poetry. Students' general knowledge of and wider reading in poetry will, however, help them to place the set text in a broader context and have a clearer understanding of how these particular poems work in relation to poetry more broadly.

The approach will differ considerably depending on whether the set text is an anthology/ selection of poems by different authors, or selected poems by one author, or a complete single volume by one author. In the first case (multi-author anthology), connections and comparisons between poems by different authors and/or of different periods or cultures will clearly be at the centre of the work. In the second case (single author selection), there is likely to be an emphasis on an overview of the author's work, style and preoccupations. In the third case (single volume), the particular preoccupations of the single volume, and the way the volume does or does not cohere, are likely to be major concerns.

When dealing with a single author, it's always good to ensure that students have a sense of how the set poems for study relate to the poet's broader work. For instance, when teaching a small set selection of poems by Auden, it's useful for students to read and discuss, if only briefly, a further group of poems by Auden, so that they can get a sense of how the set poems are or are not representative of the rest of his work. They might also be introduced to the idea of modernism, and read and discuss, again briefly, a selection of key modernist poems

– including, for instance, some Eliot and Yeats, so that they can place Auden's own brand of modernism in a broader context.

Approaches to reading poems

Whether teaching towards unseen or set text response, the reading and discussion of poems in class will form the core of the activity. There are, of course, various different ways to approach this, from relatively unstructured open reading and discussion to various kinds of structured activity such as the use of textual interventions or performance approaches. It's probably a good rule – though there's no doubt that this will depend to some extent on the style of individual teachers and classes – that the best way to approach a group of poems in class is by adopting a *variety* of different methods, to keep things lively and to avoid repetitive routines.

Why might one consider approaches other than simple reading and discussion? As we have suggested above, partly for the sake of variety. But also because other approaches can be valuable in that they stress elements of poetry such as creativity, orality, performativity – elements that help to lift poetry off the page and bring its dynamics to life. They also give students alternative, and in many respects more active, ways of engaging with texts, and appeal to different modes of learning and reception.

Below, we discuss some of the pros and cons of these various approaches. (Please note that some of these kinds of activities have already been described in relation to specific poems above; such activities can, of course, be applied to other poems if appropriate.)

Open reading and discussion of poems

The most direct approach to a poem is simply to read and discuss it, and the pleasures and benefits of this approach for both students and teachers – assuming that one has a class that is keen to talk – are considerable. It can be tremendously satisfying, and creative, to guide such critical exploration with a group of youngsters who are fully engaged in unfolding the various meanings of a text.

The role of the teacher as guide, however, is a sensitive one. Especially in the early stages of discussion, it's important to keep questions as open as possible (Dias and Hayhoe 1988: 47–50): 'Would anyone like to start us off?'; 'What are your reactions to that?'; 'What are your first thoughts about this poem?'; 'How would you describe the impact of this poem?' Once ideas start coming, it's still important not to close options off: 'Interesting idea. What does anyone else think about that?'; 'Does anyone see that differently?'; 'What do you think the implication of ... might be?' Eventually, one will almost certainly start guiding the class to particular meanings or ways of reading the text, through teacher suggestion or through affirmation of student suggestion, but it's crucial to allow the class to work their own way towards these meanings, to engage in the process of interpretation. And, of course, it's vital to remain open to the possibility that the students will notice something you've never noticed or understand something you've never understood – as has happened to us many times in class. Indeed, those moments can be particularly significant for everyone in the class, demonstrating that a teacher can only ever be an experienced guide, not the fount of all wisdom.

Whole-class open discussion is pleasurable and valuable, but it does have pitfalls. As with all whole-class work, one has to guard against a polarisation between those who always want to speak and those who never want to speak, between those who will do the work of interpretation and those who will sit back and allow others to do it. Thus, it's important to make space for everyone to be engaged in the process – and the best way to do this is to make pair or small group discussion the starting point. Sometimes, you can elicit some broad starting points from the whole class before dividing the class into groups to do more detailed work. Then you can reassemble the whole class for the main discussion once the groups have had the opportunity to thrash out some ideas.

DARTS (Directed Activities Related to Texts)

One of us once sat next to a university lecturer at a meeting who, in an outraged tone, asked if it was really true that A Level students used text completion exercises (otherwise known as cloze deletion procedure) when studying poetry. His outrage was clearly caused by the notion that a literature student might need the 'prop' of a structured activity of this sort in order to read a poem intelligently. Similar outrage was expressed by my department once when a colleague tried to use a sequencing activity to introduce students to the devastatingly moving poem by Seamus Heaney, 'Mid-Term Break'. *Their* outrage, however, was not in reaction to the provision of a learning 'prop', but because they felt that such a device was entirely inappropriate for such a powerful poem and that students should be allowed to experience the wholeness of the poem on their first encounter with it.

Activities of this kind – strategies such as completing, sequencing, labelling, restructuring, predicting texts – are a valuable staple of poetry teaching pre-16, and can be used in advanced level teaching; but they can be *over*used, and they can be used insensitively. Although *good* use of them is always directed at building student awareness of and confidence about poetic language or form, they can have less desirable effects. For instance, if not used sensitively, they can, as suggested above, destroy the experience of reading a poem, particularly if introduced before the first reading of the poem. They can also interfere with students' sense of the way that poetry is consumed in 'real life'.

That is not to say that sequencing – the exercise in which students are given a poem cut up into its constituent stanzas and have to decide what order they should go in – cannot be useful. Indeed, it can be hugely enjoyable for students, providing animated group discussion and a great sense of achievement; students are able to deploy their knowledge of poetic form, structure and language in a problem-solving situation; *and* the process of working out the logic of the poem gives them some active insight into the process of composition and the craft of the poet. Text completion equally has benefits, if used effectively. It can be an excellent way of highlighting and getting students to think closely about rhyme, imagery and pattern in poetry. However, the benefits of such activities do have to be weighed up against the benefits of hearing a poem read through the first time, allowing students to experience its impact in a way that they will never experience it again.

Other directed analytical activities, such as labelling, categorising, grouping, isolating parts of texts *after* initial reading and discussion, are perhaps less controversial, and can be extremely valuable, especially as a means of giving focus to group discussion.

Creative and performance approaches

Above, we discussed 'active reading' approaches based on creative writing and performance as ways of teaching about generic elements of poetic form and language, but they can, of course, also (and simultaneously) be used to deepen students' understanding of, response to and familiarity with set texts. All the creative writing and text transformation approaches described earlier can be adapted for use with set poems. Similarly, the performance approaches described earlier provide active ways into set texts, and can in particular highlight the imagery, structure and sound patterns of poems.

It's true that creative and performance approaches like these can be time-consuming, and inevitably they will have to be used sparingly in the classroom. However, it's important to remember that such approaches can be highly motivating and memorable for students, appealing to different styles of learning, lending variety to the work of the class, and keeping both students and teacher on their toes. They can provide insights into the work of the poet and the response of the reader that cannot be easily achieved by other means. They can also be particularly valuable with classes that are relatively reluctant to engage in extended, unstructured discussion of poems, or who are showing signs of the need for more variety in approach.

Further reading

Teaching poetry

Developing Response to Poetry (Dias and Hayhoe 1988), *The Problem with Poetry* (Andrews 1991), *Drafting and Assessing Poetry* (Dymoke 2003) and *Making Poetry Matter* (Dymoke *et al.* 2013) provide general discussions of issues in the teaching of poetry in schools, as do the special poetry issues of NATE's journals *English Drama Media* (February 2009) and *English in Education* (Autumn 2007).

The Forms of Poetry: A Practical Study Guide (Abbs 1990) and *The Poetry Pack: Exploring Poems at GCSE and A Level* (Bleiman 1995) are invaluable guides to a range of ways of looking at poetry at senior and advanced levels, whilst *Teaching Poetry* (Naylor and Wood 2012) is an excellent, comprehensive practical guide to teaching poetry from 11 to 19. Stephen Fry's *The Ode Less Travelled* (2005) is both an accessible guide to poetic form and a series of creative exercises that can be used with students. *Studying The World's Wife* (Bleiman and Webster 2007) illustrates in detail a variety of ways of approaching a poetry set text at 16–19.

Ted Hughes' *Poetry in the Making* (2008) is a classic poet's guide to poetry writing.

Critical introductions to poetry

How Poetry Works (Roberts 2000), *An Introduction to English Poetry* (Fenton 2003), *The Poetry Handbook* (Lennard 2006), *Reading Poetry: An Introduction* (Furniss and Bath 2007), *The Poetry Toolkit* (Williams 2009) and *Poetry: The Basics* (Wainwright 2011) are valuable guides to forms, varieties and elements of poetry. *Poetry: The Ultimate Guide* (Bradford 2010) surveys the history of poetry and critical approaches to poetry. *Studying Poetry* (Matterson and Jones 2011) and *How To Read A Poem* (Eagleton 2006) are extended discussions of issues to do with the nature and interpretation of poetry.

Chapter 3

Teaching the novel

Introduction: The novel in the 16–19 classroom

When students embarking on 16–19 courses are asked about their decision to study English literature, many of them will refer to their experience of reading novels. They are more likely to have a favourite novel than a favourite poem or play, and the novel is the type of text that they're most likely to encounter in their reading outside the classroom, embedded in their consciousness since childhood as a source of enjoyment and escapism. Yet its very familiarity means that the novel can be an extremely difficult genre to teach. It is often in studying the novel that the difference between reading for pleasure and reading as part of an academic discipline is felt most acutely. Some students resent the fact that the novels set for 16–19 study are not texts that they would choose to read. While the 16–19 canon has widened considerably over the past decade or so, there is still a marked difference between the literary fiction prescribed by awarding bodies and the thrillers, chick-lit and vampire romances that many contemporary teenagers might prefer. In addition, students can have strong emotional reactions to the novels they study, and while this might lead to a highly productive engagement with the text, it also risks descending into naive readings in which characters are treated as if they are real people and the development of narrative is viewed as little more than an opportunity for speculation and gossip. Because of this, it's in teaching the novel that teachers are perhaps most likely to be accused of 'spoiling' the experience of literature for students who want to enjoy their set texts on a much more simple level: there's a sense that while drama and poetry are fair game for academic analysis, the novel should be left alone.

The complex relationship between the novel and the study of English literature is nothing new. It can be understood, in part, by looking at the discipline's history. When English literature first became an academic subject, in the late nineteenth century, novels were not part of the curriculum. Degree courses revolved around poetry, drama and a wide range of non-fiction texts that included philosophy, theology and even political theory. Novels were considered to lack the rigour that was required to make them a focus for serious academic study, and were therefore consigned to what was referred to as 'home reading'. Nowadays, in contrast, the novel occupies a central part of most 16–19 courses, and makes particular demands of teachers and students 'in terms of reading time, recall of content and making connections between various strands' (McCallum 2012: 75). The novel can therefore loom disproportionately large in students' experience of 16–19 study, thus making it all the more important for teachers to have a series of clear strategies for tackling the novel and for helping their students to navigate their way through their set texts.

In doing this, teachers face a number of challenges. Most obviously, there is the sheer length of the novel. Henry James famously referred to the three-volume novels of the nineteenth century as 'loose, baggy monsters' (1908), and texts like Sebastian Faulks' *Birdsong* (528 pages) or Andrea Levy's *Small Island* (560 pages), both currently set for study in the 16–19 phase in the UK, present all manner of difficulties. As long ago as 1989, Brown and Gifford commented on the marginalisation of reading in many schools, and the difficulties faced by inexperienced readers when presented with a long and complex text. How much of the reading is it possible (or desirable) to get done in class? How can teachers support the development of independent reading? How do they check that this reading has actually been completed? What about those students – and they exist in almost every 16–19 class – who are still reluctant readers? And how can teachers help their students grapple with the cognitive difficulties involved in the long-term process of studying a novel, and the fact that, as Brown and Gifford put it (1989: 74), some novels simply cannot be 'present … in their wholeness'? Beyond these questions, there is the problem of methodology and the various critical approaches that studying the novel involves. Traditionally, studying novels at 16–19 involved a familiar plod through the certainties of plot, character and theme: the text was often read as a straightforward reflection of reality, and much emphasis was laid on what McEvoy (1999) has referred to as 'the unexamined personal response'. Nowadays, many 16–19 courses take a much more rigorous theoretical stance, articulated through clear assessment criteria that help to define what the study of literature at this level involves; students might, for instance, be asked to analyse narrative or representation, or to evaluate different interpretations of the text.

This chapter will explore some of the fundamental questions that need to be considered when teaching the novel to 16–19 students: how to introduce the text, explore narrative methods and encourage a close, considered engagement with the novel in question. It will offer examples of activities based on a range of texts, promoting a clear focus on pedagogy. It will also emphasise the development of independence. Rather than simply 'doing' their set books, students should be encouraged to use these texts as the testing-ground for a set of transferable methods and techniques that will enable them (at least in theory) to go on to study *any* novel.

It should be pointed out, of course, that many of the issues and approaches discussed in this chapter are also applicable to the teaching of short stories. Collections such as James Joyce's *Dubliners* and Angela Carter's *The Bloody Chamber and Other Stories* are frequently studied on 16–19 courses. Students may also encounter single short stories such as Oscar Wilde's 'The Fisherman and his Soul' and Charlotte Perkins Gilman's 'The Yellow Wallpaper', which can offer useful ways of exemplifying particular styles or critical issues. When studying a collection of short stories, students will need to consider how individual stories relate to the collection as a whole, and to compare narrative methods and the treatment of particular themes across the collection.

Similarly, many of the issues and approaches in this chapter might be applied to the study of literary non-fiction. Autobiography and travel writing, in particular, are increasingly popular options in 16–19 literature courses around the world, and there are strong parallels between the narrative methods used in novels and in such non-fictions – although, of course, discussion of non-fiction texts is likely to be marked by rather different discourses about the relationships between representation and reality.

Students' prior experiences of the novel

The beginning of a course of 16–19 study is daunting in any subject, but particularly so if – as in the case of English literature – there is a distinct epistemological break from the version of the subject that students will have encountered in the past. In England, Wales and Northern Ireland, students' experience of studying the novel will have been largely shaped by GCSE, and particularly by the set texts that they will have prepared for their English literature exam. These texts will have been drawn from a relatively narrow canon (the study of English literature pre-16 is still dominated by a familiar group of novels that include *Lord of the Flies*, *Of Mice and Men* and *To Kill a Mockingbird*) and its study is likely to have been heavily scaffolded by the teacher, with the latter stages of the course being geared towards preparing for the kinds of questions that students will have to face in the exam. Jacobs claims that this pre-16 study is often experienced as 'routine and numbing ... driven by an instrumentalist and utilitarian attitude towards the subject (passing the test, servicing the school league tables)' (2010: 1). Nevertheless, it is also worth bearing in mind that in spite of this focus on assessment, the kinds of texts set for pre-16 study are selected in part because of their perceived relevance to the adolescents who must read them, with their common emphasis on individual growth and struggles against oppression and injustice. This builds on a model established in the early secondary years, when students' experience of the novel is likely to have been oriented even more sharply towards a 'personal growth' model of English outlined by Cox (1989) and discussed in Chapter 1. Students may spend some time exploring an author's use of language, but exercises that focus on the constructedness of narrative tend to be relatively isolated, confined to key passages.

It is important to point out the positive value of a model of literary study that has its roots in personal growth. There are very good reasons for privileging this approach to the novel in the 11–16 phase of education, and its student-centred approach has a long and respectable history in the theory of English teaching. Back in the 1960s John Dixon wrote in the hugely influential *Growth Through English* of the power of English to 'invite us into ways of evaluating aspects of life as we experience them' (1967: 57), fostering emotional growth and an awareness of the wider world at a crucial stage of individual development. Nevertheless, the prevalence of this growth-focused pedagogy in pre-16 courses means that the study of the novel in the 16–19 curriculum represents a distinct disjunction with what has gone before, marking a shift to a different way of conceptualising the study of English (a shift similar to that recognised by Dixon [1967: 75], who noted that it was appropriate for teachers to bring about a gradual transition from a version of the subject marked by its focus on 'areas of experience' to one that also made students aware of the 'bodies of knowledge' associated with English). In this more critical model, narrative loses its transparency and gains a new importance as an object of study in itself. The challenge for the teacher of English literature at 16–19 is to think about how they will establish this new way of approaching the novel, and how they will address the questions and uncertainties that arise from it.

The transition from pre-16 to 16–19 ways of studying the novel can be articulated further using the concept of repertoires, explored by Kathleen McCormick in *The Culture of Reading and the Teaching of English* (1994). McCormick identifies one central difficulty experienced by students of literature as an adherence to the philosophy of expressive realism – a 'commonsense' way of reading underpinned by a desire for order and coherence, and privileging the development of plot and character – which, as we have noted, are often the focus of study of the novel in English pre-16. The reading strategies used by students, and the knowledge that they draw on in order to make sense of the text – in other words, the repertoires they employ in order to make meaning – will be ones that are, in general, supported by both the texts that are chosen for pre-16 study, and the teaching strategies that accompany them, referred to by McCormick in terms of:

> such well-recognized activities as creating (or, as they conventionally may assume, 'recognising') themes, identifying with characters, looking for a consistent point of view ... filling in gaps ... relating the text to personal experiences ... When reading a text, readers will tend to employ certain reading strategies in response to certain text strategies, but will employ others simply because they are familiar with them.
>
> (McCormick 1994: 86).

When the strategies employed by students enable them to make sense of a text with relative ease, a matching of repertoires can be said to have taken place. When problems start to occur, it is often because there is a mismatch between the repertoires of the student and the text. This can be in general terms (for instance, when the text demands a knowledge of a specific historical period, or an understanding of particular ideas and values) or in terms of the literary repertoire on which the text draws (for example, the use of techniques such as multiple or unreliable narrators, or the frame-breaking devices used in metafiction). A key task facing teachers is to think about how they will introduce students to the reading strategies they will need in order to make sense of the novels they will be studying – texts that will present them with far more challenging experiences than they have encountered thus far. In addition, teachers will need to consider how to introduce their students to the further complications posed by reading with theory – an issue considered further in Chapter 5.

Teaching the novel

Teaching the history and development of the novel

To understand students' tendency to treat their set texts as straightforward extensions of reality – to contextualise this desire to treat characters as real people, and to gossip about the decisions they make and the things they do – it is useful to look back at the novel's history. It is difficult, of course, to offer an overview of such a varied form, and any attempt to do so will, of necessity, be highly selective. Nevertheless, Panel 3.1 offers a brief survey of the development of the English novel that could be shared with students, and used as the basis for further independent reading and research.

Panel 3.1   The rise of the English novel

Ian Watt's The Rise of the Novel (1957) sees the defining characteristic of this literary form as its focus on the experiences of a particular individual in a particular set of circumstances. This focus on the individual (which has its roots in the philosophical changes that took place in post-Renaissance Europe) distinguished the novel from the prose fiction of the past, which drew on traditional plots derived from mythology or history and focused on stock character-types rather than unique personalities. The name of the new literary form was also significant, as novelty was crucial: from the outset, the novel was prized for its freshness and originality, rather than its adherence to literary conventions or to accepted standards of decorum.

The first novel to have been written in the English language is generally accepted as being Daniel Defoe's *Robinson Crusoe* (1719). With its story of the castaway who spends 28 years on a remote island, *Robinson Crusoe* exemplifies the desire to convey 'what purports to be an authentic account of the actual experiences of individuals' that was seen by Watt as a key attribute of the novel. Its focus on its protagonist's struggle for survival has, moreover, been linked to the capitalist society in which the novel was born. Novelists relied not on the wealthy patrons whose patronage had allowed the writers of the past to flourish, but on succeeding in the marketplace. They therefore had to appeal to a reading public; and did this by encouraging readers to identify with their central characters and by depicting places, people and events in great detail. The first chapter of Henry Fielding's comic novel *Tom Jones* (1749), with its lengthy history of the Allworthy family, and the openings of Jane Austen's novels, with their immediate and very explicit emphasis of names, family relationships, social status and location, are good examples of this desire for verisimilitude. Not surprisingly, this often led to a certain prolixity: one of the earliest English novels, Samuel Richardson's epistolary novel *Clarissa* (1748), is also the longest novel ever written in the English language, with an estimated 985,000 words.

The rise of the novel can also be linked to a number of social and economic factors. One of these was the decreasing cost of paper, which – together with developments in print technology – allowed publishers to bring out smaller, more affordable copies of books. Another was the emergence of a new leisured class who had time to read novels. Novels were, nevertheless, too expensive for most working people; and the fact that literacy levels were still relatively low meant that the target audience for the novel was essentially middle-class. It was also largely made up of women; and many early novelists directed their work to a specifically female audience, focusing on relationships and marriage, and on what Jane Austen described in a letter to her niece Anna as 'three or four families in a country village'. Men, on the other hand, were supposed to stick to more traditional works of history, biography and philosophy, or alternatively to the classics of Greek and Roman literature.

The great age of the novel in England – the nineteenth century – was also the age of the Bildungsroman or 'novel of experience', which focused on its central character's development from childhood to maturity. Examples include Charlotte Brontë's *Jane Eyre* (1847), Charles Dickens' *David Copperfield* (1850) and *Great Expectations* (1861), and George Eliot's *The Mill on the Floss* (1860). Charlotte Brontë's younger sister Emily was responsible for one of the most unusual novels to emerge from the Victorian era, *Wuthering Heights* (1847), with its complex narrative style and depiction of raw passion and brutality. The nineteenth-century novel is also notable for its minute focus on the relationship between the individual and society. Perhaps the greatest example of this is George Eliot's *Middlemarch* (1871–72), but also important was the so-called 'Condition of England' novel with its emphasis on the effects of industrialisation: examples include Benjamin Disraeli's *Sybil* (1845), Elizabeth Gaskell's *Mary Barton* (1848) and *North and South* (1854–55), and Charles Dickens' *Hard Times* (1854). Towards the end of the century, Thomas Hardy located his own exploration of the effects of society upon the individual in the semi-fictional region of Wessex, exploring the tragedy of characters in conflict with their circumstances in novels such as *The Return of the Native* (1878), *Tess of the d'Urbervilles* (1891) and *Jude the Obscure* (1895). Many famous novels of the Victorian era were first published in serial form in monthly magazines, and were issued later in three-volume format: the emergence of circulating libraries and adult education establishments such as the Mechanics' Institutes and Working Men's Colleges meant that novels could still be read by those who could not afford these relatively expensive texts.

Despite the focus on realism outlined above, another strand of the novel's history concerns experimentation. In the early years of the novel, Laurence Sterne drew attention to the impossibility of representing an individual's experiences in their entirety: his comic novel *Tristram Shandy* (1759–67) purports to tell its eponymous hero's life story, but contains digressions, repetitions and even blank pages as Tristram agonises over the hopelessness of his task. Writers of the early twentieth century, such as Dorothy Richardson, James Joyce and Virginia Woolf, extended this experimentation further through the technique of 'stream of consciousness' – an attempt to capture the flow of thoughts, emotions and sense-impressions that pass through an individual's mind. Even though works such as James Joyce's *Ulysses* (1922) and Virginia Woolf's *Mrs Dalloway* (1925) might seem very different from the novels of Jane Austen or Charles Dickens, they can still be seen as part of the novel's attempt to represent, in as much detail as possible, the experiences of particular characters in particular circumstances.

Other notable novelists of the early twentieth century, such as D. H. Lawrence, Evelyn Waugh and Graham Greene, continued to explore the relationship between the individual and his or her background and society – often through the prism of religion. Yet one of the most important developments in the history of the novel in the twentieth century was not literary, but commercial: the rise of the paperback. In 1935, the publisher Allen Lane, dismayed at the poor quality of the few paperbacks that were then available, founded Penguin Books. Its publication of series such as Penguin Classics, and the work of a wide range of contemporary authors, brought affordable, well-produced texts within the reach of millions of people.

In the last few decades of the twentieth century, the development of the English novel was marked by the work of authors from around the world – including the Commonwealth and former colonies – who used the novel to create distinctive new voices. Writers such as Salman Rushdie and Margaret Atwood brought a freshness to the novel, often using techniques such as magical realism. In the UK, experimentation with form and narrative voice continued in the work of authors such as Julian Barnes, Ian McEwan, Angela Carter and Martin Amis. As the century reached its end, however, there were fears that the richness and variety of fiction in English might be stifled by a publishing market dominated by the drive for sales rather than a desire for quality.

The first decade of the twenty-first century was dominated by the phenomenon of Harry Potter, J. K. Rowling's boy wizard whose adventures sold in their millions, and who has been credited for sparking a resurgence of interest in reading amongst people who had not picked up a novel in years. Nevertheless, perhaps the most important force in the development of the novel so far this century has been technology. The advent of the e-reader has been viewed by some as marking the decline of the printed book, and the possibilities of self-publishing offered by the internet means that new writers no longer have to struggle to find a publisher or a literary agent. Book blogs and forums provide opportunities for readers to exchange their views, and fans of particular genres – science fiction, fantasy, children's literature – have looked to the internet to provide a haven for interests not catered for by mainstream publishing. Nobody knows, yet, whether the e-reader will take over from the paperback novel, or who will write the next bestselling series to rival Harry Potter, *Twilight* and *Fifty Shades of Grey*. What is certain, though, is that readers' interest in other people, the stories they tell and the stories that can be told about them will last for a very long time.

It is, of course, possible to think of any number of counter-narratives to challenge the account given above; and students at the end of a 16–19 course – with a range of reading behind them – might even be encouraged to write these counter-narratives as a precursor to degree-level study. Nevertheless, the importance Watt places on the depiction of individual experience does offer some useful ways of helping students to understand the relationships many readers have with the novels they enjoy, and the wish-fulfilment, projections and identifications that these relationships often involve. Its emphasis on the centrality of formal realism can also form the starting-point for an exploration of whether other narrative techniques – such as stream-of-consciousness – convey these experiences more effectively. Furthermore, its discussion of wider social and economic developments – such as the gradual spread of literacy, changing patterns of leisure and the emergence of the publishing trade – might also provide students with a useful perspective on the importance of the contemporary literary market.

To extend students' thinking about the novel, it would be useful to introduce them to some of the ways in which novelists themselves have commented on the novel's form and content. Panel 3.2 contains some extracts that could be used to stimulate discussion of the craft of the novelist and the relationship between writer and reader.

Panel 3.2   Novelists on the novel

Throughout the novel's history, novelists have reflected on their craft – sometimes in prefaces and critical essays, but also in the narratives of their novels themselves. Look at the extracts below. What do they suggest about:

- the novel as a literary form – what it should achieve and how it should be written?
- the relationship between the writer and the reader?

An author ought to consider himself, not as a gentleman who gives a private or eleemosynary treat, but rather as one who keeps a public ordinary, at which all persons are welcome for their money. In the former case, it is well known that the entertainer provides what fare he pleases; and though this should be very indifferent, and utterly disagreeable to the taste of his company, they must not find any fault; nay, on the contrary, good breeding forces them outwardly to approve and to commend whatever is set before them. Now the contrary of this happens to the master of an ordinary. Men who pay for what they eat will insist on gratifying their palates, however nice and whimsical these may prove; and if everything is not agreeable to their taste, will challenge a right to censure, to abuse, and to d--n their dinner without control. To prevent, therefore, giving offence to their customers by any such disappointment, it hath been usual with the honest and well-meaning host to provide a bill of fare which all persons may peruse at their first entrance into the house; and having thence acquainted themselves with the entertainment which they may expect, may either stay and regale with what is provided for them, or may depart to some other ordinary better accommodated to their taste.

Henry Fielding, *Tom Jones* (1966 [1749]: 51)

In the beginning of the last chapter, I informed you exactly *when* I was born; but I did not inform you *how*. *No*, that particular was reserved entirely for a chapter by itself;—besides, Sir, as you and I are in a manner perfect strangers to each other, it would not have been proper to have let you into too many circumstances relating to myself all at once. —You must have a little patience. I have undertaken, you see, to write not only my life, but my opinions also; hoping and expecting that your knowledge of my character, and of what kind of a mortal I am, by the one, would give you a better relish for the other: As you proceed farther with me, the slight acquaintance, which is now beginning betwixt us, will grow into familiarity; and that unless one of us is in fault, will terminate in friendship. [...] Therefore, my dear friend and companion, if you should think me somewhat sparing of my narrative on my first setting out—bear with me,—and let me go on, and tell my story my own way:—Or, if I should seem now and then to trifle upon the road,—or should sometimes put on a fool's cap with a bell to it, for a moment or two as we pass along,—don't fly off,—but rather courteously give me credit for a little more wisdom than appears upon my outside;—and as we jog on, either laugh with me, or at me, or in short do any thing,—only keep your temper.

Laurence Sterne, *The Life and Opinions of Tristram Shandy* (1991 [1759–67]: 8–9)

With a single drop of ink for a mirror, the Egyptian sorcerer undertakes to reveal to any chance comer far-reaching visions of the past. This is what I undertake to do for you, reader. With this drop of ink at the end of my pen, I will show you the roomy workshop of Mr. Jonathan Burge, carpenter and builder, in the village of Hayslope, as it appeared on the eighteenth of June, in the year of our Lord 1799.

George Eliot, *Adam Bede* (1980 [1859]: 49)

Suffice it, to be brief, that the first person, in the long piece, is a form foredoomed to looseness, and that looseness, never much my affair, had never been so little so as on this particular occasion. All of which reflexions flocked to the standard from the moment – a very early one – the question of how to keep my form amusing while sticking so close to my central figure and constantly taking its pattern from him had to be faced.

Henry James, *The Art of the Novel: Critical Prefaces* (2011 [1934]: 320)

Examine for a moment an ordinary mind on an ordinary day. The mind receives a myriad impressions — trivial, fantastic, evanescent, or engraved with the sharpness of steel. From all sides they come, an incessant shower of innumerable atoms; and as they fall, as they shape themselves into the life of Monday or Tuesday, the accent falls differently from of old; the moment of importance came not here but there; so that, if a writer were a free man and not a slave, if he could write what he chose, not what he must, if he could base his work upon his own feeling and not upon convention, there would be no plot, no comedy, no tragedy, no love interest or catastrophe in the accepted style, and perhaps not a single button sewn on as the Bond Street tailors would have it. Life is not a series of gig lamps symmetrically arranged; life is a luminous halo, a semi-transparent envelope surrounding us from the beginning of consciousness to the end. Is it not the task of the novelist to convey this varying, this unknown and uncircumscribed spirit, whatever aberration or complexity it may display, with as little mixture of the alien and external as possible? We are not pleading merely for courage and sincerity; we are suggesting that the proper stuff of fiction is a little other than custom would have us believe it.

Virginia Woolf, 'Modern Fiction', in *The Common Reader* (1925: 189)

Yes – oh dear yes – the novel tells a story. That is the fundamental aspect without which it could not exist. That is the highest factor common to all novels, and I wish that it was not so, that it could be something different – melody, or perception of the truth, not this low atavistic form.

> For, the more we look at the story [...], the more we disentangle it from the finer growths that it supports, the less we shall find to admire. It runs like a backbone – or may I say a tapeworm, for its beginning and end are arbitrary. It is immensely old – goes back to neolithic times, perhaps to palaeolithic. Neanderthal man listened to stories, if one may judge by the shape of his skull. The primitive audience was an audience of shock-heads, gaping round the camp-fire, fatigued with contending against the mammoth or the woolly rhinoceros, and only kept awake by suspense. What would happen next? The novelist droned on, and as soon as the audience guessed what happened next they either fell asleep or killed him.
>
> E. M. Forster, *Aspects of the Novel* (1990 [1927]: 40–1)

This kind of exploration, however, will take second place in many teachers' minds. More important – and certainly more pressing – will be the novels that their classes have to study, and the day-to-day decisions they have to make about how these texts should be addressed. It is to these decisions that we will now turn.

Teaching novels

Starting the text

Teaching *any* text 16–19 involves mediating between ambitious long-term goals (plus, of course, those imposed by external assessment) and the short-term objectives that will inform lesson planning. This mediation is, however, particularly acute in the case of the novel, where the length of the text poses its own challenges, particularly at the beginning of a 16–19 course. Gibbons describes this process as being 'about relating individual lessons into the "bigger picture" of the study of a text or a group of related texts and – simultaneously – about linking day to day work with the overarching knowledge and skills in terms of developing as a critical reader and as a student able to confidently negotiate the assessment hurdles' (2010: 8). Consequently, when teachers introduce their classes to the novel they will be studying, they will need to find a way of giving them a secure foothold in the text that will build their confidence for the more detailed (and increasingly independent) exploratory work that is to come. How might they do this?

Often, teachers will begin by doing some pre-teaching: that is to say, introducing students to key concepts and issues before they actually embark on their study of the text. For instance, they might decide that students need to explore some aspects of the novel's historical or cultural context before they begin to study the text itself, introducing the 'codes' (or, in McCormick's term, 'repertoires') that students need to be aware of in order to read the text. They might approach the text by looking at the way it is 'packaged', exploring aspects such as the title and cover design, and any received impressions the students have of the text. Other teachers might want their students to discuss some philosophical questions that arise from the text, so that they have a sense of the ideas they will be discussing when they study it. Alternatively, they might anchor their study of the text by introducing students to one of the main characters. One effective way of doing this is by getting them to explore some short extracts (descriptions of this character, or examples of their speech) so that they can begin to analyse how this character is constructed.

Panel 3.3 offers two examples of pre-teaching exercises. The first is a research task that introduces Charlotte Brontë's novel *Jane Eyre*. The second is a character-focused task that introduces Stephen Wraysford, the protagonist of Sebastian Faulks' novel *Birdsong*. The tasks approach their respective texts in different ways and have different learning objectives, but illustrate the ways in which pre-teaching activities can be used to introduce students to the 'world' of the text. It is important to remember that these students may be right at the beginning of their 16–19 studies: learning activities need to be tailored to their experience, ability and levels of confidence, and, of course, to the text in question.

Panel 3.3   Pre-teaching activities for novels

Jane Eyre

This term you will be studying Charlotte Brontë's novel *Jane Eyre*. This task will introduce you to the novel's historical and biographical contexts, and help you to understand some of its themes.

First, find out as much as you can about Charlotte Brontë. Concentrate, in particular, on her childhood, her family and her education. Find out the titles of her novels and when they were published. Summarise your findings in about 250 words.

Now answer the following questions:

1   How were girls typically educated in the early nineteenth century?
2   What kinds of behaviour would have been expected of girls and young women?
3   What careers were open to young women at this time?
4   What did a governess do? How would she have been viewed by her employers?
5   What is meant by the phrase 'social mobility'? Do you think there was much social mobility in the early nineteenth century? Explain your answer.
6   In what ways was religion used to keep people in order and maintain the social hierarchy?
7   Finally, find out what Elizabeth Rigby said about *Jane Eyre* in her article in *The London Quarterly Review*. What kinds of values are reflected in Rigby's review?

Birdsong

You have been given a series of extracts concerning *Birdsong*'s (1993) main character, Stephen Wraysford. In groups, study these extracts and discuss what impression they give you of Stephen. What kind of character does he seem to be? What factual information do we gain about him? Be ready to discuss your impressions with the rest of the class.

Stephen's pale face was visible as he watched the departing guests – a tall figure with hands thrust into his pockets, his eyes patient and intent, the angle of his body that of a youthful indifference cultivated by willpower and necessity.

(p. 14)

He had kept a notebook for five years, since a master at the grammar school had suggested it. The hours of Greek and Latin study had given him an unwanted but ingrained knowledge of the languages that he used as the basis of a code. When the subject matter was sensitive, he would change the sex of the characters and note their actions or his responses with phrases that could not mean anything to a chance reader.

(p. 15)

Stephen made no judgements; he was motivated by compulsion.

(p. 28)

She was frightened of Stephen. From the day he arrived in the Boulevard du Cange with his dark face and its staring brown eyes, and his swift impetuous movements, she was afraid of him.

(p. 39)

Stephen, his eyes smarting, hit out in front of him in fury. He had lost sight of his initial aim, which was to restore peace, and now wanted only to damage the man who had enraged him.

(p. 51)

He did not exactly like Stephen; if he had asked himself why, he would have said there was something cold or withdrawn in him.

(p. 80)

'Jesus Christ!' Stephen leapt up from his seat in horror.
    Isabelle, who had been amused by the bird's fearlessness, looked up in alarm. 'What is it?'
    'That bird, that bird. For God's sake. Get rid of it.'
    'It's only a pigeon, it's just –'
    'Get rid of it. Please.'

(p. 112)

Stephen envied the innocence still visible beneath the strain that showed in Weir's open features. He felt he had already lost all connection with any earthly happiness that might persist beyond the sound of guns. The scattered grey hairs at his temples and above his ears seemed to remind him that he was changed and could not return.

(p. 153)

Stephen poured more whisky. He always hoped it would make him sleep, but in fact it made little difference.

(p. 154)

Something moved beneath his feet. It was the face of a man whose head was horribly wounded. He shouted out to be killed ... In the noise of the battle, Stephen thought, no one would know. He fired twice down by his feet.

(p. 229)

He returned to brigade headquarters. He did not want to be on the staff. He wanted to be back with the men in the trenches.
  He managed only to exist.
  His life became grey and thin, like a light that might at any moment be extinguished; it was filled with quietness.

(p. 390)

Another way of introducing the set novel is through what Elaine Showalter has referred to as 'teaching from the microcosm', drawing on Parker J. Palmer's idea that 'in every great novel, there is a passage that when deeply understood, reveals how the author develops character, establishes tension, creates dramatic movement. With that understanding, the student can read the rest of the novel more insightfully' (quoted in Showalter 2003: 36). In teaching from the microcosm, the teacher would begin with a short extract that exemplifies an important aspect of the text. This could be a moment of crisis, an aspect of language, or a key conversation. Students might even be allocated a range of different extracts, thus enabling the teacher to introduce an element of differentiation and ensure that all students participate actively in the process of learning.

Planning an exercise like this is where subject knowledge and pedagogy interact. Teachers need to know their set text well in order to be able to identify what their students will need to know about it – to find an angle that will give their students a 'way in' to what might well be the most demanding novel they have ever read. They will also need to use their knowledge about the teaching process – how to define appropriate objectives, plan activities, group students and use resources – in order to shape and support their students' developing understanding. This is a complex process.

Whether teachers decide to do some pre-teaching or not, they will soon arrive at the point where they have to tackle the first chapter. Some teachers give out copies of their set novel in advance of teaching it, and expect students to have read it beforehand – perhaps during a holiday or a period of study leave. Others like to be in control of their students' first encounters with the text, and prefer it if students' minds aren't clouded by any knowledge of what happens later – or by their perceptions of the text as a whole. Nevertheless, once they have completed this initial study, most teachers will ask students to read the whole text as soon as possible.

Work on the opening chapter will depend very much on the text in question. It might focus on how the author sets the scene and creates atmosphere: alternatively, it might explore the creation of narrative voice. It might involve a DARTS-type activity such as a cloze or sequencing exercise, as discussed in Chapter 1 (remembering that these exercises have their place in the 16–19 classroom, too). Whatever it is, it will almost certainly involve students working in pairs or small groups to share their initial perceptions and then feed them back to the whole class. This collaborative generation of meaning – the shared construction of knowledge – is both a vital part of the 16–19 experience and an important factor in encouraging students to see literary meaning as provisional, contextualised and contestable, rather than immutably locked into the text.

One way of establishing this early understanding of a text is to make use of new technologies. Two very useful tools that are available on the internet are the Cruncher facility on the Teachit website (www.teachit.co.uk), which takes a text and reorders its words so that you can look at patterns of language, and word-cloud generators such as Tagxedo (www.tagxedo.com) and Wordle (www.wordle.net), which create graphical representations of word frequency. Such tools make it very easy to focus on authorial style and can be used to encourage an exploration of choices of vocabulary, words drawn from particular lexical and semantic fields, levels of formality and so on. Students working on Ian McEwan's novel *Enduring Love*, for instance, can be introduced to the presence of vocabulary drawn from science and mathematics, and consequently speculate on what kind of narrator might use this kind of language. Alternatively, an opening lesson on *The Return of the Native* might focus on how Thomas Hardy's lexical choices create the vivid, brooding presence of Egdon Heath.

Exercises like this, based on extracts from the first few pages of a novel, fulfil a number of pedagogical roles. They demand a close engagement with the language of the text, allowing a microscopic focus on issues of vocabulary that helps to orientate students in the novel's verbal 'world'. They encourage students to talk to each other about their observations and give them the opportunity to discuss unfamiliar words in small-group settings that can seem a 'safer' environment than that of the whole class. However, they stop short of actually getting the students to read the text. They need to be followed up by introducing students to the opening pages so that they can see this vocabulary in context, with the teacher using well chosen questions to prompt an exploration of why the author begins the novel in this way. How will the students actually read the extract in question? They could, of course, read silently, or the teacher could choose a volunteer to read, but a teacher should never underestimate the power of his or her own voice – that of an experienced storyteller who knows the novel well (and therefore knows how to use appropriate intonation and pauses) and can draw the students into the text in this important first encounter.

Teachers will probably spend several lessons on the first few chapters. It's worth putting the time in on these early sections of the text, as it will allow students to establish their sense of who the main characters are and what the story is about – those basic things that we all like to get to grips with when we read a novel for the first time. On a more sophisticated level, it will enable them to inhabit the codes needed to interpret this particular text – the binary divisions, cultural archetypes and aspects of historical and biographical knowledge they need to make it 'work'. It will also enable the teachers to explore the language of prose and the concept of narrative.

Teaching the language of prose

The nature of poetry is such that issues of language, form and structure tend to be in the foreground. It's therefore arguably easier to teach students about those things in relation to verse than in relation to prose, where aspects of form, structure and language often lack visibility, melting into the background of attention-seeking narratives and arguments. Consequently, teachers and students tend to feel far more comfortable with identifying and analysing the features of poetry than prose. This is undoubtedly why examiners so often rail against students' reluctance to move away from discussion of plot, character and theme in narrative and dramatic fiction.

When they do approach analysis of language in prose writing, students are more likely to feel comfortable talking about imagery than elements of tone and style, so it's worthwhile doing some explicit work with them on close reading, and especially on helping them to see the ways in which writers might control their paragraphs and sentences in particular ways. As a preliminary, one might give students examples of prose passages that are particularly well endowed with literary devices such as alliteration, enumeration, complex sentence structures and so on: extracts from eighteenth- and nineteenth-century fiction and non-fiction are particularly good for this. Other examples of rhetorical prose, such as political speeches, can also be useful here, too.

Panel 3.4 outlines some elements of prose style that might help students to become more aware of the texture of their prose reading. With the reference sheet as a guide, students can then be given carefully chosen extracts from the novel being studied and asked to discuss whether and how the extracts conform to any of the features of prose described.

Panel 3.4   Prose features

Below are some features of prose writing that can help to determine pace, mood, atmosphere or tone.

1. Paragraph and sentence length

- **Juxtapositions** of long and short paragraphs or sentences can be used to create particular effects.
- Many short paragraphs or sentences together often have a very noticeable effect, often indicating fast pace, irony and/or humour.
- Many long paragraphs or sentences together usually result in dense writing, perhaps strongly descriptive, or perhaps very intellectual.
- However, the effects of these things can only be judged in the context of the whole piece of writing.

2. Sentence structure

- Sentences may follow conventional structures approximate to ordinary simple speech, or they may use more complex, unusual or artificial structures.
- There may be **symmetry or balance** in the structure of a sentence. Does the sentence fall into two or three deliberately balanced parts? (Some sentences can be described as *bipartite* or *tripartite*, for instance.)
- The word order in the sentence may be conventional or unusual.
- Punctuation may be used deliberately to create interest, surprise etc.

3. Rhetorical devices

Rhetorical devices are methods of arranging words in speech for particular effect. They are particularly associated with speech-making, but are often used in written prose. They may include such things as:

- rhetorical questions;
- exclamations;
- repetition;
- metaphor or simile (figures of speech);
- sound effects (alliteration, assonance, rhyme, onomatopoeia);
- symmetrical or balanced sentences (see above);
- enumeration;
- allusion.

4. Style

Use of – or lack of – any of the above devices might contribute to the overall 'style' of the writing. The style might be, for instance:

- simple, sparse, or economical;
- complex, dense or ornate;
- expansive, effusive or energetic.

Note that all these aspects of prose can also apply in verse.

Teaching narrative in the novel

In exploring narrative in the novel, it is first helpful to ensure that students are familiar with some of the main narrative methods at the novelist's disposal in relation to narrative voice and structure. Panel 3.5 provides a range of examples.

Panel 3.5   The novel – narrative, dialogue and structure

Note: Also applies to short stories and narrative poems; some parts also apply to drama.

1. Narrative voice and perspective

Narrative voice: FIRST PERSON or THIRD PERSON (omniscient)

First person:

- can share thoughts, feelings etc. directly with the reader;
- is involved in the narrative as a character;

- may be unreliable;
- cannot enter into the thoughts of other characters.

Third person:

- may be invisible, or may comment on the narrative (as if the author);
- is not involved in the narrative as a character;
- can enter into the thoughts of other characters etc. (omniscient).

Narrative perspective/point of view

- First person – point of view is always that of the narrator character.
- Third person – point of view may shift as the narrator writes from different character *perspectives*, or from a neutral perspective. Narrator may interject with personal comments, e.g.

> Mr Bennett was so odd a mixture of quick parts, sarcastic humour, reserve and caprice, that the experience of three and twenty years had been insufficient to make his wife understand him. Her mind was less difficult to develop. She was a woman of mean understanding, little information, and uncertain temper.
>
> (Jane Austen, *Pride and Prejudice*, Chapter 1)

- Where the third-person narrator not only writes from the point of view of one character but also (ironically) adopts their language, this is known as free indirect speech (or discourse), e.g.

> Mrs Bennet was quite disconcerted. She could not imagine what business [Mr Bingley] could have in town so soon after his arrival; and she began to fear that he might always be flying about from one place to another, and never settled at Netherfield as he ought to be.
>
> (Jane Austen, *Pride and Prejudice*, Chapter 3)

2. Narrative structure and time

Narrative structure

- Beginnings and endings, turning points and climaxes.
- Setting the scene (*exposition* of status quo), developing the plot (*development* – something happens to change things), resolving the plot (*resolution*, new status quo).
- Division of novel into parts and chapters.

Narrative time and structure: some important ideas

- LINEAR or CHRONOLOGICAL NARRATIVE: story moves from beginning to end in order.
- FRAGMENTED NARRATIVE: story moves between past, present and future and challenges the reader to piece the parts together.
- DUAL (or MULTIPLE) NARRATIVE: two (or more) stories intertwining or the same story with two (or more) different narrative voices or viewpoints.
- METANARRATIVE: a story within a story.

Suspense, revelation, anticipation

- FORESHADOWING (flashforward, prolepsis) – mention in a text of something which has not happened yet but will happen later. This could be in the form of a hint, which is not intended to be understood until later, or it may be an explicit reference to something which is going to happen, though we do not yet know how or why it is going to happen.
- FLASHBACK (analepsis).
- The deliberate withholding and gradual revelation of plot information by the author/narrator: manipulation of the implied reader.

With this information as a starting point, it is likely that students will need to consider some – if not all – of the questions below. This list is by no means exhaustive, but it does serve to draw students' attention to the constructedness of the text, rather than viewing it as innocently and straightforwardly mimetic. One useful way of alerting students to this is to remind them that the text does not have to be like this: what would change if the author had decided to do something different?

- What kind of narrator does the story have: First or third person? Reliable or unreliable? Is there more than one narrator?
- What kind of narrative voice is used? (For instance, if the narrative is in the first person, is the narrator a character we're supposed to sympathise with and be drawn to – or do they remain distanced?)
- What kinds of focalisation strategies are employed? Is one particular character used as the focaliser (the person from whose perspective we see things) or does the narrative switch between focalisers? What use is made of free indirect narrative?
- Are there any framing devices or external narratives (such as the story-within-a-story of Joseph Conrad's *Heart of Darkness*)? Is there an intrusive author?
- How is the narrative structured? Is it told chronologically, or are devices such as flashbacks and time shifts employed? How much time is devoted to particular events: are they described in minute detail, or glossed over as though unimportant?
- How important is the setting of the novel? Does the setting have any kind of symbolic significance or cultural resonance? If so, how is this used? Are we meant to accept it or reject it?

- How are different parts of the text connected to each other? How do chapters begin and end?
- How are characters created and conveyed? How important are names and physical appearances? Do you notice anything significant about the patterning of characters (protagonist and antagonist; foil; parallel characters in different generations or different parts of the text)?
- How is dialogue used? Is speech attributed or unattributed? Direct or indirect? Is there anything significant about which characters speak and which don't?
- What can you say about the type and length of sentences? Does the text as a whole have any distinctive grammatical features?
- Are there any significant patterns of imagery, recurring symbols or extended metaphors?

Teachers could illustrate some of these techniques by getting students to look at short extracts from a range of texts. This helps to broaden the range of their reading (which will be useful if they have to do a piece of coursework based on a free choice of texts) and also encourages them to see themselves as studying the novel as a genre – not just one particular novel. Questions – framed either by the teacher, or by students themselves – could be used to guide students' responses. What, for instance, could students say about the following?

- Charles Ryder, the narrator of Evelyn Waugh's *Brideshead Revisited* (1945), gives a detailed account of his friendship with Sebastian Flyte as an undergraduate at Oxford (an Oxford that is represented in highly nostalgic, idealised terms). However, he is much more reticent about the details of his marriage – his wife is presented almost as an afterthought, and is rarely referred to by name. How does this reflect the relative importance of the two relationships to him?
- The narrative of David Lodge's *Nice Work* (1988) is occasionally interrupted by an authorial voice that draws the reader's attention to techniques such as flashbacks and shifts in focaliser. The focaliser of the first chapter is a man called Vic Wilcox, a captain of industry who is one of the novel's two main characters: the focaliser of the second is the university lecturer Robyn Penrose. The authorial voice signals this change very explicitly: 'And there, for the time being, let us leave Vic Wilcox, while we travel back an hour or two in time, a few miles in space, to meet a very different character. A character who, rather awkwardly for me, doesn't herself believe in the concept of character.' What is the effect of this kind of authorial voice (especially one that refers to itself in the first person)?
- Kazuo Ishiguro's novel *Never Let Me Go* (2005) is set in a dystopian world in which children are brought into the world as clones to provide vital organs for their non-clone counterparts, or 'possibles'. However, the reader does not know this: it is only as the text progresses that this situation becomes apparent. The novel's narrator, Kathy H, refers to the different operations that the clones will undergo – 'first donation', 'second donation' and so on – and also to their 'completion', or death, but we are never explicitly told what these terms mean. Kathy's narrative voice is flat and calm, with little ornamentation or emotion. How does this kind of narrative voice draw us into the novel's world?
- Andrew O'Hagan's *Personality* (2003), loosely based on the life of the Scottish singer Lena Zavaroni, is about a child star, Maria, whose existence is dominated by what other people want for her. The narrative is divided between a number of different voices, as Maria's mother, agent, boyfriend and fellow celebrities – and, later, her stalker – are all given the opportunity to tell the story. It is only in the very last chapter that Maria takes

over the narrative. This coincides with the point where she escapes her stalker and sets out to create a new life for herself. Why has O'Hagan used this polyphonic technique and what does it tell us about Maria's life?

- Christopher Boone, the narrator of Mark Haddon's novel *The Curious Incident of the Dog in the Night-Time* (2003), is a fifteen-year old boy with Asperger's syndrome. Many of the sentences in the novel begin with conjunctions – 'And', 'But', 'So'. What effect does this create? Why has this kind of narrative voice been given to this character?
- Many novels make use of locations to represent different values or stages in a character's life. Think about the way that Wuthering Heights and Thrushcross Grange are used in *Wuthering Heights* (1847), or Talbothays and Flintcomb-Ash in *Tess of the d'Urbervilles* (1891). What does each location symbolise? How do the authors use language to create these impressions?

In addition to these questions, there might be other critical terms and concepts that students need to know, depending on the text they are studying: magical realism, dystopia, epistolary novel, Bildungsroman, metafiction, polyphony, the American dream, and so on. These concepts could form the basis of some student-led research and wider reading: a group studying *Jane Eyre* might be directed to read *Great Expectations* and *Oranges Are Not The Only Fruit* to compare different examples of the Bildungsroman, while students working on *Small Island* could explore other texts with multiple narrators, such as Sebastian Barry's *The Secret Scripture* and Barbara Kingsolver's *The Poisonwood Bible*.

Creative writing approaches are also extremely valuable in teaching about narrative technique and style in the novel. Rewriting a scene of a novel in script form, for play or film, highlights the role of the narrator in a very concrete way. Rewriting a narrative in a very different style forces students to foreground elements of style in their thinking. (A simple example, used many times to great effect whilst teaching Jane Austen, is to ask students to rewrite a scene from a current soap opera or television drama in the style of an Austen novel. It's surprising how the domestic settings and scenarios of many soap operas lend themselves to this exercise, whilst helping students to see the crafted formality of Austen's narrative and dialogue.) Similarly, elements of narrative voice and perspective can be taught by asking students to rewrite a scene from a different perspective, in a different narrative voice or adopting a different tone. Adding new scenes, characters or settings can also help students to come to terms with narrative and style.

Most importantly, of course, students will need to comment on the effects of the techniques that they identify. In the early stages of a 16–19 course, teachers will probably need to refer back to the point-example-analysis structure that students will have encountered in previous phases of their education. As they become more sophisticated critics and writers, they will develop ways of refining this technique, but it is nevertheless a useful framework to use when making notes and developing analytical skills.

Structuring independent reading

At some stage, teachers will reach the point where their students need to strike out on their own, where their shared exploration of the text needs to be supplemented by independent reading and study. Ideally, teachers should prepare students for this point before they actually reach it. There is no way that either the teacher or their students should expect to cover everything in class, and students (and, potentially, their parents) will probably need reminding of this. However, students who have studied relatively short novels (such as *Of Mice and Men*) in the past, and who have had their encounters with these novels heavily scaffolded in lesson time, will find this independence a shock. Teachers will need to set out their expectations clearly, and think carefully about the support that they will give their students as they get to grips with what might well be the longest book they have ever read.

Different teachers have different ways of managing this process, which will, of course, need to take into account the experience and abilities of their students and the kind of assessment they are preparing for (a novel being studied in preparation for external examination will demand a different kind of approach to one being assessed by coursework). Nevertheless, there are some common techniques that can be adapted for use in most situations.

Comprehension questions can be particularly useful in the early stages of a novel, especially at the beginning of a 16–19 course when they can be used to establish the depth of analysis necessary. When followed up by discussion in class, they ensure that students have a clear grasp of the key points that emerge from specific chapters or sections of the text, and also help to scaffold the understanding of less able or less confident students. However, they can become tedious and repetitive – and can also limit students' interpretations by making them focus only on what the teacher considers to be important. For these reasons, we recommend that they should be used judiciously and sparingly.

A more effective approach, particularly with regard to building students' independence, is to help them to develop their own **systems and structures for note-making**. This might involve making brief notes in the margin or in a separate notebook whilst reading and expanding on these later, keeping a running note of relevant page numbers under different subject headings, or using sticky notes to mark key pages and then revisiting them for further exploration. What students actually make notes on will depend to some extent on how they will be assessed (some specifications, for instance, focus exclusively on narrative technique; others will require an understanding of historical and cultural contexts, or different critical interpretations). It can be useful to get students to explore and discuss *what* they need to make notes on, rather than simply prescribing this for them. It is also useful to model the process of note-making, and share examples of students' notes, to demystify a process that many students find difficult.

Reading journals offer an alternative to this kind of structured note-making. Brown and Gifford argue, in fact, that reading journals represent a more effective way of personalising the study of the novel, being 'the record of each student's active participation in the construction of meaning over a period of time' (1989: 93–4). Reading journals allow students to record their 'first impressions, random thoughts, flashes of insight … doubts, changes of mind, and uncertainties because these are crucial stages in genuine personal learning' (1989: 93, 97). Nevertheless, students will benefit from suggestions as to what they could include in their journals, to ensure that they move from unexamined personal response to a more considered and analytical mode of reflection. As with note-making, modelling and sharing of high quality work will help to guide students in the right direction.

Finally, many teachers and students are making increasing use of **new technologies** to support their study of the novel. Electronic texts can be highlighted and annotated very easily – and, if different colours are used to highlight, for instance, different patterns of imagery or narrative techniques, then these can be called up for close comparison by simply pressing a key. The reading journals described above could easily be completed in electronic form and, if students agree, they could be shared with the rest of the group so that peers (and teachers) can add their thoughts and comments. Discussion forums can be used to promote reflection and stimulate debate, and the fact that these can be accessed in students' own time can be a very effective way of keeping the text 'alive' in students' minds.

With all of these approaches, promoting independence and encouraging students to take responsibility for their learning is crucial – both in the short term, with regard to their study of the text in question, and in the long term, with a view to preparing them for life beyond 16–19 study. Two ways of doing this – one building students' independence through getting them to teach a lesson, the other drawing on new technologies – are outlined in Panel 3.6.

Panel 3.6   Building independent learning

Peer teaching

Richard gets his students to prepare and teach a short lesson on a section of their set novel. He begins this phase of their work by getting students to identify the main elements of a lesson (starter, main activity, plenary) and to discuss the kinds of questions that are asked in English literature lessons, exploring the different functions of closed and open questions. He then puts the students into mixed-ability groups (three students is a typical number) and assigns each group a chapter. They then have time to analyse their chapter and plan and prepare their lesson, identifying the key aspects of the narrative and thinking of activities that will enable the rest of the class to understand the effects of these techniques. The rest of the class must also read the chapter and come to the lesson with a list of questions that they want to ask.

This approach has a number of important benefits. First, it builds students' independence by getting them to take control of the learning. It encourages cooperative working and allows space for risk-taking and divergent, often creative approaches. It also enables students to develop confidence in standing up in front of a room and taking charge of a situation in which they have to think on their feet and respond to questions and ideas that they might not have anticipated. In terms of preparing students for the transition to HE, or the workplace, these skills are vital: students find these activities difficult at first, but are unanimous in recognising how valuable they are.

Discussion boards

Natasha has set up a discussion board for her students on the school's VLE. Each week there is a new focus for the discussion (a new chapter, character or issue) and students are expected to post at least three contributions to that week's discussion. The discussion begins with a personal reflection and a series of questions designed to prompt further thought and debate. Natasha initiated the first two weeks' discussions herself, but then made individual students responsible for leading future discussions. This allowed her to introduce an element of differentiation: the first student-led discussion was assigned to the most able member of the group, and other able students were given more complex chapters and topics on which to post. As the course progresses, students can refer back to these postings to see how their understanding of the text has developed.

In encouraging use of the VLE, this approach means that students gain confidence in handling the new technologies that will shape their experience of further study. It also means that they can be directed very easily to critical material, reviews, film clips and other online resources. It helps them to develop the ability to recognise and evaluate different points of view. Importantly, it emphasises that there are not necessarily correct responses to the questions that are raised. In doing this, it helps students to become accustomed to the 'messiness' of learning in English literature: the fact that questions cannot always be resolved neatly, and that one's understanding of a particular text will inevitably change and develop during a course of study.

Ranging around the text

Many examiners' reports refer to the need for students to 'range around the text': to have the confidence, in their written work, to draw on different parts and aspects of their set novel rather than plodding through it chronologically. How can teachers help their students to develop the ability to do this?

One way of encouraging this flexibility is by getting students to find short extracts that exemplify a particular theme or technique. Can they identify, for instance, six key quotations that show the development of tension, or the representation of character? This will get them to evaluate and prioritise. Limiting the number of extracts that they have to find is crucial. When they come to write on their set novel, students will always be working within limits – either the word count of a piece of coursework, or the time constraints of an exam. Conscientious students, in particular, often struggle to recognise what they can leave out as well as what they should put in. The confidence to recognise that success often rests not on how *much* you know but how effectively you can *use* what you know is something that students will need to develop.

Novels on screen and stage

Screen adaptations of novels are a resource used by many English teachers to accompany work on fiction texts. Less commonly used, but nevertheless a useful resource for teaching, are stage adaptations of novels. Both screen and stage adaptations are very useful pedagogical tools but, as discussed in Chapter 4 of this book, need to be approached thoughtfully. In transforming a substantial work of prose fiction for the screen, significant textual changes are required, even in the case of a lengthy serialised television adaptation. The language of prose fiction and the multiple 'languages' of the screen and stage, each with their own distinct grammars and conventions, vary widely, and as such teachers and students need to develop appropriately critical approaches to the use of screen adaptations. There are also substantial differences between film and television adaptations. Fay Weldon notes, for example, that:

the structure of [a television] series is much like the structure of a novel: you can follow the book practically chapter by chapter – page by page almost [in the case of my *Pride and Prejudice*] – putting the text into the mouths of the various sisters. A film has no sense of chapter: it drives through to its end like a short story, so changes to plot and even character may well be needed to capture the gist of the novel.

(Weldon quoted in Green 2009b)

In looking at adaptations of novels for the screen, therefore, it is important to consider with students the possibilities and limitations which come with such textual transformations. As observed in Chapter 4, the demands and methods of screenwriting are substantially different from the methods of writing prose fiction, and such contingent demands mean that texts may look and feel very different in these media.

Pedagogically it is important to be clear why screen or stage versions of the text are being used. If the answer is simply to cover for reading that has not been done or to limit the amount of reading that students need to do, then the use of such adaptations can be problematic, especially in the light of Fay Weldon's observations. Additionally, any visual representation of a text will make certain assumptions and encode certain critical interpretations, which may or may not form a part of students' personal visions of the source text (but which, nevertheless, constitute alternative readings of the text that can be discussed alongside other interpretations). Narrative sequences may be reordered, removed or conflated to meet the demands of televisual or stage production, but these may create aesthetic tensions with the very different demands of the source novel. When teachers choose to use a film, television or stage adaptation of any text, this choice needs to be made on sound pedagogical grounds and needs to be made an explicit focus of classroom discussion – the screenplay or stage play and the resultant productions are, after all, critical-creative responses to the source text and should be treated as such.

Panel 3.7 suggests a number of ways of approaching screenplays, both for critical and creative purposes, in the 16–19 classroom. Such activities may feed into either formal analytical work on set fiction texts or into re-creative and transformative writing (as discussed more fully in Chapter 7).

Panel 3.7   Working with screen and stage adaptations

1   Still images from screen adaptations are an effective way of focusing students' discussions on the ways in which the text has been interpreted. What do particular images, for instance, suggest about the way a particular relationship has been portrayed?

2   Similarly, the trailers for screen adaptations – condensed versions of the whole production – offer useful 'snapshots' of a director's interpretation of the source text and can prompt debate on which aspects of the text have been foregrounded. The official trailer for Cary Fukunaga's 2011 version of *Jane Eyre*, for example, emphasises the novel's Gothic elements. How does it compare with the trailer for the 2006 BBC version of *Jane Eyre*?

3   Consider with students the production activities that go into the creation of adaptations for the big screen and the small screen, e.g. screenwriting, costume, props, make-up, selection of locations, use of composite locations, music, sound effects, publicity. How

do these affect viewers' reception of the text? How is this likely to differ from their reception of the text in its original form?

4   Explore with students the function of the literary heritage for the media, publishing, broadcasting and other cultural industries, and the impact of new media technologies on audiences' reception and interpretation of the literary heritage. Consider why canonical literature is so frequently adapted and the ways in which it is approached.

5   Compare adaptations over time. Watch extracts from a range of screen and stage adaptations of a single text (silent movies to contemporary; for film and television). Consider how media 'language' and convention has developed over time. How does this affect the way we view the text? How does the relationship between the original text and the adapted text change between adaptations? What does this tell us about the social and cultural context of the adaptation and its meanings? If studying a classic text such as Mary Shelley's *Frankenstein*, for example, the novel could be compared to a variety of film adaptations (e.g. James Whale's 1931 production with Boris Karloff as the monster, Ken Russell's *Gothic* of 1986, and Kenneth Branagh's *Mary Shelley's Frankenstein* of 1994) and a stage version of the play from 1823 entitled *Presumption*, by R. B. Peake.

6   If possible, attend a staged version of a fiction text. Ideally this will be an adaptation of a text the students are studying, but it need not be. Prior to the performance, read the original, then use the staged version as the basis for a critical evaluation of what happens to texts in adaptation. Think carefully about how this reflects back upon students' understanding of the source text. Remember, not all adaptations will be straight plays. *Wuthering Heights*, for instance, has inspired several ballets – *The Brontës* by Dominic Muldowney, *Wuthering Heights* by Claude-Michel Schönberg of *Les Misérables* fame, and *Sturmhöhe* by Dave Maric – and other novels exist in operatic versions, such as *The Handmaid's Tale* by Poul Ruders, *The Turn of the Screw* by Benjamin Britten and *Heart of Darkness* by Tarik O'Regan.

The sense of an ending

One aspect of narrative not mentioned earlier in this chapter, but which is nevertheless vital, is how the novel ends. Students will need to consider what kind of closure is arrived at by the final page of the text. Does the novel reach a satisfying conclusion, or are the reader's expectations frustrated? Would a different ending have been more effective? Does the ending seem convincing, or are there loose ends that still remain – ones that perhaps threaten the resolution that seems to have been reached? McCormick (1994) argues that students should be taught to embrace these ambiguities and resist the notion that interpretive difficulties always need to be resolved. Students will also need to be taught how to handle these difficulties in writing; and a lesson spent focusing on the use of discourse markers to structure a discussion of these complexities will not go amiss.

A useful way of encouraging students to explore endings is offered by David Lodge's novel *Changing Places* (1975). In the novel, the lecturer Morris Zapp finds a book called *Let's Write a Novel*, which contains the following advice:

There are three types of story, the story that ends happily, the story that ends unhappily, and the story that ends neither happily nor unhappily, or, in other words, doesn't really end at all. [...] The best kind of story is the one with a happy ending; the next best is the one with an unhappy ending; and the worst kind is the story that has no ending at all. The novice is advised to begin with the first kind of story. Indeed, unless you have Genius, you should never attempt any other kind.

(Lodge 1975: 87–8)

Interestingly, *Changing Places* itself is a novel that lacks a clear sense of resolution: its final chapter, told in the form of a film script, ends by freezing the action in mid-frame just as a character is reflecting on the artificial nature of endings. (Lodge plays around with endings in other novels, too. Robyn Penrose, a character from *Nice Work*, tells her students about the endings of Victorian novels, whose plots are typically resolved by means of 'a legacy, a marriage, emigration or death' [1988: 83]. At the end of the novel, the first three of these are offered as ways of resolving the uncertainties in Robyn's own life). How would students categorise the ending of their set text? And do they agree with the view that the worst kind of story is one that has no ending at all? The teacher might want to get them to reflect on other novels they have read, and to see how they react to novels that resist the simplistic closure of 'happy ever after'.

Teachers will also need to think about another kind of ending: how they will conclude their study of their set novel. In one sense, of course, their students won't stop working on this text until they've sat their exam or submitted their coursework, and if it is an exam text, the class will invariably need to return to it as part of revision and exam preparation. However, teachers will probably want to mark the end of their formal teaching of the text in some way. This might be through giving students the opportunity to reflect on their personal experience of the text – what it has meant to them, what they enjoyed about it or what they found most puzzling or frustrating. Such an activity will help to counteract the feeling of anti-climax identified by Brown and Gifford, who highlight the tension inherent in guiding students through texts that are likely to be both intellectually and emotionally demanding – and then having to prepare them for an assessment regime whose requirements might well seem extremely reductive when compared with the richness and multivalency of the texts being studied (1989: 74–5). One UK A Level specification uses the concept of 'destinations' to sum up this idea of reading as a journey through the text, getting students to reflect on the way its meanings emerge and develop and the ways in which it challenges its readers and makes them think. This notion is a very powerful metaphor to share with students, and might help them to articulate some of the frustrations and breakthroughs they have experienced in studying their particular set novel.

Further reading

Teaching the novel

Teaching Literature (Showalter 2003) offers some interesting perspectives on teaching the novel, including some approaches to teaching longer texts. The English and Media Centre has produced a range of resources to support the teaching of prose fiction, including *The Modern Novel* (Bleiman *et al.* 2001), *Studying Narrative* (Bleiman and Webster 2008) and guides to studying a range of individual texts, including *The Road*, *The Great Gatsby*, *Wuthering Heights* and *Wise Children*. *The Forms of Narrative: A Practical Study Guide* (Abbs and Richardson 1990) is a useful guide to a range of ways of looking at narrative fiction, with many well chosen extracts from novels.

Critical introductions to the novel

The Rise of the Novel (Watt 1957) remains the classic introduction to this literary form, tracing the relationship between the novel and its social, economic and philosophical contexts. *Aspects of the Novel* (Forster 1927) explores issues such as story, plot, character and narrative structure, and offers insights into the craft of novel-writing. *The Art of Fiction* (Lodge 1994) and *How Novels Work* (Mullan 2006) explore aspects of prose narrative in more detail, ranging across a variety of texts. *Studying the Novel* (Hawthorn 2010) is an excellent introduction to the form and approaches to studying it.

Chapter 4

Teaching drama

Introduction: Drama in the 16–19 classroom

> In a written story, context is defined through words alone. In drama, however, it is actually constructed from space, objects and people as well as words.
>
> (Winston 2004: 26)

The quotation above summarises very neatly the challenges of teaching drama texts as part of the study of English literature in the 16–19 phase. Much literary study presupposes a relationship between a solitary reader and a text. Drama, which presupposes plurality and shared, lived experience, challenges such a relationship in unique ways, and in so doing raises some particular issues for teaching and study. Drama is a mediated and mediatory form in ways that prose fiction, literary non-fiction and poetry (the other staples of English literature courses) are not, and this requires that drama texts be approached and read differently. Drama texts written for stage production depend upon a dynamic interaction between the producer of text (the playwright), the mediators of text (a plethora of directors, designers, technicians and actors) and the receivers of the text (an audience). The 'space' of the text is thus uniquely interactive, and as such provisional and liminal. Even if students cannot see productions of the texts they are studying, an awareness of the range of processes that go into the 'making' of drama as it lifts from the page, and the range of demands this places upon the notion of 'reading' enormously enriches their engagement with dramatic texts.

As a direct consequence of this, teaching literary dramatic texts involves certain tensions. The prime impulse for writing drama is generally for it to be viewed on stage: to put it simplistically, plays are written to be watched, not read. Nevertheless, reading is central to the study of drama texts, and will be of obvious importance to the experience of 16–19 students of English literature, whose work on drama will mostly take place in the same classroom settings that shape their experiences of poetry and prose fiction. In any case, it could be argued that drama texts are most objectively approached in their written form rather than in mediated (and possibly manipulative) produced versions, where many of the possibilities of interpretation are taken away from the individual reader. As soon as we see a drama text performed, that production becomes a benchmark and will automatically predispose us to 'see' certain things in the text as we read it. In reading, the text can be given a life – an interpretation – that might never be realised on stage, but that exists nevertheless in the realms of potential.

It should be clear from these introductory ideas that the study of drama texts involves – for teachers and students alike – a reconceptualisation of the notion of 'reading'. 'Reading' is commonly taken to denote the act of decoding and making sense of words (and, in some cases, images) on a page. When studying drama, however, the act of reading acquires an extra dimension that comes from being able to visualise the play in performance, to imagine the effects of staging and stagecraft and to be able to 'hear' and weigh up different performances of particular lines in one's head. Howard observes how audiences encounter 'a particular succession of sights, sounds and events that create a unique theatrical experience with its own tempo, rhythm, and pauses, its own moments of engagement and detachment, and its own natural points of emphasis' (1984: 178–9). Students need to learn how to 'read' the stage as well as the page; and this chapter will offer some ideas as to how they can be introduced to what, for many, will be a very new conception of 'reading'. This 'reading' also needs to have a dimension that belongs to the realms of the subjunctive. Students should be encouraged to consider not just how their set play has been produced, but how it might be produced – developing their own interpretation as part of what Fisher (2007) has referred to as as a 'Menippean dialogue' with the text. Studying drama texts, and working with this 'extra dimension', is therefore a process of keeping multiple versions of the text, both actual – drawing on productions that have already taken place, and potential – alive in one's mind simultaneously, weighing up the possibilities that these different versions might offer.

Students' prior experiences of drama

Conceptually, then, the study of drama has layers and dimensions not shared by the study of other literary forms. Drama also has a complex relationship with the discipline of English itself, overlapping in some ways but retaining its own distinct identity in others; and an understanding of the position of drama in the pre-16 curriculum can help to contextualise some of the difficulties that students have with this form.

In the pre-16 English curriculum in England and Wales, 'drama' tends to feature both as a major aspect of the study of literature *and* as a separate, specialised area of study comprising aspects of theatre studies and educational drama (sometimes referred to as 'process drama'). As well as studying drama within the requirements for literary study, students embarking on 16–19 courses should have had opportunities to 'use different dramatic approaches to explore ideas, texts and issues'; 'use different dramatic techniques to convey action, character, atmosphere and tension'; 'explore the ways that words, actions, sound and staging combine to create dramatic moments' and 'evaluate drama performances that they have watched or taken part in'; they should also have had the chance to devise, script and perform plays, watch live theatre and take part in drama workshops (QCA 2007a, 2007b). In some schools, these experiences of drama will have taken place entirely within the English curriculum. In others, however, drama exists as a separate subject with its own timetabled lessons, and might be taught by entirely different staff. Some students will have had the opportunity to take a separate course in drama pre-16, and some might be pursuing a 16–19 qualification in theatre studies alongside their study of English literature. Courses in drama and theatre studies will, of course, include a substantial performance element; but they will also include the study of drama texts, although this study will focus much more on texts-in-performance than the study of drama texts in English literature courses. It is theoretically possible for a student to be studying the same drama text in both English literature and theatre studies – but taking a different approach in each.

Students might also have experienced drama as a set of pedagogical methods that are drawn on in other areas of the curriculum. This approach has been theorised most widely by Heathcote and Bolton (1995) and is described by Neelands in terms of a 'classroom resource' used to facilitate personal, social and emotional development, as opposed to 'the formal study of plays, performances and dramatic criticism' (2000: 74). It includes activities such as hot-seating, teacher-in-role and mantle of the expert, and can be used to illuminate and explore topics across a range of subjects: debates about urban regeneration in geography, say, or the decisions taken by different historical figures. Such approaches are, of course, used widely in English as well, and will be useful for exploring aspects of other literary forms, in addition to drama texts.

Students are likely therefore to approach the study of drama 16–19 with a variety of experiences. Some students will be accustomed to using drama-based approaches as a way of exploring both literary texts and other areas of the curriculum. Others will be less confident with these approaches; and this lack of confidence will need to be borne in mind when planning classroom activities. Some students will also have little experience of seeing live theatre, and this will pose additional challenges. In an ideal world, all students of 16–19 literature would have the chance to see a wide range of plays being performed, including (but not restricted to) those being studied. The benefits of this would be multiple: students would be able to broaden their experience of drama, compare different productions of their set plays and observe the possibilities made available by different theatrical spaces. However, issues of distance, cost and time – not to mention the likelihood of particular set texts actually being in production in any given year – often make this impossible. Furthermore, many students find the social world represented by theatre intimidating: as Neelands acknowledges, the model of drama-as-arts-subject (as opposed to drama-as-process) has been accused of resting on an elitist conception of theatre (2000: 80). It is worth remembering that some 16–19 students might never have been to the theatre before, and that some will come from backgrounds where a visit to the theatre is a completely alien experience. Helping students to feel comfortable in this environment is often a vital stage of the learning process.

Teaching drama

Teaching the history and development of drama and the theatre

Neelands and Goode describe theatre as having 'a traditional role as an educative form of entertainment, which responds to a basic human need to interpret and express the world through symbolic form' (1990: 5). Yet students with little experience of drama often lack a sense of the conventions and rituals of theatrical performance, expecting theatre to be more realist than it frequently is. As with poetry or the novel, it is clearly not necessary or possible at this level to teach a comprehensive overview of the history and development of drama; an understanding of this, however, helps students to see the plays they study as having their roots in symbol and ritual, rather than being attempts to represent 'reality' in straightforwardly mimetic ways. The relationship between the real world and the world of the play is a complex one, and can be difficult for 16–19 students to grasp unless they have some sense of the wider context of dramatic history. It is also only too easy for the set text to dominate students' experience of literary study, losing sight of the bigger picture.

There is real benefit to students in introducing them to the broader sweep of a genre's history, enabling them to locate the text they are studying in relation to other major literary works. It also gives teachers a useful chance to introduce the skills of independent research – a vital part of students' 16–19 experience. In the run-up to the study of a set text, students could be set independent or small-group research tasks relating to the broader sweep of literary drama as a way of engaging them with the 'shape' and history of literary drama, perhaps focusing on types or aspects of drama that will be particularly relevant to the play to be studied. Such tasks might include researching the development of a major genre or the performance history of a major play, or producing an illuminated timeline of key dramatists and texts. Clearly such tasks will need to be structured and will be limited in nature, but they will serve the purpose of introducing students to the contexts of drama and the factors shaping the texts they are studying. Panel 4.1 offers a very brief summary of some of the major developments in the history of theatre, which could be given to students to form the basis of further research and exploration, and to stimulate discussion about where a set text features in a broader historical context.

Panel 4.1   History and development of drama in the West

In the Western dramatic tradition, the first dramatist and actor is generally acknowledged as being the Greek musician Thespis (sixth century BCE). Thespis, from whose name the term 'thespian' is derived, composed a series of musical 'dialogues' between a solo singer and a chorus of singer-dancers. These works, often performed during religious celebrations or rites, came to be known as tragedies and provided the basis of hundreds of works produced by Greek tragic playwrights. Comparatively few of these early plays have survived, but those that are still extant – 32 plays by the three major dramatists, Aeschylus, Sophocles and Euripides – have been enormously influential, focusing on the interaction of the human and divine worlds and so establishing a close relationship between drama and religious ritual. In ancient Rome, the art of tragedy was developed principally by Seneca, and comedy – previously popular in ancient Greece too, especially the plays of Aristophanes – emerged as a significant form with the works of Plautus and Terence.

After the collapse of the great classical civilisations of Greece and Rome, drama in the West did not re-emerge until hundreds of years later. Ironically, when it did so, it was from a quarter that had traditionally opposed any form of theatre: the Christian church. It became a tradition at Easter, and later at Christmas, to interpolate short dramatisations of biblical narratives into religious services. These short dramas were elaborated over time and were eventually presented on their own by secular actors outside the church, shaping themselves into the morality, miracle and mystery plays of the medieval era. Cycles of plays from York and Wakefield (the 'Towneley plays') are perhaps the best known. The connection of theatre to religious ritual is again transparent, but from this point on, secular elements increasingly found their way into drama until it emerged as an art form in its own right from the mid-sixteenth century.

By the beginnings of the early modern period, drama was well established as a form – albeit one that was regarded with a great deal of moral scepticism. The theatre had by now moved far from its original religious roots and was perceived as a threat to moral rectitude. Shakespeare is the titanic figure of the theatre of the Elizabethan and Jacobean eras. The excesses of revenge tragedy (major examples of which were produced by Shakespeare, but also by John Ford, Cyril Tourneur, John Webster, Thomas Kyd, John Marston, Philip Massinger and others) no doubt added to the perceived immorality and amorality of drama as a form. There was also a thriving comic dramatic scene, however. Shakespeare, Thomas Dekker, Ben Jonson and others produced a large body of intelligent 'city' comedies (e.g. *The Shoemaker's Holiday, Volpone, The Alchemist* and *Bartholomew Fair*). Whilst both these comedies and the revenge tragedies make a significant shift towards realism – characters in these works are much more developed and defined than those in the medieval drama – theatrical 'types' and the role of declamatory verse are still highly significant (in the way that recitative and the formal aria still are in opera). The formal properties attached to such elements of Renaissance drama frequently pose difficulties for students.

Drama went into an enforced decline as the theatres were closed under the Puritans and throughout the Civil War, but with the return of Charles II from exile in France and the restoration of the monarchy in England in 1660, the theatre was able to emerge once more. At first this relied on the pre-Civil War repertoire, but the new French influence of Molière was more fitted to contemporary tastes than the works of Shakespeare and his contemporaries. Consequently, a form of social comedy emerged that was witty, brittly satirical and often bawdy – a reaction to the cloying Britain of the Puritans. Drama and the Restoration stage therefore took a further step towards the concerns of the 'real' world. Early in the eighteenth century, however, a Puritan resurgence fettered the free spirits and broad humour of the Restoration stage (George Farquhar, William Wycherley, William Congreve, George Etherege and others) and turned towards more sentimental comedy and moralising domestic tragedy. After a brief resurgence of drama in the hands of Colley Cibber and Henry Fielding, the Licensing Act (1737) brought the theatres under the personal censorship of the Lord Chamberlain.

Although domestic theatricals were very popular in the Victorian era and adaptations of many of the major fictional works of the era (such as Charles Dickens' *The Pickwick Papers, Great Expectations* and *The Christmas Books*, Charlotte Brontë's *Jane Eyre* and Wilkie Collins' *The Woman in White* and *The Moonstone*) were very popular, few writers of serious drama emerged again in Britain until the beginning of the twentieth century.

Developments in drama over the last 150 years have marked a shift towards realism, particularly under the influence of Scandinavian and European dramatists such as Ibsen, Strindberg and Wedekind and practitioners such as Stanislavski. Nevertheless, the hugely important work of Bertolt Brecht challenged the notion that drama should offer a window onto reality, disrupting audience expectations and discouraging spectators from identifying with the characters on stage as if they were 'real' people. In the second half of the twentieth century, the Theatre of the Absurd – associated with playwrights such as Samuel Beckett, Harold Pinter and Tom Stoppard, as well as Continental dramatists such as Eugène Ionesco, Jean Genet and Václav Havel – took this sense of estrangement to new extremes, depicting a world apparently lacking in meaning and resisting any straightforward interpretation.

Note: Whilst this summary focuses on Western traditions, it must be remembered that ancient and equally rich traditions of drama also developed in Africa and Asia.

Teaching about text and performance

An important aspect of the history of drama is, of course, the development of theatrical spaces themselves. Understanding the broad move of theatre from outdoor to indoor performance, and the way this, along with such developments as electric lighting, gradually changed the nature of theatre, is crucial to understanding the historical development of the theatre; grasping the implications of such performance conditions is perhaps particularly important in understanding the way classical, medieval and Renaissance dramatists (such as Shakespeare) shaped their texts, for instance through the use of verse. All students, but particularly those with little experience of visiting the theatre, will benefit from exploring the physical environment of the theatre and considering the potential and limitations of different performance spaces. This will give them a set of visual reference points for their interpretation of drama texts, enabling them to work within the 'extra dimension' represented by imagined performances of particular plays and moments within these plays. Panel 4.2 contains four suggestions for activities that will encourage students to consider the development of different theatrical spaces. Variations on these activities might, for instance, be used as part of a scheme of work on a set Shakespeare play or Greek tragedy in order to highlight the rather different ways in which performance spaces have shaped texts and determined the nature of the interaction between performers and audience at different stages in history.

Panel 4.2   Considering the theatre space

1   Give students a sequence of images depicting different stages in the history of drama: the amphitheatre in Epidaurus; an image of a modern, open-air production of a medieval mystery play, using a traditional wagon; the reconstructed Globe Theatre in London; a nineteenth-century proscenium arch theatre, such as the Theatre Royal in York; and an example of theatre-in-the-round, such as the Royal Exchange Theatre in Manchester. Students could begin by putting these images into chronological order and justifying their choices, then discussing the kind of relationship with the audience that these particular kinds of stage would encourage.

2   As a variation on the above, look at still images to explore how productions of one of Shakespeare's major plays have reflected developments in theatrical history. How, for instance, might present-day productions of *Macbeth* draw on the methods of Theatre of the Absurd?

3   Take students to a theatre – both to see a production (regardless of whether or not it is of a text they are studying) and when the theatre is empty – or use a DVD of a live theatre performance, such as one of the recent live performances from Shakespeare's Globe. Ask them to reflect on the following:
— What do they notice about the way the theatre is laid out? What might this suggest about the relationship between the audience and the stage?
— How and when is the audience 'permitted' to interact with the performance?
— When is it acceptable to make noise and when is it not?
— What kinds of noise are acceptable and what are not?
— What kind of set is used? Is it realistic or symbolic? Does the set change? If so, how are set changes carried out?
— What did they notice about sound, lighting and special effects? What is it possible to do with these in this particular theatre?

4   Introduce students to the names given to different types of stage, and to the different parts of the stage. Students could be asked to research definitions, either singly or in pairs, and share these definitions with the rest of the group. The following terms are a useful starting point: *proscenium arch, apron, thrust stage, theatre in the round, gallery, black box theatre, locus, platea, fourth wall*.

5   It is also useful to encourage thinking about how the theatre at different times has worked with staging (e.g. considering how the following would have been used in Shakespeare's theatre: the location and use of musicians; the use of the heavens and the space under the stage; theatre in the open air etc.). How does this differ in the contemporary theatre?

Students will also need to consider what they do when they 'read' live theatre productions, and how this process relates to and differs from the other kinds of reading they do – when they watch a film or television adaptation or read the published version of a drama text. It is often useful to start with general questions to make students reflect on their understanding of their reading processes in the three different contexts where they are likely to encounter drama texts:

•   What do you 'read' when you attend a theatre performance?
•   What do you 'read' when you watch a film or television adaptation of a play?
•   What do you 'read' when you read the text of a play?

Specific elements of these different reading processes can then be approached through more tightly focused questions, such as the following:

•   How do we 'read' costume?
•   How does incidental music influence our 'reading' of dramatic situations?
•   How does lighting influence the mood of a scene?
•   How do we 'read' the set?

- How does the use of close-up in a film or television adaptation both assist and limit our 'reading' of particular scenes and characters?
- Does your set playwright alert readers to the visual dimension of the text? If so, how?

Some of these questions can be addressed in very general terms, but all are most effectively approached through specific examples. Consider, for example, Trevor Nunn's 1999 production of *The Merchant of Venice* for the National Theatre, in which Jessica remains on stage alone at the end of the play, singing a Jewish Kaddish: students observing this may feel that this gives the character a depth that may not otherwise emerge, leading to a revised interpretation of her relationship with Shylock in consequence. Particularly powerful discussions can also emerge where multiple versions of a particular scene or dramatic moment (such as Hamlet's entrance in *Hamlet,* Act 1, Scene 2) are considered alongside one another. Such comparisons are now easily resourced with the proliferation of materials available on the internet. Further discussion of ways of engaging students with aspects of the translation of text from page to stage are explored later in this chapter.

Teaching about symbolism, realism and convention

Exploring different theatrical spaces, and the kinds of productions that take place in them, will help students to recognise that drama remains a ritualised form of interaction between the real and imagined worlds and between actors and audiences, and that playwrights will often appeal to their audiences' awareness of symbol, ritual and theatrical history. As suggested in the historical account above, it is valuable in this regard to teach students about the continuum of dramatic style from stylisation to realism (well illustrated for instance by comparing the conventions and methods of relatively stylised ancient verse drama with those of relatively realist modern prose drama). This gradual historical shift can be linked with developments in theatre buildings, lighting and stage technology, printing and mass literacy. The associated move away from verse to prose as the principal means of telling a story (as signalled particularly by the rise of the novel) might be highlighted here to raise awareness. A further link can be made with the modernist reaction *against* realism in surrealism, the Theatre of the Absurd etc.

A simple but effective exercise is to ask students to weigh different plays up against some features of the two extremes of the stylisation/realism continuum:

STYLISATION	REALISM
Poetic language, music, dance	The language and movement of ordinary social life
Explicit symbolism in character and setting	Psychologically and socially specific characterisation and settings
Traditional fables, myths, legends	'Original' stories about invented characters

Even when a play appears to represent 'reality', students should be encouraged to look beneath the surface for elements of ritual and convention, from Arthur Miller's reworking of elements of classical tragedy in *A View from the Bridge,* to the ceremonial disrobing of Hector at the beginning of Alan Bennett's *The History Boys.* The symbolic aspects of drama might also be emphasised further in production, adding another dimension to the possibilities that students should be encouraged to envisage when they study drama texts. Drama can be seen, then, as a liminal space where a number of different worlds meet: the fictional world of the play, the real-world event that is witnessed by the audience and the alternative worlds represented by the different possible interpretations of the play.

Just as students need to be introduced to the elements of poetic form that make up the backbone of the poet's repertoire, so students should be made aware of aspects of the artifice behind dramatic narratives. Some key dramatic conventions and devices, along with examples of them from the plays of Shakespeare and other dramatists, are outlined in Panel 4.3. A useful exercise here is to ask students to discuss three dramas they are familiar with – for instance a Shakespeare play, a modern play and a television drama or soap opera – and to decide which of these conventions are used, and how, in each.

Panel 4.3   Dramatic conventions and devices

Convention/ device	Function	Examples
Aside	When a character effectively steps out of their immediate dramatic context in order specifically to address the audience. The drama effectively freezes for a moment, allowing the playwright through the character speaking the aside to comment (often ironically) on the events that are taking place or to provide a necessary gloss on the events that are unfolding. Asides are an example of the breaking of the 'fourth wall', the imaginary barrier between the audience and the events unfolding on stage.	Shylock in *The Merchant of Venice*, for example, whilst addressing his rival Antonio politely in public, observes in an acerbic aside, 'How like a fawning publican he looks! / I hate him for he is a Christian, / But more for that in low simplicity / He lends out money gratis and brings down / The rate of usance here with us in Venice.' Similarly, Iago in *Othello*, overseeing a conversation between Cassio and Desdemona which he plans to use to create dissension between the Moor and his wife, observes aside, 'He takes her by the palm: ay, well said, / whisper: with as little a web as this will I / ensnare as great a fly as Cassio. Ay, smile upon / her, do; I will gyve thee in thine own courtship.'
Soliloquy	When a character speaks alone. This often takes the form of a direct address to the audience in which the character unfolds hidden motivations or provides us with a true insight into their emotional state or gives a personal perspective upon the events unfolding in the surrounding drama.	A particularly famous sequence of soliloquies occurs in *Hamlet*, but other significant examples are also found in *Macbeth* and *Othello*.
Chorus	A device often used to provide a commentary on the events of the play, or to move the events of the play through space or time.	This may take the form of narrative steers (e.g. the opening choruses of *Romeo and Juliet* and *Henry V* or the famous intervention of Time in *The Winter's Tale*). Alternatively, the dramatist may use it to provide some kind of observational, didactic or moral gloss upon the events unfolding on the stage, as in Arthur Miller's *A View from the Bridge*.

Convention/ device	Function	Examples
Masque	A theatrical form in its own right, but sometimes used within plays too, the masque is a kind of courtly musical theatre, highly stylised in form and often sumptuous. Characters hide their faces under masks, which are often representative of certain stock types. It is taken, perhaps because of the concealment of the face, to represent deceit.	Good examples by Shakespeare can be found in *The Tempest* and *The Merchant of Venice*. Milton's *Comus* and Ben Jonson's *The Masque of Beauty* and *Oberon, the Faery Prince* are also interesting examples.
Song	Songs in plays often reflect (seriously or ironically) on the main events of the drama.	Songs are found throughout the works of Shakespeare, and many of these are available in recorded versions. They are particularly prevalent in the comedies, and well known sequences of songs can be found in *As You Like It* and *Twelfth Night*. They are often pithy and satirical and are frequently used to provide a reflection on the concerns of the drama. 'There was a lover and his lass', for example, from *As You Like It* reflects on the play's concern with romance and marriage as it plays out in the lives of the characters.
Cross-dressing	Where characters of one gender dress (for a variety of reasons, comic and serious) as the opposite. The proscription of female performers in Shakespeare's theatre, however, doubles the irony in that it would have been a man playing a woman playing a man. As with the example of plays within plays, this illustrates the self-referential nature of drama as a form. This kind of irreverent reversal is characteristic of Bakhtin's conception of 'carnival' (1984).	Shakespeare frequently employs the device of cross-dressing, where his female characters take on the guise of males (e.g. Rosalind and Ganymede in *As You Like It* or Portia and Nerissa in *The Merchant of Venice*).
Disguise	Characters frequently appear in plays as that which they are not – an ironic metatheatrical device. The disguises adopted on stage are a representation of the broader philosophical idea of disguise and deception that underpins the whole notion of theatre.	Jessica in *The Merchant of Venice* escapes from her father's house disguised in the masque her father so despises, and female characters, as has been observed above, frequently disguise themselves as men. Edgar in *King Lear* appears as Poor Tom. Hamlet, whilst himself to some extent 'acting' madness, reflects upon the deceit of actors. Macbeth adopts a theatrical metaphor for life, as does Jaques in *As You Like It*. A good contemporary example occurs in Richard Bean's *One Man, Two Guvnors*.

Convention/ device	Function	Examples
Dramatic irony	This is when an audience is aware of information as yet undisclosed to some or all of the characters on stage. This is often a device employed to create humour, but it also has more sinister uses in tragedy.	Possibly the most famous example occurs in *Macbeth*, where Macbeth is hailed as Thane of Cawdor by the three witches. Macbeth protests that this is impossible – 'The Thane of Cawdor lives' – yet the audience knows that the current Thane of Cawdor has been sentenced to death, and that Duncan has proclaimed that Macbeth will be given his title.
Unities	Three principles derived by French classicists from Aristotle's *Poetics*. They require a play to have a single plot (unity of action) represented as occurring in a single location (unity of place) and within the course of a day (unity of time). These three unities were redefined in 1570 by the Italian humanist Lodovico Castelvetro in his interpretation of Aristotle, although Aristotle emphasised only one unity, that of action.	*The Tempest* comes very close to observing the three unities, taking place on a single day, in a single place (the island) and focusing on the restoration of Prospero's power. A modern example is J. B. Priestley's *An Inspector Calls*, whose action – the investigation of the events leading up to the death of Eva Smith – takes place in the Birlings' dining room and occurs in real time.

Screenplays and other forms of dramatic performance

We discuss screen versions of stage plays later in this chapter. For the purposes of this book, however, we otherwise restrict our discussion of drama to scripted plays produced in the theatre, since these are central to the 16–19 literature curriculum. This is not to suggest that other forms of drama, especially film and television drama, do not have a legitimate place in that curriculum. Indeed, the longstanding neglect of film and television drama in literature courses is in many respects hard to understand. One issue is the existence of film and media studies as a specialised discipline; another is the relatively uncertain status of film/script as an authored work; another is the question of the identification of what UK syllabuses call 'texts worthy of literary study' in a form where there is perhaps even less agreement about what constitutes literary quality than in fiction and poetry. Even leaving those arguments aside, however, many 'literary' dramatists have opted to write for television and the big screen (e.g. Tom Stoppard's *Shakespeare in Love* (an original screenplay) and his adaptations of Tolstoy's *Anna Karenina* for the big screen and Ford Madox Ford's *Parade's End* for the BBC; or Stephen Poliakoff, whose *The Lost Prince* won an Emmy); and some, such as Dennis Potter, have written almost exclusively for that medium.

A valuable discussion might be had with students about the differences between theatre, film and television drama. This might touch upon the different approaches each of these dramatic media adopts to authorship and production, the varied presentational conventions of each, and the different status they accord to script and performance. Cultural value is also a useful area for discussion, considering how each medium straddles conceptions of literary and popular culture. Enabling students to see that the boundaries between literary and media study are blurred is also a valuable outcome in itself.

Similarly, it is helpful to explore the overlap that exists between literature, drama and theatre, in particular the differences between scripted/authored plays and other forms of improvised, physical and community theatre. Students will thus recognise that not all theatre is authored and scripted in the mode of the formal drama that is usually the focus of literature courses; that interactions between writers, directors and actors in the theatre can shape drama as much as – or instead of – scriptwriting; and that the potential of drama for powerful social impact goes considerably beyond the realm of the conventional literary play.

Teaching plays

Reading drama texts

It is a truism to say that plays are meant to be watched, not read. Nevertheless, reading is both a crucial part of the literature student's experience of studying drama texts and the first stage in an actor or director's engagement with a playscript. What actors and directors do with their reading is to go on and create a 'production' of the text for the benefit of themselves and a live audience. They produce, in other words, their own 'reading' or interpretation of the text. As stated at the beginning of this chapter, a key skill that students need to acquire is that of visualising a range of different interpretations of their set play during their reading and study. Teachers of drama in the 16–19 literature classroom will need to develop a repertoire of techniques that will encourage students to carry out this visualisation, drawing not only on their knowledge of the text itself but also on their developing understanding of theatrical history and stagecraft.

Unlike texts of prose fiction, a full read-through of some drama texts, especially shorter modern texts, can be achieved in class within a few hours. This might be done in one sitting, providing students with an unbroken overview of the play as a whole, giving them a clear concept of the time over which an audience will engage with the drama, and allowing them to gain an insight into the narrative(s) of the drama without the inevitable fragmentation of a scene-by-scene approach. However, there is also a great deal to be said for a reading which builds in periods of discussion between scenes or sections of the play, so that students have a chance to share their developing reactions to the drama, make predictions, reflect on shifts in character and emphasis in the narrative, and so on.

Whichever of these methods is chosen, this first read-through is likely to need supplementing with a more detailed reading and exploration of the text. Teachers will need to weigh up for themselves how to balance teacher-led reading with more structured autonomous reading. Students, especially early in their courses, will need support in approaching a complex literary text, especially in an unfamiliar form (whereas most students will read prose fiction in their spare time, very few students will read plays). Teachers have to balance the need for a detailed and nuanced reading of the play with the need to complete the reading within a limited amount of time. A detailed reading and discussion of every scene of a play – especially one of Shakespeare's plays – could not possibly be achieved in the 20 or 25 hours of teaching time available – even if such an approach were desirable. Nevertheless, students need to be familiar with the whole text and its implications. How, then, does one balance detail with a broad overview, especially given the range of ability that might be present in a 16–19 class?

A detailed set of approaches to reading drama texts can be found later in this chapter, in relation to reading the plays of Shakespeare – an aspect of literary study that poses particular challenges to teachers and students alike. There are, nevertheless, several key issues that are relevant to the study of any drama text. One is the extent to which students can and should be left to read the play independently – whether in parts or as a whole. If dealing with a high ability class this will be easier, but even able students can struggle if left to their own devices. This is not to say that they might not get the gist of what is going on – especially if helped by watching a performance – but moving beyond the gist to a detailed understanding of the language is often harder. In this context, reading together in class is an important strategy, but it is also important to vary approaches to reading in order to develop students' confidence and independence.

The traditional strategy of sharing the reading of scenes in class, with students taking parts, and the whole class (guided by judicious questioning by the teacher) working together to construct a shared interpretation of the scene, is an important part of the teacher's armoury. It can work well, and is important in establishing the class's relationship with the reading of the play. However, it can also be problematic. For one thing, it depends on having enough students who feel confident both in reading fluently and in offering interpretations of language and concepts that are often relatively complex. It is time-consuming and can become routine. There can also be a tendency for the less able to become passive, relying too heavily on the contributions of the most able. A class with a number of less able and/or less motivated readers might struggle to maintain sufficient energy to make this an effective strategy, especially if it is used too frequently. An alternative strategy is to read scenes from the play in conjunction with watching a film version or listening to an audio version, with books in hand. (It's worth noting too that the DVD 'subtitle' option can be used so that students can read the words of the text on screen as they watch the film.) Whether audio or video is used, this strategy has the obvious advantage that students hear a good reading of the text, but it also means that students approach the text with a prior interpretation already in mind, which might – unless handled carefully – place a limit on students' own interpretations of the play.

The language and structure of dramatic narrative

The dynamic qualities of dramatic narrative are so powerful that examination of its literary language is sometimes at risk of neglect.

At a fundamental level, students need to consider whether a play is written in verse or prose (or both), why that is, and the impact of the choices authors make in this regard. These are questions that are sometimes overlooked, but they are significant in terms of understanding individual texts and in terms of the broader development of the genre.

Many of the techniques already described for close reading of prose and verse language in Chapters 2 and 3 of this book are, of course, also applicable to the study of drama texts. Particularly significant in drama, however, is the concept of voice, since it is through characters' voices that the narrative is chiefly propelled. In a rather different fashion to the narratives of prose fiction, story in drama is 'told'. This is an issue worthy of careful consideration, as differing voices provide varied inflections upon the unfolding narrative. A fascinating possibility here is to compare the narrative of stage drama with passages from the novels of Ivy Compton-Burnett, whose prose narratives largely eschew convention and are carried forward almost uniquely in dialogue. By comparing prose dialogue with dramatic dialogue some very interesting parallels and differences emerge. A crucial question is the extent to which characterisation is achieved through voice.

Another issue to consider is the narrative interventions playwrights make in the drama in the form of stage directions and narrative background. These interventions hold an interesting place in drama texts. They play a central function in establishing the literary world of the text, but how and to what extent should teachers and students actually consider them part of the text? Certainly they contribute to the play's 'literary' qualities and feed into the 'extra dimension' of drama texts alluded to previously. The audience for these interventions, however, is not primarily the viewing audience but actors, directors and others involved in a play's production. The language and style of these interventions is obviously very different to the remainder of the text and raises some very interesting questions. Is the language of such textual interventions any the less literary and any less important? How and when should students talk about such language and the interaction between it and the overtly literary language of the drama script itself? How and when do audiences engage with this element of texts? How do we discuss this language and its parallel existence to the main text?

The question of stage directions also highlights one of the key issues in understanding narrative in drama: how narrative direction is achieved without an over-arching narrator. Here, a key concept is dramatic purpose. One powerful way of helping students to understand the qualities of dramatic narrative is transformational writing – getting students to transform a dramatic scene into narrative prose, or vice versa, so that they can experience how writers must convey information to the reader/audience in different ways according to the demands of different genres. Informative comparisons can again be drawn by considering works of prose fiction – in this case works with multiple narrators. Good examples can be found in the epistolary novels of the eighteenth century (e.g. Henry Fielding's *Shamela*, Samuel Richardson's *Clarissa*, or Tobias Smollett's *Humphry Clinker*) or in the sensation novels of Wilkie Collins (*The Woman in White* and *The Moonstone*) and Bram Stoker (*Dracula*). In each of these examples a single narrative is carried forward in multiple voices, and the writers achieve considerable effects of drama and irony through the interactions of the various voices in relation to the story they share. The similarities and differences between prose narrative and dramatic narrative emerge through such a comparison.

Panel 4.4 summarises issues relating to the particular nature of dramatic narrative. This could be given to students as a reference sheet.

Panel 4.4   Dramatic narrative

Drama uses many of the same narrative techniques as other narrative forms – the novel, the short story and narrative poetry. However, what is unique about drama is its social, physical nature, and the way it is mediated through actors, directors and so on. The Greek word 'drama' comes from a word meaning 'to do, to act'.

Some of the features of drama that distinguish it from other genres include the following:

1   The narrative in drama is often more small scale than the drama in novels and epic poetry. The limitations of the theatre mean that it is likely to employ *fewer characters* and *fewer settings*.

2   With a few exceptions, there is no narrator in drama. One of the things that makes drama dramatic is that the stories are told almost entirely through *dialogue*. Settings, characters, costumes etc. are not described – they are seen. In addition, *non-verbal actions* can be performed physically rather than described as in a novel, and these can have a very powerful effect in the theatre. *Stage directions* are often used to supply narrative instructions.

3   Another thing that makes drama dramatic is the presence of an audience. It is not designed to be consumed in private like the novel or, often, poetry. Although novelists and poets try to create an emotional impact on their readers, this can be more direct in drama because of the direct communication between actors and audience, and the emotional effect of the live performance on the audience. Techniques such as *asides* and *soliloquies*, which enable actors to address the audience direct, are a major feature of drama.

4   Although writers in all forms let readers know information which is not known by all the characters, thus creating irony and a sense of suspense or tension, *dramatic irony* – where one character knows something that another doesn't – is particularly strong because the irony is shared directly by the actors with the audience.

5   Similarly, although all writers insert scenes in narratives for a particular purpose, we talk about *dramatic purpose* in plays to describe the reasons why playwrights insert particular scenes to move the narrative on and to reveal information to the audience. There is no narrator to reveal information, so it must all be done through dialogue.

Remember also that drama may be written in *verse*, or *prose*, or *both*. So we can talk about:

1   *Drama, poetry, the novel*, and *the short story* as major forms of literature.
2   *Verse* and *prose* as the modes of language used in literature.

Panel 4.5 illustrates how students might work with such issues in detailed study of a set text.

Panel 4.5   Language, form and structure in *A View from the Bridge*

1. Dramatic form and structure

We have already seen how the play reflects elements of the narrative structure of Greek tragedy. Now, we need to look at how the play works as a dramatic narrative.

a   The role of Alfieri is crucial in the narrative. Reread the passages of Alfieri's narration, and the scenes between him and Eddie, then think about the following questions.
   (i)   Narration: Why do you think Miller decided to use a narrator? Why did Miller choose Alfieri as narrator? What is the significance of what Alfieri says as a narrator? How does Alfieri influence the way we experience the narrative?

(ii)   Dialogue: What role does Alfieri play? What is the significance of his scenes with Eddie?

b   Dramatic irony is where the audience knows something the characters don't. Where is this important in this play?

c   Dramatic purpose is the way in which the playwright places scenes within the narrative to reveal new information to the audience. Think about how Miller uses dramatic purpose to further the narrative.

2. Dramatic language

Both the dialogue and the stage directions are characteristic of realist drama.

a   Look carefully at the use of stage directions and notice how Miller uses these to convey characters' feelings and relationships, as well as to describe the scene. Find some examples.

b   The dialogue attempts to portray the way people really speak. It is written in American dialect, and tries to recreate real speaking patterns. Look through the play and identify:

(i)   some of the main features of the dialect

(ii)   some examples of realist dialogue.

How does realist dialogue differ from the language of older, more poetic drama?
How does Alfieri's language differ from that of the other characters?

From script to stage

As suggested earlier, when teaching any drama text teachers will need to think about how they can balance their study of the words on the page with an awareness of the 'extra dimension' of drama – the ways in which the play has been, and could be, actualised on stage. The watching of live performances (and preferably multiple live performances) of drama is, of course, beneficial wherever possible. Such performances provide access to the plural possibilities of interpretation to which drama texts are subject. There is, of course, no guarantee that a stage performance of a set play will be running over the period a text is being taught, or if it is, that it will be accessible; it is sometimes, however, a good idea (if circumstances allow) to choose a set drama text with the availability of such performances in mind. It's worth noting here the increasing availability of very high quality DVDs and online streaming of live performances, such as those issued by Shakespeare's Globe and Digital Theatre, which are highly recommended, and a very economical way of bringing live theatre to a class.

Whether a class sees a production live in the theatre or watches a film of a live theatre performance, the experience inevitably provides a great opportunity to explore the translation of the script to the stage, and it is always worthwhile devoting some time in class to exploring responses to the production. Often the best time to see such a production is when students have already read at least part of the play, if not the whole thing, as they will then be very keen to discuss the ways in which the stage version has brought the script to life, changed their view of the play, or conflicted with their expectations. Class or group discussion is likely to focus on the following kinds of question:

- Was the play in performance as you expected it to be, or did it feel different from what you expected?
- Did any aspects of the play come to life or make sense to you that hadn't done so when reading the script?
- Did the director or actors make any changes to the play in performance? Did they add anything or leave anything out, or change things round?
- Were you surprised by any of the decisions made by the director or actors in relation to how to stage or act the play?
- Did you feel that the stage version supported your understanding of the play, or made you think about it differently?
- Did you feel that the stage version took liberties with the script or presented it faithfully?
- Do you feel that the director chose to interpret the play in a particular way or to emphasise or highlight a particular aspect of the play?

Another very valuable activity following a class viewing of a production is to gather together reviews of the production, and press articles about it, and allow students to discuss the issues that emerge from these. It's also worth remembering that many theatre companies produce very interesting education packs, or accompanying web pages, through which students can explore various aspects of both the play and the production.

Where no live productions are available, it is quite possible that teachers and their students might only experience their set play in its written form. Thomas Hardy, in his 1903 preface to *The Dynasts*, questions 'whether mental performance alone may not eventually be the fate of all drama other than that of contemporary or frivolous life' (2007: x). The kind of 'mental performance' Hardy envisages here is perhaps not so far from the experience of many students of literature. It is important, therefore, to provide students with access to the processes by which performances of drama texts are constructed, so that they are able to explore for themselves the kinds of interpretive choices that underpin the staging of drama texts. In undertaking such tasks, students of literature enact dramatic methods of 'reading', and consider the multiple 'literacies' involved in the experience of watching performed drama.

One particularly effective technique is to engage students with the processes of drama production. At a textual level, directors may have to decide between variant texts (as is often the case when working with Shakespeare), nuances of interpretation, whether and what to cut from a text, and the particular emphasis to be placed upon certain themes or political agendas. In addition, as Antonin Artaud reminds us, it is not only the words on the page that constitute the language of theatre. When approaching drama texts, students need to think about a variety of stage 'languages'. In making choices about how the written text will be presented on stage – the nature of the scenery and props that will be employed, the decision about whether to present a play in period or whether to produce a modern version, the costumes characters will wear and how their hair and make-up will be done, the role of music and sound effects – those working with a play text significantly influence the way in which the drama text will be 'received' by an audience. Reading drama texts as if they were directors, producers and actors makes students authorial collaborators.

An obvious starting point for this kind of exploration is the way that the play is established right at the start. A useful concept to introduce here is that of the *mise en scène* – a term derived from French theatre that literally means 'put in the scene'. Some dramatists are very specific – even prescriptive – in setting out the details of what they want to happen on stage, even extending to precise information regarding set design. John Osborne, for instance, provides very detailed stage directions at the opening of *Look Back in Anger*, as does J. B. Priestley at the start of *An Inspector Calls*. Other writers, such as Shakespeare, provide notoriously little in the way of stage directions – most of the stage directions in his plays are editorial, based on textual suggestions.

The two activities in Panel 4.6 offer some examples of questions that can be used to prompt students' explorations of the beginnings of plays. The first focuses on the differences between the opening of *The Tempest*, which contains very little textual direction, and *Look Back in Anger*, which contains a great deal. Such differences open rich veins of discussion and pedagogic opportunity in the 16–19 classroom. The second explores the *mise en scène* of Arthur Miller's *A View from the Bridge*, in which a detailed description of setting is followed by the opening monologue of the lawyer Alfieri – a speech that functions as a chorus, giving the audience important information about the nature and significance of the events that will follow.

Panel 4.6   Exploring *mise en scène*

Activity 1

Give students the very different opening pages of *The Tempest* and *Look Back in Anger*.

1   What different demands do these openings place upon directors and actors?
2   What choices are left open to the directors and actors in each case?
3   How much more 'mediated' is the experience of the audience of one play compared to the other?
4   How would you approach these scenes as a director or actor? What would you want to achieve?

Activity 2

Give students the opening pages of *A View from the Bridge*, from the beginning of Miller's stage directions to the end of Alfieri's opening monologue.

1   How does Miller establish a sense of the play's geographical and social setting?
2   How important are the stage directions at the beginning of the play? Do you need to read them?
3   What role does Alfieri occupy in the community that Miller depicts? What role does he occupy in relation to the audience?
4   What kind of atmosphere does Miller establish through Alfieri's opening speech?

An effective way of building on this kind of activity and encouraging students to think about the play in performance is to get them to produce a set of resources based upon the play they are studying. This might include set designs, costume designs, potential props, incidental music (whether pre-composed – e.g. Mendelssohn's *A Midsummer Night's Dream* or Finzi's music for *Love's Labour's Lost* – or music the students select themselves), colour schemes for use in the production, and concepts surrounding contemporary, other historical, modern-day or futuristic productions of the play and rationales for these. The gathering of such resources (and others) involves students creatively in the processes of reading and interpreting drama texts and can be used as a stimulus for debate with the class about the varying potentials of the text. Students can be encouraged to explore the varying effects that would result from the use of the resources they collect and how these would affect the audience's response. Such tasks can be undertaken at a whole-text level, at the level of a single scene or in relation to very specific elements. For example, how would we understand Blanche in *Cat on a Hot Tin Roof* differently at this point if she wore different kinds of dress? Or, knowing what you know about Falstaff, what kind of drinking vessel would you have him use in *Henry IV*? The discussions emerging from this kind of discussion can immerse students deeply in the minutiae of the text, as they think in detail about the nuances of their reading and the ways in which information is passed on to audiences in the drama.

This kind of engagement with the processes undergone as a play makes the leap from script to stage is fruitful in enabling students to access the 'extra dimension' implicit in drama texts to which we've already referred. It is important, in other words, that students explore some of the processes by which drama texts are activated. Panel 4.7 suggests a number of activities that allow access to these dimensions of working with text.

Panel 4.7   Drama texts – from script to stage

There are many ways in which this aspect of texts can be brought to life in the classroom, but some successful strategies are as follows:

1   Students are required to consider any character in the play as if they were the actor to play that part. They read the play in full (or perhaps at selected key points) and then have to answer in as much detail as possible the following questions:

    a   What does my character say about him/herself?
    b   What does my character say about other characters?
    c   What do other characters say about my character?
    d   What does my character do (e.g. entering, exiting, shaking hands, drinking, kissing etc.) and how would he/she do these things?
    e   What does the playwright say about my character (e.g. in notes on the cast list, in stage directions etc.)?

2   Read a range of reviews of stage performances of the play covering as wide a range of productions and time periods as possible. What do the reviewers say about the play and its production? How does this provide an insight into ways of reading the plays?

3 Read relevant extracts from the biographies and memoirs of famous actors or directors, or interviews with actors, directors or stage managers. What do they say about particular plays, particular characters and particular types of characters? This can often provide an interesting insight into how characters are brought to life.

4 Examine photographs of stage productions or 'stills' from filmed live productions. Link this back closely to the source text. How do these images reflect the content of the text? What has the director or designer brought to the text? How are these 'bringings' likely to affect audience response?

5 Listen to the incidental music to a play (e.g. recordings of songs from a Shakespeare play, Grieg's incidental music for *Peer Gynt* or Mendelssohn's for *A Midsummer Night's Dream*) and then read the relevant extract of the source text. How is such music likely to shape the way a play appears on the stage?

6 Look at pictures of a range of costumes for particular characters in a set text – these should cover 'period' performances through to modern updates and experimental productions. How would the decision to clothe a character in these different ways bring to life certain aspects of a character and text, and in what ways would it lessen or remove other possibilities?

Developments in digital technology have made available a number of additional resources for exploring the production of drama. Many of these resources focus on Shakespeare. The *Designing Shakespeare* collection (www.ahds.rhul.ac.uk/ahdscollections/docroot/shakespeare/playslist.do) is an extensive archive of production photos that allow students to explore costume and setting. The Globe Theatre's Resource Library (www.globe-education.org/discovery-space/resource-library/document) contains a series of downloadable 'Research Bulletins' that explore the rehearsal process behind the staging of various plays, including decisions about set design, props, costume and music. Also available on the Globe's website is an 'Adopt an Actor' facility (www.globe-education.org/discovery-space/adopt-an-actor) containing journals and interviews that offer fascinating insights into the demands of working in this most unique of theatres. The Royal Shakespeare Company, meanwhile, has its own archive of production photographs (www.rsc.org.uk/education/resources/bank). Other resources can be accessed through the education pages of theatres and companies such as the National Theatre (www.nationaltheatre.org.uk/discover), the Royal Court (www.royalcourt theatre.com/education) and the Royal Exchange in Manchester (www.royalexchange.co.uk). Such resources allow students important access to the thinking behind theatrical productions and the multiple possibilities opened up when plays are 'activated' on stage, broadening the range of interpretations to which they are exposed. They allow students to enter into an imaginative exploration of the details and potential meanings of dramatic texts – often uncovering perspectives that they might not have considered if using more conventional approaches.

From stage to screen

Although films of live theatre are increasingly available for classroom use, film and television adaptations are the visual representations of drama texts that students are perhaps still most likely to encounter. There is great value in using well-selected screen adaptations of plays and appropriate extracts. As mediated interpretations of drama texts they provide easily accessible, widely varied and flexible 'performance' versions, and, like films of live theatre, can be used with students to assist reading, prompt interpretation and promote discussion of the representation of texts. Film and television adaptations, however, cannot be seen as substitutes for live productions. Whilst providing a useful visual medium version of drama texts, these media cannot reproduce the 'lived experience' of theatre.

It is important to remember, too, that drama texts (like novels, short stories or films based on poetry), when not filmed live on stage, have to be adapted for the screen. It is easy to assume that because the text was written for performance it is the same text that we see on the screen, but this is an unwarranted assumption. Drama texts and screen adaptations of those texts must not be conflated or unfairly compared. Criticising a film for not being sufficiently true to its source novel or play is as unreasonable as blaming a dog for not being a cat. In fact, exploring such differences provides excellent stimulus for critical discussion and is of great benefit to students. Consider, for example, how a text has been adapted in order to function on the screen. Here are some suggested points for discussion:

- Most films are of 90 minutes' to two hours' duration, whereas most plays are longer than this. Consider what is cut and why. What is the effect of this on the viewer and on the pace, impact and balance of the drama? What is gained and what is lost by such treatment of the original text;
- Look at the sequence of scenes in the screen adaptation. Are these presented in the order in which they appear in the play, or has the narrative been reorganised? Why have any changes been made? What is the impact of these changes on the meaning of the narrative and the ways in which an audience might respond?
- Screen versions are 'air-brushed' in ways that stage productions cannot be. Where in live performance mistakes will out and become part of the performance and the actors' interaction with each other, the text and the audience, such errors rarely (if ever) find their way into final cut versions of screen drama. How is this likely to affect impact and response?
- Film and television adaptations of plays (and films of live theatre) make use of a wide range of televisual possibilities – the close-up shot, the bird's-eye view or the long shot, for example. Perspective and distance can thus be varied very quickly and in ways not open to those working with the text on stage. How do directors of screen and stage versions of plays approach texts and how do they use such approaches to affect viewers' responses? Whilst an audience may gain great insight into a character through a close-up shot, for example, they simultaneously lose the choice of what to look at and cannot see the reactions of other characters involved in the same scene;
- Film and television, like the stage, have their own representational codes, such as the voice-over, the flashback, slow motion and a wide variety of shot angles. How do such devices compare to the possibilities of live theatre, and how do they affect the way in which an audience interacts with the text at key moments? Much is gained, for example, in our fine understanding of a character's emotions if we see a full-face close-up;
- The experience of watching a film in the cinema, which involves something of the shared experience of being in the theatre, is quite different to the experience of watching a film on the small screen in the more intimate settings of the classroom or at home. How do small screen and large screen adaptations of drama texts (and the experience of watching them) differ?

The activities in Panel 4.8 are very useful for getting 16–19 groups to consider the possibilities and limitations of film.

Panel 4.8   Exploring drama on screen

1   After discussing with students the range of techniques available to the film director, set them the creative task of adapting a scene or section of a scene for the large or small screen. This could be presented as a storyboard, or they could actually make the film if time and resources allow. The 'screening' of the film or presentation of the storyboard should be accompanied by a detailed rationale relating to the original text and what the students were hoping to achieve through their adaptation.

2   View multiple versions of screen adaptations of either the whole play or selected scenes, looking closely at how the different directors have approached the process of screen adaptation. What is gained and what is lost in each case? How does each contribute to our reading of the play and its impact upon the audience? How would this have to appear differently if it were performed on stage? (A useful list of film adaptations of Shakespeare's plays, ranging from traditional adaptations such as Franco Zeffirelli's *Romeo and Juliet* and Michael Radford's *The Merchant of Venice* to more creative rewritings such as Gil Junger's *10 Things I Hate About You* and Billy Morrissette's *Scotland, PA*, can be found online at srufaculty.sru.edu/derrick.pitard).

3   Make three separate viewings of a chosen sequence from a film or screen adaptation. The first viewing should be sound only – what effects do the music, dialogue and the sound effects alone create? The second viewing should be visual only – what impression do the visual dimensions of the text alone make upon the viewer, and how does the lack of sound affect what we see and how we see it? The third viewing, which follows a discussion of the different levels of reading undertaken in the first two viewings, should be conventional, allowing for an exploration of the text as a whole. This activity allows students to explore the impact of multimodality – an effect that is to some extent available both in the theatre and on screen.

4   As a variation on activity 3, reverse this viewing sequence, allowing the students to deconstruct the visual and aural components of the film in response to a pre-formed 'meaning'.

5   Compare drama script and screenplay versions of the same scene from a play in order to gain insight into the creative transformational processes adapters go through in modifying a play for the screen.

6   A variant on activity 5 is to compare a drama script with a play originally written for the screen in order to explore the differing demands of writing for the stage and for the screen.

It's worth pointing out here that there are also countless opera, musical and ballet versions of drama texts. To take Shakespeare's *Romeo and Juliet* as an example, there is Tchaikovsky's *Overture-Fantasy Romeo and Juliet*, Frederick Delius' opera *A Village Romeo and Juliet*, Leonard Bernstein's dramatic reworking of the play in *West Side Story*, Prokofiev's monumental ballet *Romeo and Juliet*, and other musical treatments by Hector Berlioz, Vincenzo Bellini, Charles Gounod and Nino Rota. *Macbeth* boasts interesting and varied musical interpretations by composers as diverse as Giuseppe Verdi (opera), Dmitri Shostakovich (*Lady Macbeth of the Mtsensk District* is a taut modern retelling and its libretto is easily available online), Sir Arthur Sullivan (overture), Richard Strauss (symphonic poem), Collin Simon and Liz Muller (musical), and Mitch Benn (comic song).

While there is much to be gained from considering stage and screen adaptations of texts, however, teachers must always remember that their students are, primarily, students of literature. While assessment requirements will vary from one course to another, students need to be able to respond to and write about drama texts as *literary* texts. Students who are also studying theatre studies or media studies sometimes struggle with this distinction; and it is not uncommon – even in the 16–19 phase – to find students writing about the film adaptations of their set texts as if these are the 'real' versions. Bringing students back to the words on the page and their multiple possibilities can be a delicate process, but it is one that needs to be negotiated.

Teaching Shakespeare

It is impossible in a chapter dedicated to the teaching of drama texts to ignore the work of Shakespeare, whose texts figure so prominently in literature courses. It should be stressed here, however, that there is nothing uniquely different about the teaching of Shakespeare as dramatic text. The approaches one would adopt in teaching *Othello* or *Much Ado About Nothing* are substantially similar to the approaches one would adopt in teaching *The Confidential Clerk*, *Hedda Gabler* or *Juno and the Paycock*. Nor are there difficulties attendant on the teaching of Shakespeare that are not found in the teaching of other drama texts. The difficulties students face in approaching the language and context of Shakespeare are equally present in the works of his contemporaries (e.g. Christopher Marlowe, Ben Jonson, John Ford, John Webster and others), which are often found on examination syllabuses. Similarly, the issues surrounding verse drama are difficulties faced in the dramatic works of both Shakespeare's contemporaries, and of Shelley, Byron, T. S. Eliot and Christopher Fry. Plays dealing with conceptually advanced material, such as Samuel Beckett's classic *Waiting for Godot* or Ibsen's *Peer Gynt*, present students and teachers with challenges equal to anything Shakespeare has to offer. In fact, in many ways Shakespeare is arguably easier for students to access and teachers to teach than any other dramatist, given the almost endless wealth of materials available to support the study of his plays. This said, however, it is worth spending some time specifically considering some of the issues faced when approaching a text by Shakespeare, if only because he is the dramatic figure above all others that students are likely to encounter in the course of their 16–19 literary studies.

Reading Shakespeare

As stated above, the approaches that teachers might use when teaching Shakespeare's plays have much in common with those that might be used when teaching other drama texts. Nevertheless, Shakespeare's archaic language and relatively unfamiliar verse form can present even able students with problems: the metaphorical density, multiple allusion and wordplay Shakespeare engages in add their own levels of complexity.

In this context, reading in class together is an important strategy, but it is also important to vary approaches to reading in order to develop students' confidence and independence as readers of Shakespeare. Therefore, we need to consider explicitly what strategies we might use to make students more confident in tackling Shakespeare's language, so that we can assign them selected passages, then scenes, then sequences of scenes, and ultimately full texts to read independently in the knowledge that they are developing the necessary abilities to work with such text and its nuances.

There are several general strategies that can be employed at an early stage of the reading of the play to boost student confidence and independence in reading Shakespeare in a nuanced way, sensitive to the ways in which Shakespeare uses language for particular effects. Panel 4.9 offers some suggested ways in:

Panel 4.9   Reading Shakespeare

1   Teach students explicitly about the elements of Shakespeare's language and stagecraft – archaic grammar and vocabulary, classical allusion, use of verse and prose, soliloquies and asides etc. Don't assume they understand what these are or what they mean, or why Shakespeare uses them. These can be explored in relation to a set of short extracts from across Shakespeare's oeuvre in order to build confidence. John Haddon's book *Teaching Reading Shakespeare* (2009) is very useful here, and for teachers less familiar with the academic content relating to Shakespeare's language, Frank Kermode's *Shakespeare's Language* (2001) is an excellent starting point.

2   Teach students explicitly a range of literary/rhetorical devices (from questions and exclamations to long and short sentence lengths) that Shakespeare employs for effect. Ask students to write a commentary on how Shakespeare uses these devices in a particular speech.

3   Get students to prepare, in small groups, a group reading or performance of a short section (say 60 lines) of a scene, and provide them with questions to frame their discussion relating to the action, the kinds of language used and its implications. This activity is particularly useful in getting less confident readers to 'find their voice' for reading Shakespeare, by helping them to read as active meaning-makers. Regular group discussion and reporting back is vital throughout the reading of the play to ensure that all students engage actively with meaning-making and overcome residual reluctance to engage with the nuances of the text.

4   Work at word level. Take a significant speech from a play – perhaps a soliloquy – and allocate each line (or a pair or trio of lines, depending upon the number in the class) to each student. Ask them to select a single word from their line(s) that for them seems to be the most interesting or important word. Around the class read out these words and then look for emerging patterns of meaning that the students can then apply to the speech as a whole to access possible meanings.

5   Take a speech. Ask the students to remove from it all adverbs, adjectives and articles, leaving only the nouns, pronouns and verbs behind. Use this 'skeleton' speech to gain the gist of meaning, then return to the speech as a whole.

6   Take a speech or a whole scene. In small groups, students select images and collect them together into families of images. What do these images and groups of images suggest on their own (e.g. disease imagery may suggest discomfort, anger, corruption etc.)? What do they suggest when brought into combination (e.g. the combination of disease and plant imagery in *Hamlet*)? Use these emerging connotations and connections as a way of reading back into the text for fuller meaning and compare the use of these image trains in scenes drawn from across a particular play.

As students gain confidence, they can be given increasing levels of responsibility for leading class responses to reading, either in groups or individually. This will, of course, require support, especially in the early stages of a 16–19 course. Panel 4.10 provides an example of how guided group reading, which provides a halfway house between whole-class reading and fully independent reading, can be used to explore *Hamlet*, Act 2, Scene 2.

Panel 4.10   *Guided group reading:* Hamlet, Act 2, Scene 2

Work in groups to prepare a performance reading of an extract from Act 2, Scene 2 looking at both the meaning of the extract, and what you were trying to show from the way you read it. Guiding comments and questions are provided.

First, read the lines and discuss potential interpretations. At this stage, just try to get the gist of what is going on. The idea is to become familiar with the extract so that interpretations will emerge in reading. Then practice the performance reading in line with your discussion. At this stage, you might want to think more about the exact meanings of some of the less obvious lines. Read the whole of Act 2, Scene 2 from the beginning to line 277 so you can place your passage in the relevant context.

You will find it useful to compare Hamlet's behaviour and language in your extract with his behaviour and language in other extracts.

Groups 1 and 2 – Claudius, Gertrude, Polonius
Group 1: Line 80 (It likes us well) – line 127 (Received his love?)
Group 2: Line 128 (What do you think of me?) – line 170 (O give me leave)

Ophelia has told Polonius that, after she rejected his continued advances according to Polonius' instructions, Hamlet came to see her in a disturbed state of mind, apparently acting madly. Polonius assumes that Hamlet has gone mad because Ophelia has rejected him. In this part of Scene 2, he goes to Claudius and Gertrude to report these events...

• What is Polonius trying to achieve here, and does his behaviour fit with what we already know of him, and of Claudius?
• Does the language Shakespeare gives Polonius here suggest a particular interpretation of his character?

- How might Claudius and Gertrude react to Polonius here? How might you play all three characters if you were acting them?
- What might be the dramatic purpose of this part of the scene, i.e. why might Shakespeare have included this scene?

Group 3 – Hamlet, Polonius
Line 171 (How does my good Lord) – line 220 (God save you Sir)

In this part of Scene 2, Polonius agrees with Claudius that together they will watch an encounter between Hamlet and Gertrude to see how he behaves. Meanwhile, as he finishes speaking to Claudius and Gertrude, Polonius sees Hamlet coming and decides to talk to him...

- How do you interpret Hamlet's behaviour towards Polonius here? To what extent does it fit with what we know of Hamlet, and Polonius, already?
- What kind of language does Shakespeare give Hamlet here, and how does it affect your interpretation?
- How would you describe Polonius' reactions to Hamlet? How might you play both if you were acting them?
- What might be the dramatic purpose of this part of the scene, i.e. why might Shakespeare have included this scene?

Groups 4 and 5 – Hamlet, Rosencrantz and Guildenstern
Group 4: Line 221 (My honoured Lord!) – line 268 (What make you at Elsinore?)
Group 5: Line 268 (What make you...) – line 323 (What players are they?)

Claudius has asked Rosencrantz and Guildenstern, two old friends of Hamlet, to try and find out what is wrong with him and report back. In this part of Scene 2, Hamlet meets and greets Rosencrantz and Guildenstern, and later tries to find out why they are there.

- How do you interpret Hamlet's behaviour towards and relationship with Rosencrantz and Guildenstern here? To what extent does it fit with what we know of Hamlet, and of Rosencrantz and Guildenstern, already?
- What kind of language does Shakespeare give the characters here, and how does it affect your interpretation?
- What do you make of Rosencrantz and Guildenstern's reactions to Hamlet? How might you play all three of these characters if you were acting them?
- What might be the dramatic purpose of this part of the scene, i.e. why might Shakespeare have included this scene?

Group 6 – Guildenstern, Hamlet, Polonius
Line 364 (There are the players) – line 413 (where my abridgements come)

Hamlet concludes his talk with Rosencrantz and Guildenstern, reflecting on his state of mind; he then mocks Polonius, who comes to announce the arrival of the Players (actors) to the castle.

- How do you interpret Hamlet's behaviour towards Rosencrantz and Guildenstern, and towards Polonius, here?
- What kind of language does Shakespeare give the characters here, and how does it affect your interpretation?
- What do you make of the reactions of Rosencrantz and Guildenstern, and Polonius, to Hamlet? How might you play these characters if you were acting them?
- What might be the dramatic purpose of this part of the scene, i.e. why might Shakespeare have included this scene?

Activities such as these can appear time-consuming during the early stages of reading the play, but investment in them can pay dividends as students quickly become more confident and independent during the latter part of the reading, and more alert to the implications of Shakespeare's style.

Teaching about Shakespeare's theatre

Alongside a detailed focus on the nature of Shakespeare's language, it's also useful to explore with students the functional aspect of Shakespeare's theatre, looking with them at the major theatrical conventions he uses and how these operate.

It is important to remember the differences between a theatre-going audience in Elizabethan England and the theatre-going audience of today. Shakespeare's audience, as McEvoy (2006: 12–13) points out, would have accounted for approximately 15 to 20 per cent of London's population. The Elizabethans were regular playgoers who would have been used to dealing with lengthy text and as such would have been much more attuned to the demands of the theatre as listeners than we are today. The comparative lack of technical theatre and stage machinery then available meant that certain things (such as the weather, time of day, location), which are nowadays reproducible by stage sets, sound effects, music and lighting, were much more frequently presented as part of the spoken text in Shakespeare's day. The use of open-air theatres and daytime performance also meant that night-time had to be indicated in words (e.g. Portia's observation of the light of the candle as she returns to Belmont at the end of *The Merchant of Venice*).

Shakespeare's stage was in many respects very different to the proscenium arch theatre with which we are so familiar. Pictures of Shakespeare's Globe (e.g. Walter Hodges' reconstruction diagrams) and other Elizabethan and Jacobean theatres are easily available online. Look closely at such pictures, or even better go to Shakespeare's Globe in Southwark. Use these to identify the constraints and the possibilities of Shakespeare's stage.

Resourcing Shakespeare

A plethora of excellent (and many not so excellent) resources for the teaching of Shakespeare exists. This is both to the advantage and the disadvantage of teachers and students. Evaluating the relative merits of such a vast bank of potential materials is, in itself, a significant amount of work, and as such careful guidance by the teacher may be required to assist students as they learn to make good selections of their own (a skill that will be essential to them as they progress either into HE or into the world of employment). It is well worth investing in quality editions of the texts, such as the outstanding Arden Shakespeare, New Cambridge, and Oxford World Classics series, all of which come with extended notes and commentaries and are reliable versions of the text.

Many online versions of the plays also exist, and these are an excellent resource for teachers and students alike, providing downloadable text versions that can be cut and pasted, adopted and adapted at will within a wide range of classroom activities (e.g. textual adaptations, programme construction, creating actors' or directors' versions of text, blogging notes, and so on). The quality of these versions varies considerably, however, and teachers would be well advised to make specific recommendations (or even supply links) to desirable versions. Particularly good online texts are available at Project Gutenberg at www.gutenberg.org, and http://shakespeare.mit.edu provides another good complete set. Other interesting sites to visit are www.shakespeareauthorship.com, which explores the fascinating and thorny issue of who actually wrote the plays that are attributed to Shakespeare. A set of contextual documents related to Shakespeare and his life, including a set of prefaces to historical editions of Shakespeare's works, can be found at http://shakespeare.palomar.edu and a good site for exploring the original quarto versions of the plays is to be found on the British Library's website at www.bl.uk/treasures/shakespeare/homepage.html.

Further reading

Teaching drama

There are many excellent introductions to issues in the teaching of drama – for instance *Making Sense of Drama: A Guide to Classroom Practice* (Neelands 1984), *Education and Dramatic Art* (Hornbrook 1998a) and *On the Subject of Drama* (Hornbrook 1998b) – which contain valuable insights for the 16–19 literature teacher; there are very few, if any, however, on the teaching of drama as literature, although *Teaching Literature* (Showalter 2003) has a useful chapter. The English and Media Centre provides a range of resources to support the teaching of plays, including *Studying Comedy* (EMC 2012), *Tragedy: A Student Handbook* (McEvoy 2009) and *Pre-1770 Drama: Elizabethan and Jacobean* (EMC 2001). On teaching Shakespeare, *Teaching Reading Shakespeare* (Haddon 2009) is invaluable, and *Teaching Shakespeare: A Handbook for Teachers* (Gibson 1998) is a classic general introduction.

Critical introductions to drama

The Life of the Drama (Bentley 1964) is a classic text on how drama works. More recently, *The Crafty Art of Playmaking* (Ayckbourn 2003), *The Secret Life of Plays*

(Waters 2010) and *How Plays Work* (Edgar 2009) offer dramatists' views on the creation of drama texts and the ways in which dramatic narrative functions. *The Drama Handbook: A Guide to Reading Plays* (Lennard and Luckhurst 2002) and *Studying Plays* (Wallis and Shepherd 2010) are excellent overviews of all aspects of drama from narrative and genre to theatre production. *The Oxford Illustrated History of the Theatre* (Brown 2001) and *A History of the Theatre* (Wickham 1992) are excellent historical overviews.

There are far too many books on Shakespeare to list more than a few: *Shakespeare: The Basics* (McEvoy 2006), *Doing Shakespeare* (Palfrey 2011), *Shakespeare's Language* (Kermode 2001), *The Genius of Shakespeare* (Bate 2008) and *The Shakespearean Stage* (Gurr 2009) are some of the most useful introductions.

Chapter 5

Teaching theory and criticism

Introduction: Exploring context and interpretation

The previous three chapters of this book have dealt separately with poetry, prose fiction and drama – and have focused on ways of contextualising set text study by teaching students about aspects of those forms beyond the set text, thus deepening students' understandings and strengthening their interpretations. In this chapter and the next, we broaden our focus on teaching texts in context by examining a number of issues that cross the boundaries of specific literary forms.

These issues – some of which have already been touched on briefly in previous chapters – allow us to focus on ideas about literature as a discourse, an art form and a subject, and to investigate some of the ways in which literary texts and forms can be connected through such ideas, again broadening students' knowledge about literature, contextualising their textual study and refining their skills of interpretation. We hope to suggest that helping students to develop a range of contextual understandings and to explore the nature of interpretation can make them more confident students of literature, enabling them to see more of 'the bigger picture'.

This chapter explores the place of theory and criticism in the teaching of English literature, looking broadly at how the social and educational contexts in which texts are read, studied and evaluated – and in which literature as an idea is formulated – affect our interpretations and help us to think about the nature of literary meaning, value and education.

Meanings and values in the classroom

Back in 1989, Brown and Gifford commented that many teachers of English were 'bewildered that a course which represents the pinnacle of English studies in school' – the A Level English literature course – 'remains unaffected by recent developments in critical theory' (1989: 1). These developments – concerning how meaning is generated from the body of texts referred to as 'literature', and how this body of texts is defined – have continued to have an uncertain place in 16–19 study. There was certainly no trace of these 'recent developments in critical theory' in many current English teachers' own experiences of studying English literature in the 16–19 phase. Nor was there any formal requirement to study the different interpretations of texts generated by literary critics, although the more assiduous amongst us might well have ploughed dutifully through the dusty critical texts available in our school libraries. Contexts – in the form of 'background research' into authors' lives and the periods in which they wrote – would be more familiar to many, although the information gleaned through this research is likely to have remained as 'background', its role in shaping the interpretive process unexamined. At university, many (though by no means all) of us encountered a very different state of affairs, with texts such as Terry Eagleton's *Literary Theory: An Introduction* (1983) – a mainstay of many an undergraduate reading list – challenging the foundations on which our existing understanding of literary study was based.

Some of us, however, would have had our most successful introduction to literary theory through fiction – through texts such as David Lodge's novel *Nice Work* (1988), in which a lecturer in feminist literary theory takes part in a job-shadowing scheme with the managing director of an engineering company. Through *Nice Work,* readers were introduced to debates about the nature of the canon, the representation of women in literature, and the possibility that texts could be interpreted in more than one way. Perhaps most importantly, they were also introduced to questions about how and why we study literature and the value of a degree in English – questions that all students of English literature in the 16–19 phase should have the opportunity to explore, whether they are part of the syllabus or not.

This chapter offers some suggestions as to how questions relating to theory and criticism can be approached. It gives a brief survey of debates about the teaching of theory and criticism in 16–19 English, focusing on arguments about the reform of English literature at A Level, where recent debates have been intense. Nevertheless, whilst the following discussion is rooted in the UK context and explores the development of a particular group of qualifications in 16–19 English literature, the issues raised are of relevance to a variety of other national contexts, reflecting similar debates that have happened in other countries – for instance Australia (Beavis 1997; Golsby-Smith 2013). They also echo longstanding international debates about English in higher education (see for instance, Graff 1987 and Scholes 1998 in the US). We will outline some of the difficulties involved in teaching these areas of literary study, most notably the bewilderment that ensues when students are introduced to them in inappropriate ways. Finally, we will explore a range of approaches to the teaching of theory and criticism, placing the emphasis very firmly on beginning with students' existing understanding of how literary texts are studied and interpreted.

Context and interpretation in the UK: the situation at A Level

The controversy that has surrounded the place of context and interpretation at A Level, the main 16–19 qualification in England, Wales and Northern Ireland, offers some particularly interesting perspectives on the troubled relationship between these aspects of literary study and the 16–19 curriculum. It illustrates, in particular, the disjunction between the study of English at 16–19 and in HE, raising questions about responsibility for curricular reform, political involvement in the teaching of English and the pace of educational change. It also highlights a number of important issues concerning the implementation of educational reforms, particularly their implications for teacher education and in-service training.

In 1999, widespread changes were announced to the system of 16–19 education in England, Wales and Northern Ireland, as part of a series of reforms known as 'Curriculum 2000'. In most subjects, these changes were largely structural, involving the modularisation of subject content and the introduction of an additional set of public examinations taken after the first year of 16–19 study. In English literature, however, they also involved some significant philosophical changes to a subject that had, in the words of Robert Eaglestone, 'been pickled in educational aspic for far too long' (1999). The new specifications in English literature engaged explicitly with the teaching of interpretations and contexts for the first time. For many commentators, this engagement was long overdue. Back in 1983, the year in which Eagleton's *Literary Theory: An Introduction* was published, Brian Hollingworth noted that while 'tertiary levels of education are riven by structuralist and post-structuralist debate ... literature courses in the schools go on much as usual' (1983: 3). The following year, Barnes and Barnes commented that A Level was dominated by a heavily didactic pedagogy in which 'pupils were passive receivers of instruction that transmitted a single interpretation of set books' (1984: 395). Six years later, a report by NATE, the National Association for the Teaching of English, argued that:

> teachers of English need to engage in the debate which [critical theory] has encour-
> aged about the nature of literature; they need to recognise the importance of consid-
> ering a text's means of production, its historical and social context, literature's place
> in different cultures, the effects which our gender, race and class have on the meanings
> we make from a text, and the insights critical theory offers us into plural readings of
> any text.
>
> (NATE 1990)

Yet the prospect of a theoretically-inflected 16–19 curriculum was still very remote. English at secondary level was reeling from the unprecedented amount of political influence that had been brought to bear on the National Curriculum when it was introduced in 1989, seeking to impose a version of the subject that was explicitly heritage-based (Cox 1995). It was only in 1999 that changes to 16–19 English offered to bring the subject into line with the theoretical perspectives that had had such a powerful influence on the study of literature in HE, challenging the 'certain certainties' that had shaped the curriculum for so long. Students would now be expected to show an understanding of the cultural and historical contexts within which texts had been produced, and of 'the ways in which texts have been interpreted and valued by different readers at different times, acknowledging that the interpretation of literary texts can depend on a reader's assumptions and stance' (QCA 1999).

The changes that were announced in 1999 were initially met with enthusiasm, but their implementation was far from straightforward. There was disquiet from some corners of the teaching profession as to the version of literary study that they sought to introduce; and specifications that were praised for offering to close the gap between 16–19 and degree level English literature were soon being criticised for the reductive, assessment-driven framework they imposed on students' experience of the subject. The troubled history of these specifications has been documented elsewhere (see, for example, Atherton 2003, 2004, 2005; Snapper 2007), but it is worth pausing to consider some of the objections to the teaching of interpretations and contexts that were raised in opposition to them. Some (Craddock 2001, 2003) focused on the values that they felt were disappearing from the English curriculum, arguing that students should be able to 'turn to English literature to find answers, possibilities, consolation, new horizons' (2003: 118). The possibility that students might find such answers and possibilities through the exploration of interpretations and contexts was not examined: nor were the assumptions on which these liberal humanist views rested. Others concentrated on the importance of what was often referred to as an 'informed personal response', contending that such responses were threatened by the new emphasis on interpretations and contexts. In an opinion column in the *Times Educational*

Supplement, one English teacher argued that students would end up 'studying books about books and not books', implying that they would end up unable to think for themselves (Hoyes 2000).

The strength of these views can be ascribed to journalistic hubris, but they echo a concern raised in much more serious form by Brown and Gifford in 1989. Noting that A Level had barely begun to address the question of how to use literary theory and criticism in the classroom, they drew attention to the difficulty involved in 'offer[ing] advice about the use of critics' (1989: 66). They also made a clear distinction between the use of criticism to offer different interpretive perspectives on a text (and therefore to *problematise* the question of meaning) and the reliance on notes and study guides to iron out uncertainties (and therefore to *simplify* the question of meaning) (1989: 43, 66). For Brown and Gifford, the latter acted as an obstacle to a sense of personal engagement with the text, leading to 'a distancing from the imaginative experience … in the effort to categorize, classify and create a neat, well-ordered essay' (1989: 66). In order to combat this, teachers would need to 'encourage the tentative and hesitant voice', creating opportunities for students to 'be critically responsive to … perceived meaning and its implications' (1989: 9, 11).

The concerns raised by Brown and Gifford are important, then, not because they put forward a case as to why interpretations and contexts should *not* be taught but because they give some indications as to the way in which they *should* be taught. They emphasise the need to acknowledge 'where students are' and teach them the skills they need to engage with, evaluate, play off and, if necessary, reject different interpretations. There has been a lack of such teaching at undergraduate level as well as in the 16–19 sector. In his study of the transition from school to university, Snapper (2009, 2011) observed first-year degree students being asked to apply concepts such as Marxism and feminism to literary texts when they had little idea of what these concepts actually involved: 'little allowance seemed to be made for the palpable difficulty these students might experience in dealing with abstract theoretical material' (2009: 199). In this particular environment, a course that aimed to challenge the assumptions about literature that students had acquired in school became a run-through of a series of literary theories that remained undigested and unassimilated by students. This course was pitched inappropriately and little attention was paid to pedagogy, meaning that 'substantial dialogue never developed, and there were frequently uncomfortable silences' (2009: 198). While the theories included were clearly considered important by the course convenor, they did not reflect the agendas of the students themselves. Such a mismatch between course content and student needs can potentially lead to a paradoxical situation in which concepts and theories that notionally challenge the status quo – that support radical social and political agendas, and thus might be viewed as reflecting the concerns of the student body, freeing them from the stultifying values of the past – are experienced in practice as alien, confusing and irrelevant.

Similar arguments were raised in the 1980s against early proposals for a radical theorization of the secondary English curriculum, when critics noted that the approaches that sought to facilitate agency in students often ended up by denying this agency. Millard, for instance, observed that the attempt 'to create a more relevant form of English study imposes even more teacher-led material, and appears to condition the students' responses as much if not even more rigidly than traditional approaches' (1988: 8). If not handled carefully, the teaching of literary theory can become just as monologic as the approaches it seeks to challenge, substituting one adopted voice for another.

The approaches advocated in this chapter take much more of a 'light touch', building on the constructivist methodology outlined in previous chapters. Crucially, they are based on issues and questions that might already have been forming themselves in students' minds. Robert Eaglestone reports that a colleague of his once commented that 'all seventeen year olds are natural theorists. They ask the big questions of literary texts because they really care about what they mean' (2001: 7). For Eaglestone, such questions are central to the discipline of English: 'English is not just "reading literature": surely it is an informed reflection on that literature too ... English should be a reflection on literature as it forms, interacts with and mirrors the world we all share' (2001: 7). Teaching criticism, theory and contexts is, then, a process of enabling students to engage in this act of reflection and developing their metacognitive awareness of the study of literature, allowing them to consider what kinds of texts we study and what is involved in studying them. Such an engagement – which involves the questioning of value-judgements and received ideas, and encourages students to negotiate their own interpretations rather than simply accepting those handed down by others – also has an important part to play in our students' wider education, and can be seen as part of 'our responsibility to ensure that students can [...] articulate and thus defend their own interests, opinions and priorities' (Wright 2006: 15). It is, in short, a way of preparing them for their role as citizens able to play an active role in and reflect critically on the world in which they live. What is important is not the theories and interpretations they explore, but the *act* of theorising and interpreting itself.

Questions of value

What do we do when we study literature?

A very effective starting point for the exploration of different interpretations is to get students to consider their own experiences of literary study. This roots their introduction to literary theory – a concept that can seem intimidating because of its abstraction – in something that is very familiar. Outlined below are three exercises that could be used to get students thinking about the study of literature, introducing them to the idea that English is 'not only about *reading* literature but *thinking about how we read*' (Eaglestone 2000: 26). These exercises could be used independently, but they also represent a clear sequence of activities – a 'hook' to introduce the topic, a range of questions to encourage group discussion and a series of quotations that will extend students' thinking by getting them to consider some additional perspectives. They therefore offer clear scaffolding for students' thinking.

The first activity concerns the nature of the canon and the judgements that have been made about the kinds of texts that should be taught in school. In 2011, Michael Gove, the UK Secretary of State for Education, argued that the majority of texts taught in state schools in England and Wales lacked intellectual challenge and that teachers ought to choose authors from the more traditional canon. The text in Panel 5.1, an excerpt from an article in the *Daily Telegraph*, offers an excellent stimulus for debate: teachers in other countries may be able to find examples that relate directly to their own education systems.

Panel 5.1 Michael Gove on the study of literature in schools

Teach Jane Austen, state schools to be told

State schools will be told to teach the classic English novels they currently ignore in a radical overhaul of what is taught in the classroom.

The move comes after a survey carried out for ministers found state secondary schools tend to teach children aged 11 to 14 works by contemporary writers such as Louis Sachar and John Boyne, rather than classic authors such as Jane Austen and William Golding.

Ministers now want to see more challenging texts introduced in state schools to mirror what is taught in private schools, where pupils are much more likely to read dead authors whose work has stood the test of time.

Changes to English lessons will form a central plank of the proposals to be made in a sweeping review of the national curriculum which will report in the New Year.

They are expected to specify the key authors, as a minimum, that pupils should read in each year of schooling.

The survey by the Department of Education shows that two thirds of the books studied in a sample of more than 100 state secondary schools had been written in the last twenty years.

Plans to make English more challenging underline the determination by Michael Gove, the education secretary, to deal with what he believes is a lack of rigour in schools.

"The academic demands placed on children in state schools have been too low for too long," said a Government source. "Schools need to raise the bar by requiring pupils to read a larger selection of books."

Bethan Marshall, a senior lecturer in English education at King's College, London, said forcing children to read the classics too early could backfire.

"I think getting children to read more books is a very good move but it should be books that children want to read," she said.

"Putting too much emphasis on the classics too early can be a mistake. I read the pre-20th century literature at grammar school and hated it."

(Henry 2011)

A useful way of approaching such a resource is to give students time for initial reading and thinking, and then to ask them to formulate just one or two comments or questions as a basis for discussion. This will ensure that all students have points to contribute, minimising the risk of the kind of uncomfortable silences described by Snapper (2009). One very effective method of getting students to engage with a text like this is to project it onto a whiteboard and ask them to write their responses on sticky notes which they then place on the relevant points of the text: the teacher can then use these responses to open up a wider discussion. (Of course, students should be encouraged to spot the flaws in arguments such as Gove's: why is 'contemporary' automatically equated with a lack of rigour?)

This kind of discussion will inevitably raise further questions about the nature of both literary study and 'literature' itself. These can be explored further through group work. Panel 5.2 contains a number of questions that will get students thinking about a range of issues relating to the canon, the study of texts and the concept of 'meaning'. Some of these questions are more complex than others, meaning that there is scope here for differentiation.

Panel 5.2   Exploring literature

1. What is literature and what is it for?

- How would you define 'literature'?
- What is the difference between 'literature' and 'fiction' or 'drama'?
- Is soap opera literature? Is *Harry Potter* literature?
- Is there a particular kind of language that is only found in literature?
- What is the purpose and/or value of literature?
- What view of literature does the course you are studying give?

2. What is the study of literature and what is it for?

- What do you learn from studying literature? What skills and knowledge does studying literature give you?
- How are those skills and knowledge similar or different to other subjects?
- Is it more important to study old texts or new?
- What benefit is there for society in the study of literature?
- What benefit is there for the individual in studying literature?
- What might the study of literature have to do with the following areas of study: history, politics and sociology, media studies, linguistics, philosophy, gender studies, psychology?

3. How do we interpret and evaluate literary texts, and why?

- What knowledge do you need to interpret a text?
- How important is it to know the author's intention when interpreting a literary text?
- Do literary texts have only one meaning, or many potential meanings? Can a text mean anything you want it to mean?
- How do you evaluate whether a literary text is good or not?
- Is it possible to dislike or disapprove of a text but still think it is 'good' (or to enjoy a text but still think it is 'bad')?
- Why might interpretation and evaluation be important, both in studying texts and in society more generally?

When approaching such questions, it is worth remembering that students' thinking might well be very tentative. It might be useful to turn this into a teaching point, getting students to reflect on their uncertainties and recognise that some of their answers might be provisional and subject to change. Teachers whose students have access to a VLE might be able to use electronic discussion boards to pose questions and encourage further reflection on questions raised earlier in the course. Alternatively, a 'question wall' in the classroom is an effective way of recording topics that require further debate and keeping them 'live' in students' minds.

The third activity in this sequence encourages students to engage with some other views about the study of literature, embodied by the quotations in Panel 5.3.

Panel 5.3   Statements about the study of literature

All pupils, including those of very limited attainments, need the civilising experience of contact with great literature, and can respond to its universality.

(Newsom Report, CACE 1963)

Any belief that the study of literature is the study of a stable, well-definable entity, as entomology is the study of insects, can be abandoned as a chimera. Some kinds of fiction are literature and some are not; some literature is fictional and some is not; some literature is verbally self-regarding, while some highly-wrought rhetoric is not literature. Literature, in the sense of a set of works of assured and unalterable value, distinguished by certain shared inherent properties, does not exist.

(Eagleton 1983)

Because it is such a profound and universal experience, Literature must be taught to school pupils, whereupon it becomes an instrument within the whole apparatus of filtering whereby schools adjust young people to an unjust social order.

(Sinfield 1985)

Is literature an ideological instrument: a set of stories that seduce readers into accepting the hierarchical arrangements of society? ... Or is literature the place where ideology is exposed, revealed as something that can be questioned? Both claims are thoroughly plausible.

(Culler 1997)

The complexity of some of these excerpts means that they will need careful handling: again, teachers might want to differentiate which quotations are given to which students. Nevertheless, 16–19 study should give learners the opportunity to engage with texts that place considerable cognitive demands on them; and a judicious teacher will be able to use a range of different strategies to give students access to such texts. One obvious technique would be to get students to paraphrase these statements; but they could also be asked to rank them in order of how strongly they agree or disagree with them, or to imagine how Eagleton, Sinfield, Culler and the authors of the Newsom Report would answer some of the questions contained in the previous activity. How would Sinfield, for instance, define the benefit to society of the study of literature? And how would his response differ from that of the authors of the Newsom Report?

Why do we study Shakespeare and the canon?

Another way of introducing some of the central issues of literary theory is by exploring the place of Shakespeare in the curriculum. Often the greatest difficulty that students and teachers face when approaching Shakespeare is *the perception* that they are going to be doing something that is both exceptionally difficult and a vital part of the English literary heritage. The mystique that surrounds the study of Shakespeare can have an undesirable impact on students' receptivity and self-belief. If time allows, it is worth exploring (and perhaps even exploding) this mystique. Students in the 16–19 phase can often make extremely thoughtful observations, frequently rooted in personal experience, about the place Shakespeare occupies in the curriculum. The activities in Panel 5.4 can be used to provoke debate and challenge some of the unexamined beliefs about Shakespeare, both positive and negative, that can cloud students' experiences.

Panel 5.4   Investigating Shakespeare

Activity 1

Give students the following statements on slips of paper. Get them to discuss the statements and put them into three piles: 'Agree', 'Disagree' and 'Undecided'. Then ask them to choose the statement that they felt most strongly about, and explain their choice. Their responses can often uncover some interesting beliefs and experiences. Be prepared to be surprised!

- Shakespeare is really really boring and completely incomprehensible.
- Shakespeare is intimidating – if you don't understand Shakespeare, you'll never be any good at English.
- Every schoolchild in the country should learn about Shakespeare.
- Shakespeare was writing 400 years ago – his works are completely irrelevant to people today.
- Reading Shakespeare will make you a better person.
- Shakespeare is the preserve of the rich and well educated – that's why people find him off-putting.
- Shakespeare is often taken too seriously.
- The issues in Shakespeare's plays are matters that affect everyone.
- Shakespeare should be treated carefully, like a national treasure.
- Rather than putting Shakespeare on a pedestal, we should think more carefully about what his works mean to people today.
- Making Shakespeare a compulsory part of the curriculum is just about the worst thing you could do to him.

Activity 2

The following questions could be used as a plenary to pull together students' responses to the previous exercise.

- How do you feel about studying Shakespeare?
- Why do you think the study of Shakespeare is compulsory?
- Do you think it should be optional? If so, who should get to choose – teachers or students?
- What kind of associations does Shakespeare hold for you?

Activity 3

The following extracts could be used as a follow-up to the previous discussions to give students examples of the ways in which Shakespeare's place in the education system has been spoken of and written about. Students could be asked to find their own examples.

I   There are now several GCSE English literature courses that prescribe no Shakespeare at all. There is at least one A Level English literature syllabus on which Shakespeare is not compulsory. Thousands of intelligent children leaving school at sixteen have never seen a play of Shakespeare on film or on the stage, and have never been asked to read a single word of any one of his plays. Even the Bank of England has caught the disease, with last week's news that the bard's picture is to be removed from the £20 note!

As we move towards a National Curriculum for our schools – sometimes known as an entitlement curriculum – I find myself wondering why the students of our schools are not as entitled to Shakespeare as to other parts of the syllabus? Do those who disapprove of Shakespeare, arguing for some extraordinary reason that he is elitist, wish to deprive those not already familiar with his work from acquiring an understanding of it – or of other great literature?

I don't want my children – or anybody else's – to be deprived of Shakespeare, or of the other life-enhancing elements which I have suggested should be part of the schooling entitlement of all the children of this country. And I don't want our future generations to be the poor relations in a Europe in which there will be less and less room for those who can't keep up. But I fear that these are real dangers if we evade those key questions about the nature and purpose of education which I have touched on today, and if we fail to give our schools and our teachers the resources, and the philosophical framework, they need to produce the right results.

(HRH Prince Charles, Annual Shakespeare Birthday Lecture 1991)

2   The preservation of a canon against neglect ... cannot be done by forcing *Julius Caesar* or *A Midsummer Night's Dream* on fifteen-year olds.

(Frank Kermode, literary critic)

3   Candidates, particularly the less able, should be steered away from 'The Works of William Shakespeare'.

(North West Regional Examination Board:
Certificate of Secondary Education,
Reports on the 1983 Examinations, quoted in Sinfield 1985)

4   Every pupil should be given at least some experience of the plays or poetry of Shakespeare.

(Brian Cox, chair of the Working Group that set out the first version
of the National Curriculum in English, governing what should be taught
in state schools in England and Wales, in 1989; Cox 1991: 82)

5   Dame Helen Mirren has suggested that schools should stop making children read Shakespeare. The actress said that pupils should be introduced to the Bard through live performance or cinema rather than the texts of his plays.

'Honestly, I don't think kids should be made to read Shakespeare at all,' she said. 'I think children's very first experience of Shakespeare should always be in performance, in the theatre or on film – mostly in theatre. But it should be a performance because that makes it alive and real.'

The study of Shakespeare's works is a compulsory part of the national curriculum, but Dame Helen's thoughts echo those of the Royal Shakespeare Company, which has warned that children are being turned off the subject because of the 'boring' way in which it is taught.

(Singh in *Daily Telegraph*, 4 March 2011)

An alternative exercise for looking at these questions of literary value, and one that also engages students in extended reading of accessible literary journalism, is to collect together a set of newspaper articles which address issues about what is considered valuable in literature in schools and in society more generally. Students can then be asked to read the articles in groups, perhaps reporting back to each other about what different articles argue, what issues they collectively raise, and what the students themselves feel about them. The following articles have been successfully used, but of course there are many others available in newspaper archives online:

Group 1: What about genre fiction and bestsellers?
- *Populist prejudice:* Crime books easier to write than 'serious' novels? That attitude is frankly, cobblers. (Mark Lawson, *The Guardian*, January 2008)
- *Why does crime still have such unpardonably low literary status?* (Stuart Evers, *The Guardian* Books Blog, July 2009)

- *Science fiction author hits out at Booker judges*. Kim Stanley Robinson, one of science fiction's contemporary greats, accuses the Booker prize judges of ignorance. (Alison Flood. *The Guardian*, September 2009)
- *A word of mouth success*: Why are people lining up to rubbish *The Da Vinci Code*? Simple – it's a bestseller that doesn't know its place. (Lucy Mangan, *The Guardian*, August 2004)

Group 2: What about 'the classics'?
- *A bit of Brontë does you good*: Victorian novels may be hard going, but they are a proper education in broadening the mind. (Libby Purves, *The Times*, May 2005)
- *Canon fodder*: It's madness to force-feed the classics to teenagers – it could put them off reading for life. (Stephen Moss, *The Guardian*, August 2006)
- *Reading ruined by classroom dissection*. (Shereen Pandit, *TES*, December 2005)
- *Highly literary and deeply vulgar*: If James Kelman's Booker novel is rude, it's in good company. (Robert Winder, *Independent*, October 1994)

Group 3: What about Shakespeare?
- *Save us from a winter of discontent – ban the bard*. (Miranda Sawyer, *The Guardian*, September 2005)
- *Shakespeare: Time for a moratorium?* (Dominic Dromgoole, Richard Bean, *Time Out*, April 2006)
- *Plays for today*: If we do not adapt Shakespeare for our times, the richness of his work will be lost. (Michael Bogdanov, *The Guardian*, November 2003)
- *Bard not that hard to follow*: Stop teaching the plays as literature; that is what they have become, but it is not what they were. (Paul Innes, *The Scotsman*, November 2009)

Group 4: What about Harry Potter?
- *Harry Potter attack starts war of words*. (Hugh Davies, *The Telegraph*, July 2003)
- *Harry Potter course to be offered at Durham University*. (Alison Flood, *The Guardian*, August 2010)
- *Is Harry Potter classic children's literature?* (Daniel de Vise, *Washington Post*, July 2011)
- *You can't be serious about Harry Potter!* (Sarah Rainey, *The Telegraph*, May 2012)

Questions of value: what is 'literary'?

As the previous sections demonstrate, notions of what constitutes literature, and what should be included in the study of literature, are frequently hotly contested. As well as examining the cultural values that attach to the literary canon and ideas about the nature and purpose of literary education, students might be introduced – often in passing, when discussing texts more generally rather than in the form of a dedicated activity – to a number of other ways of thinking about the nature of literariness, and the ways in which 'literature' intersects with a number of other fields of related study and activity.

Whilst syllabuses make certain distinctions relating to what constitutes the study of English 16–19 (e.g. English literature, English language, English language and literature), such distinctions are inevitably problematic in reality. When teaching literary texts, it is valuable to acknowledge their cultural, linguistic, language and (increasingly) media contexts. To explore literary texts without reference to such issues is to remove powerful forces both in terms of the texts' construction as language/cultural artefacts and in terms of their reconstructed meanings for readers.

Literature and language

Elsewhere in the book, we have spoken of the way in which literary study in the 16–19 phase tends to be defined through set text study rather than through conceptual study, and we have argued for a more systematic approach to teaching literary concepts. A fundamental part of learning to read and write literary criticism is learning to understand literary concepts and use literary terminology. Here, we address the concept of literary language. In particular, we wish to draw attention to the rich possibilities for teaching which are offered by ideas such as imagery, tone and style, all of which cross the boundaries of form and genre, and indeed of language and literature too, and which are easily neglected.

The question of whether there is a particular kind of language that is 'literary' is worth exploring with students. The simple question, 'How would you define literary language and what are its elements?' focuses students valuably on language analysis, but also raises further questions about the nature of the literary. In the discussion that ensues, students are most likely to suggest that literary language is characterised by metaphor, description and various patterned structures such as alliteration and repetition. It is not at all difficult, however, to show that all these language features are far from restricted to literary uses.

Advertising and political rhetoric use many 'literary' devices; and indeed the relationship between 'rhetorical' and 'literary' language valuably suggests that what is considered 'literary' might in fact be more to do with context and value than differential definition. Less obviously, recent research into creativity and language (for instance Carter 2004; Pope 2005) shows that many verbal strategies traditionally regarded as literary are in fact common in everyday talk. It has long been recognised that metaphor, far from being a purely literary device, is at the heart of everyday language (Lakoff and Johnson 1981). There is much to be gained from attending to this idea, and broader ideas about literal and figurative language, in some detail. The idioms listed below serve both as an introduction to the essentially metaphorical nature of much language, and to discussion of the differences and similarities between everyday and literary language. Can students think of further examples?

---

anger → heat
he makes my blood boil
she got all steamed up
you're a hothead

emotion → madness
he's out of his mind with grief
I'm mad with jealousy
she's crazy about him

---

light → liquid
sunlight poured into the room
the stage was flooded with light
he soaked up some sun

life → journey
he was travelling down life's path
she just sails through life
they're headed for great things

words → weapons
she used some sharp words
that was pretty cutting language
he hurled insults at her

Beyond this, there are, of course, numerous creative writing exercises that can help students to understand and experience the power and pleasure of metaphor, and many texts that lend themselves particularly to the study of metaphor.

Conversely, a fascinating question which students will respond to with great interest is whether 'non-literary' language, when used in literature, is actually 'literary'. A classic example of this is James Kelman's novel *How Late It Was, How Late*, whose first-person narrator is a heavy-drinking, heavy-swearing, working-class Glaswegian, and which caused national outrage when it won the Booker Prize in 1994.

Clearly there are many other ways in which linguistic terms and concepts can be brought to bear on students' understanding of literature, raising their awareness of both stylistic features (lexis, grammar, syntax, cohesion, phonology, graphology, modality etc.) and issues relating to the social, cultural and political implications of particular uses of language. What is important is to try to find time and space to privilege these concepts rather than to hide them away.

Literature and media

Increasingly texts are produced and consumed in, allude to, and make use of a plethora of media. Exploring with students the range of media versions of texts and the different ways in which they are presented, consumed and read in various media is an important context for the production and reception of literary texts.

More broadly, just as the discourses of linguistics can enrich literary understanding, so can the discourses of cultural and media studies, which often take a more sociological approach to understanding the nature of text (Buckingham and Sefton-Green 1994). A key issue for literature here, already touched upon earlier, is that of cultural value. It is worth asking students directly whether they think 'literary' texts are more 'valuable' than 'media' texts, and if so how. Are literary texts 'better' or just different and, if so, how are they different? Again, questions of definition will arise here: to what extent, for instance, can there be any meaningful division between 'literature' and 'media' texts? Of particular interest, though, is the question of the social functions of texts. Asking students to talk about the social functions of soap opera, on the one hand, and literary drama in the theatre, on the other, opens up a discussion which draws on a set of ideas about culture which students will have a great deal to say about, but which are too rarely considered in the literature classroom.

A related issue, and again one that students will enjoy discussing, is the nature of narrative, explored further in the next chapter. Narrative not only crosses literary genres, but also unites literary, non-literary and media texts: what makes certain narratives 'literary' and others not? To what extent is 'literariness' dependent on words, or does it reside somewhere else?

Literature and publishing

Whereas media and cultural studies emphasise the idea of culture as a commodity, the 16–19 literature classroom rarely considers the nature of publishing, the process of bringing a literary text into being, and the commercial viability of such texts. Discussion of modes of textual production and consumption can easily be included in the work of the 16–19 classroom and reminds students powerfully that literature has a life outside the classroom and a purpose beyond study.

It also raises their awareness of the fact that literary texts are not 'fixed' but are subject to differing forces in their commodification, which might have a significant impact on how they are read. Students will naturally think of set texts as very particular 'packages' – a physical object of so many pages, such a size and with a particular design on its cover. It is interesting to consider with them that this is yet another of the contexts within which they receive a literary text and is by no means the only form in which the text has had its life.

When reading Victorian fiction, for instance, students might consider the journal publication of much Victorian fiction and the impact of this on structure, form and content, with writers taking into account cumulative audience response as they went along and adapting accordingly.

Knowledge about the production of text in the theatre of Shakespeare's age – from cue scripts to folios and quartos – and the existence of variant versions of texts provides crucial insights as does the existence of variant and revised texts of, for instance, Blake's poetry and Shelley's *Frankenstein*. Seeing illuminated medieval texts, and learning about the early history of books and printing, never fails to interest students, and can bring the study of medieval and Renaissance literature to life for many.

A related issue is the relationships between literature, journalism, bookselling and publishing. For instance, at various points in their study, students might consider issues such as the function of book reviews in the media, the coverage of literary issues and authors in the press, the role of advertising in selling books or the influence of reading groups on literary culture. Furthermore, all these questions can lead to an important discussion about the difference between 'reading' and 'studying' literature.

Literature and politics

Finally, there are questions about the intersection between literature and politics; not just the political issues that literary texts address, but the ways in which they might become involved in 'real' politics. Issues about censorship and freedom of expression are central here as is discussion of the ways in which texts might actually contribute to social and political change, or spark controversy in the press, suggesting to students ways in which literature might be seen as a dangerous social and political force.

In the USA, the annual Banned Books Week encourages schools to discuss issues of censorship and freedom of expression. A consideration of the powerful (and disturbing) images of book-burnings that occasionally make the news always leads to interesting discussions, as does thinking about the rationale for and implications of the systematic exclusion of certain artworks (e.g. the *entartete kunst* – degenerate art – of Nazi Germany, the works proscribed by Stalin in the Soviet Union in the 1950s or by Joseph McCarthy in the USA). There are also important questions, touched upon earlier, about the ways in which governments might promote certain values through education.

In the light of this, it's worth making time to discuss topical issues with students – 'literature in the news'. Julie Blake, a teacher of English language A Level in the UK, ran a very popular blog about 'cool stuff happening in the world of words' for several years (http://languagelegend.blogspot.com) to encourage her students (and others around the world) to take a broader view of language. It doesn't have to be a blog: occasional informal discussion in class can benefit students by alerting them to the ways in which literature of the past and present functions in society today.

Questions of 'meaning'

The view that 'seventeen-year-olds are natural theorists' is illustrated neatly by the number of questions that students themselves ask about the interpretation of texts. Does a text have to mean what the author wanted it to mean? Can't a text mean whatever the reader wants it to mean? Such questions are a good way of introducing students to the exploration of 'meaning' itself, and therefore to the notion of different critical positions.

Where is the meaning of a text? This question might perplex students initially – they are more used to thinking about *what* the meaning is – but it is one that will get them thinking. Is it locked into the words on the page, or is it in the reader's head? Or is it somewhere in between?

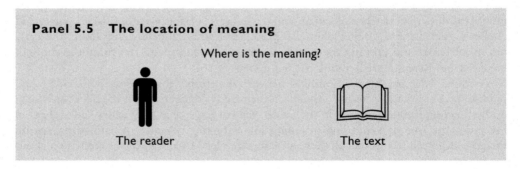

Panel 5.5   The location of meaning

Where is the meaning?

The reader   The text

One way into this question has already been described in the 'poetry and art' activity in Chapter 2. Panel 5.5 offers another effective and accessible way of engaging students in this debate. First, project or copy it onto a whiteboard. Next, ask students to put a cross on the board to represent the location of the text's meaning. Teachers might get their classes to consider the location of different conceptions of meaning: one that sees meaning as completely subjective, for instance, or one that insists that there is only one 'correct' meaning of a text. Students should be asked to explain their choice of location and – perhaps – to relate their choice to particular texts that they have studied. The next stage in this exercise is to introduce the concept of the author. Does the author decide what the text means? Is literary criticism simply a matter of trying to work out what the author intended? Finally – and importantly – what sorts of factors might govern the production of 'meaning', by both the author and the reader? Can the students think of contextual factors that have influenced their own interpretation of particular texts? Students in a rural area, for instance, found it fascinating to consider how their reactions to Philip Larkin's poem 'Going, Going' had been shaped by their experience of living in a part of the UK that had lost a lot of agricultural land to new housing estates, and to think how they might have read the poem differently if their families' livelihoods had depended on the new development so feared by Larkin. Students from more urban backgrounds might interpret this poem very differently. This kind of discussion can alert students to the 'situatedness' of their own readings and the fact that no interpretation is ever context-free.

From here it is a relatively short step to getting students to explore the notion of different critical positions. One particularly effective way of introducing this is to get students to read 'in role'. Gibbons (2010: 9–10) outlines an activity called 'What's My Line?' in which students are asked to interpret Rupert Brooke's poem 'The Soldier' from a number of different viewpoints, including those of an army general, a conscientious objector, a politician, the mother of a young man who has recently died in the trenches and so on. Such an exercise reinforces the idea that texts can be read from different perspectives: if students are asked to refer to particular lines from the poem in formulating their responses, they can produce some very sharp analytical work. Teachers should also ask students to consider what kinds of contexts might have influenced these readings, to avoid presenting them simply as reflections of different personal opinions. What political views might shape the views of the conscientious objector, or the patriotic general?

An exercise that builds on this 'reading in role' activity, and develops students' awareness of different schools of literary criticism, is offered by Ogborn *et al.* (2000: 34–46). Their exercise involves the use of 'critical positions' cards that give brief summaries of different critical approaches. Students are asked to read a text through the lens of a particular approach, and to consider what the text gains and loses by being read from these varying perspectives. Ogborn *et al.*'s exercise focuses on a short story by Flannery O'Connor, but teachers might find that their students engage with this kind of activity more effectively if they are asked to apply the critical positions cards to a text that they already know. Students who have studied the poetry of the First World War, for instance, can explore 'The Soldier' from Marxist, feminist, formalist and psychoanalytic perspectives, considering the gendering of England, the idealised portrayal of the country and Brooke's use of the sonnet form. The English and Media Centre has also very successfully used Maurice Sendak's picture book *Where the Wild Things Are* to demonstrate the potential of different critical approaches. This progressive 'layering' of interpretation – in which a text is revisited and reconsidered from different angles – builds students' confidence and helps to give them a real sense of 'possessing' the text. A useful example is offered by Barry (2008), who uses the concept of 'reading with' theory to describe the way in which students are asked to approach a text (in his example, the poem 'To the Man After the Harrow' by Patrick Kavanagh) 'with gender' and 'with history'. Barry's argument – that teachers of English literature should teach theor*ising*, rather than theory – helps to maintain a focus on the active construction of meaning.

Debating representation: class, gender and race

Working with different critical positions as suggested above helps students to understand the polysemic nature of texts and to recognise the critical role of the reader in making interpretations that might seem a long way from the putative intentions of the author. A key concept here is representation. The writer represents the world and its social relationships through a narrative that organises experience in a shapely and inevitably stylised way; through narrative, the writer guides and even manipulates the reader through this world. The reader may be entirely transported by this journey; however, the reader is also able to challenge this representation in a number of ways, seeking to reveal the social and political ideologies that underpin the narrative, the way these ideologies are embedded in language, and the ways in which the narrative has been valued and understood. Different critical positions represent different ways of examining and challenging literary representations; indeed, literary theory might be defined as the science of literary representation – in some senses a branch of linguistics, the science of language.

The theory of literary representation is complex, but teaching some of the fundamental issues need not be. Indeed, examining the ways in which certain social relationships – for instance class, gender, sexuality and race – are represented in literature is now a standard move in 16–19 literary study, and can provide an excellent introduction to some of the basic elements of literary theory.

It is, of course, perfectly possible to examine the representation of aspects of, say, gender in any particular text without recourse to broader discourses about gender and its representation in literature. There are many reasons, however, why introducing students to such discourses is a good idea. In purely literary terms, understanding the key tenets of associated critical positions – particularly Marxism, feminism and post-colonialism – broadens students' critical base and anchors their analyses more firmly. In terms of preparing students for further study, whether in English literature or in other subjects, a basic grasp of these discourses is likely to be invaluable, especially if students are thinking of going on to study English or other arts, humanities or social science subjects.

We might also ask ourselves whether our students will have the opportunity – in any context other than their English literature lessons – to discuss the crucial issues about social relationships which underpin these critical positions. Teachers in 16–19 and HE often make unwarranted assumptions about students' social and political awareness; many students who go on to read English at university find themselves suddenly expected to read complex texts of Marxist, feminist and post-colonialist theory when, in fact, many have never even had the opportunity to discuss formally in a systematic way issues about class, gender, sexuality and race in society, let alone how such ideas might be applied to literary texts. Literature teachers at 16–19 might protest (as they often have done) that these social issues are not the concern of the subject 'literature'; but, even if they were not in the past, they have categorically become so now.

Access to a foundational understanding of these issues is crucial both for citizenship and for continuing study, and if it is not provided in English, it might not be provided elsewhere. Here, then, we suggest some introductory approaches, taking gender issues as an example. These approaches can all be successfully customised for dealing with issues of class and race, too, focusing on Marxist and post-colonialist theories.

Gender: Positions and definitions

However basic the question may seem, it's essential to ask students what they know about gender issues as a starting point.

- Start by asking students to discuss briefly what they know about feminism, and gather together responses, establishing briefly a very simple statement of definition.
- Next, ask students to discuss what they understand by the term 'gender'. Again, gather responses. A number of issues are likely to arise. In particular, there will almost certainly be discussion of the difference between 'gender' and 'sex', a question of definition that will need to be cleared up straight away.

WHAT IS GENDER?

Whilst 'sex' refers to the physical sexual characteristics we are born with (i.e. in the vast majority of cases, 'male' or 'female'), 'gender' refers to the socio-cultural behaviours which we display: 'masculine' or 'feminine'. Whilst sex is biologically determined, ideas about gender – in particular what behaviours are considered typical or appropriate for the different sexes, what is masculine and what is feminine – are unfixed and culturally constructed. The idea of gender is crucial to feminism; feminism argues that power structures are perpetuated through the perpetuation of certain gender roles assigned to men and women in society.

Having established this, students can then begin to explore what they think about the idea of the construction of gender.

CONSTRUCTION OF GENDER: SOME QUESTIONS

- What gender behaviours and characteristics does our society encourage/validate/ discourage/invalidate for men and women/girls and boys?
- How does it encourage or discourage them?

In our experience, the discussion that emerges from these questions could go on for several lessons, so it's important to shape and direct it carefully, and judge an appropriate time to summarise and wrap it up. At some point, it might also be necessary to clarify other key issues, notably the relationship between nature and nurture, and the relationship between gender and sexuality.

NATURE V. NURTURE

Whilst some gender roles might be related to sexual difference ('nature'), this position is often overstated. The role of cultural construction and environmental factors ('nurture') is vital, most obviously in relation to the way men and women are expected to dress and look, but arguably in many other aspects of behaviour, too – including, for instance, elements of emotional and psychological character, where, many sociologists argue, people 'perform' the gender roles that are expected of them.

GENDER AND SEXUALITY

The idea of gender is related to the idea of sexuality as well as sex. Ideas about masculinity and femininity are clearly linked with ideas about heterosexuality and homosexuality – though it is vital to note that there are no simple correspondences between gender and sexuality. 'Queer theory' – a branch of feminist/gender theory – suggests that ideas about sexuality, like ideas about gender, are often culturally constructed. But queer theory is not just about sexuality: it is a broader set of ideas about the functioning of social norms, and the ways in which 'deviant' or minority behaviours operate within society.

From here, one can move on to consolidate a basic factual grasp of the history and concerns of feminism as a social and political movement, perhaps asking students to research the topic on the internet.

Gender: Literary representations

The next stage is to introduce the idea of feminism as a critical position, and some of the ways in which questions about gender might be applied to literature and other cultural forms. The most effective way of doing this is to ask students to discuss freely the representation of gender and sexuality in a range of types of literature. A successful activity, for instance, is to divide the class into groups, with one group discussing traditional folk tales and fairy tales, another discussing children's literature, another discussing Hollywood film and so on.

Finally, a set of more structured questions might be applied to literary texts that students have studied, for instance Shakespeare.

REPRESENTATIONS OF GENDER IN SHAKESPEARE

In your group, decide on one Shakespeare play you all know well (e.g. *Macbeth, Romeo and Juliet, Hamlet, King Lear, Much Ado About Nothing*) and then discuss the following questions:

- How many male characters and how many female characters are there? How significant are the male/female characters? How much space is given to each in the play? Are there any homosexual characters?
- How are the relationships between male and female characters presented? What do you notice about the way they speak to and behave towards each other, and what about the way they speak about each other?
- To what extent can you see gender stereotypes at play in these characters and relationships? To what extent are women portrayed as 'feminine' and men as 'masculine'? What roles do men and women perform in the society represented in the play?
- To what extent do women exercise social and/or economic power in the world of the play? How much of that power is inside the home and how much outside?
- Do you think gender roles are fairly and/or accurately represented? What might the play tell us about the way people have thought about gender roles?
- What difference does it make that the author is a man?

There are, of course, many ways in which this work can be developed from this point, depending on the amount of time the class has available and the context in which the topic is being considered. Here, we have had room only to sketch ways of helping students to acquire a firm grasp of key issues. We recommend that at some point students are asked to read and discuss carefully selected extracts from an undergraduate introduction to literary theory (see 'Further reading' section for suggestions) as a crucial step in helping them to make the adjustment to the kind of secondary reading they might be expected to do at university (whatever subject they go on to study).

However they complete their study at this level, it's important that they should be aware that they have only scratched the surface of a complex theoretical debate, and that there are many other ways in which gender theories might be applied.

FEMINIST LITERARY THEORY

Feminist literary theories are concerned with analysis of the representation of women and gender roles in literature and culture, and the way gender is constructed through language and culture.

At a simple level, feminist approaches to literature are interested in:

- the balance of power between men and women in the literary world, e.g. equality of opportunity for women writers;
- the representation of women in literary texts.

More complex approaches may look at the ways in which texts hide and reveal patriarchal power structures, for instance:

- through the use of male narrators, voices and viewpoints;
- through the construction of gender through language patterns and imagery;
- through representations of social, sexual and emotional behaviours.

Using literary criticism

Introducing critical texts

Some teachers might argue that it would be more logical to introduce different critical interpretations by starting with critical texts, getting students to read critical essays and extracts and using these to illustrate the ways in which the texts they are studying could be interpreted. This is, in fact, the way in which many teachers had their own introduction to literary criticism and theory. However, this approach has some significant drawbacks, as alluded to earlier in this chapter. One is the fact that students often view published criticism as offering a 'right answer', a solution to their own interpretive problems, rather than an interpretation that is provisional and contestable. The other is that students often experience critical reading as difficult, written (as it frequently is) for a much more experienced readership. If students are to make sense of literary criticism – if they are to use it as a tool against which they can test out and hone their own interpretations, rather than feeling they should simply bow to its authority – then teachers need to think carefully about how to introduce these skills and incorporate them in their programmes of study.

Many students of English literature will begin their 16–19 courses with very little idea as to what literary criticism actually is, and will benefit from exploring some fundamental questions about literary criticism: what it is, what it is for and who it is written by. The most effective way of doing this is to begin with what students *do* know. Most students will have encountered study guides (printed or online) during their pre-16 courses, although they will probably have read these sources to assist their understanding of their primary texts rather than to offer a range of interpretive possibilities. Many students will also have encountered more discursive forms of writing about literature, such as book reviews and blogs, and will therefore be able to draw on their knowledge of how texts are explored, debated and evaluated in these forums. In addition, they will almost certainly be experienced readers (and perhaps even producers) of other kinds of criticism, most notably film and music reviews. It is worth spending some time discussing these forms of analysis and getting students to share what they have internalised about the conventions they follow and the values they encode. Wright draws attention to the ways in which 16–19 courses in film studies, for instance, require students to see that 'the newspaper, magazine or internet review site [is] contingently placed, text in amongst lots of other text' (2006: 17): students discuss 'possible audiences, purposes and the perceived cultural capital of each publication, considering contexts for reading' (2006: 17). Making students aware of the fact that, in Wright's wonderful description, 'the critical space can swarm with voices' is crucial if they are to see themselves as agents within this space, able to argue with and even reject particular voices rather than simply having to 'revere the hushed tones of one or two hallowed guides' (2006: 17).

A practical activity that introduces this multiplicity of voices involves exploring short extracts from a wide range of responses, both written and spoken, to a literary text with which the students are familiar. These responses might include:

- explanatory texts, such as York Notes or SparkNotes;
- reviews of theatrical productions;
- essays aimed at 16–19 students (the English and Media Centre's *e magazine* and Philip Allan Publications' *The English Review* are good sources, and can also be used as models of critical writing that students can refer to in developing their own writing skills: see Chapter 6 for a further discussion);
- newspaper articles and reviews (John Mullan's weekly 'Book Club' column in the *Guardian*, which explores a text over a period of four weeks, is an excellent and very accessible example);
- extracts from book blogs;
- specialist academic criticism that explores the text from different perspectives;
- short excerpts from radio and TV discussions such as Radio 4's *Open Book* and *A Good Read* and BBC2's *Newsnight Review*.

Students should be asked to consider each text in the light of the following questions:

- Who is the author of this text? What kind of knowledge enabled them to author it?
- Who is it aimed at? How much does this person need to know about the primary text in order to understand the critical text?
- Does the critical text give you any additional factual information about the primary text or the context in which it was written?
- Does the critical text help you to make sense of the primary text?

- Does the critical text offer you a different way of interpreting the primary text?
- How is the primary text perceived? As sacrosanct? As a target for destruction? Something in between?

Such activities offer an initial grounding in the range of critical texts students might encounter. They also provide a good opportunity to remind students of the need to use the internet with care. The internet will give students access to a much wider range of critical material than was available in the past, but some of it will be of extremely dubious quality. Time spent teaching students how to search for critical material and assess its provenance will not be time wasted: students need to know that the material they find online will not necessarily have been subjected to mechanisms of peer review, editing, revision or quality control, and that they need to approach it critically rather than simply accepting it at face value and treating it as a short-term solution to complex interpretive problems.

Once students have carried out this initial exploration of some short critical extracts, they should be asked to think about what use they will make of literary criticism. The aim of this discussion should be to alert them to the different perspectives and interpretations offered by critical texts, and to the ways in which these can be debated, evaluated and played off against each other: any suggestion that criticism offers an authoritative, 'correct' reading must be avoided. As Ogborn *et al.* put it, 'increasing ... students' awareness of how texts can be read differently will be of more use to them than a limited amount of reading of single critics' (2000: 5).

Using critical texts

How can students be taught how to make use of the literary criticism they read? The objections to literary criticism in the 16–19 phase that were discussed earlier in this chapter posit a worst-case scenario in which students spend hours dutifully poring over 'books-about-books' but fail to incorporate any of this material into their own essays with any kind of success. In this scenario, students quote chunks of this critical material simply because it sounds good: it says what they want to say themselves but expresses it so much more precisely than they ever could. (They might even fall into the classic student trap of quoting interpretations that contradict each other without actually spotting the contradictions.) Criticism effectively becomes a substitute for the students' own voices – and, ironically, a substitute for critical thinking.

One way of avoiding this situation is by getting students to read criticism more actively, concentrating on the quality of their engagement with it rather than on the quantity of criticism they read. This involves the judicious selection of material that will stimulate discussion, offer a range of interpretations and encourage students to become aware of (and refine) their own critical stances. Time spent exploring relevant material is invaluable. The internet has made a rich variety of critical material available online, but traditional print sources still have a lot to offer. The Macmillan Casebooks, introduced in the late 1960s under the editorship of A. E. Dyson and updated more recently to take account of developments in literary and cultural theory, are a fantastic resource for teachers seeking to introduce their students to literary criticism, as they offer extracts from a variety of key critical texts and represent a range of approaches. Better still is the fact that the early editions are still widely available from second-hand bookshops and online sellers, meaning that students can explore the ways in which literary criticism has changed over time.

The exercises outlined below are based on extracts from the two Macmillan Casebooks on *The Merchant of Venice*, the first edited by John Wilders (1969), the second edited by Martin Coyle (1998). These exercises were developed to introduce students in their first year of 16–19 study to the ways in which critical material could be used to develop their understanding of the play's performance history and the different ways in which particular characters, scenes and speeches could be interpreted. Rather than getting students to read lengthy critical texts, they encourage them to engage with short excerpts – in some cases just one or two sentences. Their aim was to build students' confidence in handling critical material, but also – crucially – to maintain a focus on the primary text, directing students to return to specific parts of the text and reconsider these in the light of their critical reading.

Exercise 1: Information retrieval

The first exercise focused on the Introduction to the original 1969 Casebook. It was the first piece of critical reading that the students had been asked to do, and therefore took the form of a straightforward piece of information retrieval, designed to introduce students to the play's cultural context and performance history. These questions were as follows:

- Which event might have prompted Shakespeare to write a play with a Jewish central character?
- Where did the tale of the pound of flesh come from?
- Where did the tale of the caskets come from?
- How did the following actors depict Shylock?
  — Thomas Doggett
  — Charles Macklin
  — Edmund Kean
  — Henry Irving.

This exercise does not seem particularly sophisticated. Nevertheless, it fulfilled its aim of getting a mixed ability group of students to read and process some relatively complex critical material. It also meant that they had a basic knowledge of some key aspects of the play's history, and introduced them to the debates surrounding the character of Shylock – an important focal point of our subsequent work on the play.

Exercise 2: Introducing different interpretations

The next two panels outline activities used to get students to compare and evaluate different interpretations of particular scenes. The first focuses on the character of Launcelot Gobbo in Act 2, Scene 2. The students were told that some productions of *The Merchant of Venice* cut this scene altogether, and were asked to think about why they might do this. After some initial discussion, the students were then asked to consider two different views of Gobbo – one from Harold C. Goddard, the other from Kiernan Ryan. As shown in Panel 5.6, students first had to explain what these critics actually said – thus allowing their comprehension to be assessed. They then had to consider the different views of this scene offered by these critics, and which of them would be most likely to support the cutting of the character of Gobbo.

Panel 5.6   Interpreting Launcelot Gobbo

The Merchant of Venice: Act 2, Scene 2

In this scene we meet Launcelot Gobbo for the first time. Launcelot is the nearest we get in *The Merchant of Venice* to a clown or fool. However, some people argue that his character plays quite an important role.

In his article 'The Three Caskets' (1951), Harold C. Goddard describes Launcelot as 'merely a parody and reduction to the absurd of the loquaciousness that infects the main plot'. What do you think this means?

Kiernan Ryan gives a different interpretation:

> The clown's monologue [in Act 2 Scene 2] presents him as torn back and forth between his conscience's demand that he stay with his master the Jew and the devil's insistence that he abandon him. This apparently inconsequential scene can now be seen to convey more than mere comic relief. As in other plays, especially *King Lear*, *As You Like It* and *Twelfth Night*, the fool acts as a personified index of the text's evolving viewpoint. Gobbo gives us a condensed comic version of the crisis of allegiance provoked by Shylock throughout *The Merchant of Venice*.

What does Ryan mean by this?

Points to consider:

- Why do you think Shakespeare included this scene at this point? Is it just comic relief, or does it serve another purpose?
- What does Launcelot say about Shylock and the way he has been treated by his Jewish master? How could Launcelot be played in a way that would make us a) sympathise with him or b) sympathise with Shylock?
- Which of the two critics quoted above do you think would be most likely to cut the Launcelot Gobbo scenes from a production of the play? Why?

The activity in Panel 5.7 focuses on Shylock's famous 'Hath not a Jew eyes?' speech in Act 3, Scene 1, seeing this as a pivotal moment in the depiction of this character and asking students to consider the play in the post-Holocaust era. The critical excerpts were kept relatively short, but students were asked to engage very closely with them and the interpretations they offered. Note that some of the activities invite students to consider how particular aspects of the play could be interpreted on stage: students should be encouraged to see theatrical performance as another kind of critical interpretation, and indeed their work on plays (as discussed in Chapter 4) should include the opportunity to compare different productions of the text in question.

Panel 5.7   Interpreting Shylock

'Hath not a Jew eyes?'

This famous speech exemplifies the ambiguities that surround the depiction of Shylock. Some critics see it as offering scope for a sympathetic portrayal of the character, claiming common ground and a shared sense of humanity. Others contend that it can be played as opportunistic and ingratiating. You are going to explore the views of E. E. Stoll and Kiernan Ryan.

Stoll argues that the 'Hath not a Jew eyes?' is the speech 'of a villain', 'beginning on a note of thwarted avarice and revengefulness and ending on one of rivalry in revenge, of beating the Christians at what, however justly, he chooses to think their own game. Certainly it is not the plea for toleration that it has generally been taken to be'. He points out that Shylock's words are spoken not to Antonio, but to Salerio and Solanio, two 'minor and unresponsive characters' who prevent the speech from having the pathos with which it is often invested.

Ryan contends that with this speech 'there erupts into the play an irresistible egalitarian attitude, whose basis in the shared faculties and needs of our physical nature indicts all forms of inhuman discrimination. The speech provokes a sharp shift of emotional allegiance, from which our perception of the Christian protagonists never recovers'.

- Which of these interpretations is closest to your own view of this speech?
- In your groups, work out a reading of this speech that would support your chosen interpretation.
- How might Salerio and Solanio behave in a way that supports a) Stoll's interpretation b) Ryan's interpretation?
- Stoll was writing in 1927, Ryan in 1995. How might their interpretations of Shylock have been influenced by their own historical contexts? You might like to think, in particular, about David Nathan's view that in the shadow of the Holocaust, *The Merchant of Venice* should no longer be produced.

Exercise 3: Broadening the range

When students have gained confidence in the structured close reading of secondary and primary sources, they can be introduced to a wider range of interpretations. The extracts in Panel 5.8 were used to encourage students to think about the role of Jessica in *The Merchant of Venice*.

Panel 5.8   Interpreting Jessica

Graham Midgley calls Jessica 'callous', saying that her elopement strikes a blow 'at all that Shylock holds dear, his pride of race, the sober decency of his household life and the dear sanctity of the family and family bonds'.

John Drakakis contrasts Shylock's attempt to constrain Jessica with the marriage-test that was established by Portia's father: 'The "will" or law of Portia's dead father represents a secret meaning which it is the task of her prospective suitors to prise from the caskets; this practice is underwritten by patriarchal goodness and virtue which resists the temptation to align itself with shows of material wealth. [...] By contrast, Shylock's patriarchy is shown to be not one of provision, but rather one of tyranny and restraint.'

W. H. Auden says that 'Lorenzo and Jessica, for all their beauty and charm, appear as frivolous members of a leisure class, whose carefree life is parasitic upon the labours of others, including usurers. When we learn that Jessica has spent fourscore ducats of her father's money in an evening and bought a monkey with her mother's ring, we cannot take this as comic punishment for Shylock's sin of avarice; her behaviour seems rather an example of the opposite sin of conspicuous waste'.

Sigurd Burckhardt comments that, 'As lovers, Jessica and Lorenzo stand in the sharpest imaginable contrast to Portia and Bassanio. Their love is lawless, financed by theft and engineered through a gross breach of trust.'

Kim F. Hall sees Jessica's desire to marry a Christian as setting her apart from 'her father's alienness', a way of increasing Shylock's isolation in the Christian world of Venice.

Alan Sinfield argues that Jessica's elopement has to be seen in the context of wider power relations within the play, stating that Jessica can only 'get away from her father' because 'he is very unpopular and Lorenzo has very powerful friends'.

Extracts like this could be used in a number of ways. Students could be asked to do any or all of the following activities, all of which emphasise an active engagement with both the critical extracts and the primary text.

- Rank the extracts in order of how sympathetic they are towards Jessica.
- Choose an interpretation that they agree with most strongly (or disagree with most strongly) and explain their choice, using evidence from the text to support their argument.
- Consider whether the extracts represent particular critical approaches.
- Select moments within the play that could be used to exemplify particular interpretations, and consider how these moments could be acted and directed.

Such activities lend themselves well to active approaches such as think-pair-share (in which students work first on their own, then with a partner, then with a larger group) or jigsawing (getting students to work in groups, and then reform in different groups to report back on their initial discussions). These approaches will help to develop students' familiarity with critical material, reinforcing the view that it is there to be grappled with and argued against rather than representing an alien yet authoritative voice.

Students will, of course, need to learn how to use this material in their writing. This process could begin with the composition of short responses to the primary text that draw on one of the extracts discussed in class, with students using this extract to support their own interpretation or arguing against it. Students might benefit from having this process modelled for them: they will undoubtedly find it useful to read examples of other students' work so that they can look at how critical arguments are constructed. Panel 5.9 contains an example of an exercise that can be used to highlight the composition of a paragraph that addresses two contrasting critical perspectives.

Panel 5.9   Incorporating critical views in writing

The following paragraph is taken from a student's essay on Shakespeare's presentation of the conflict between Antonio and Shylock in Act 1 of *The Merchant of Venice*.

You are going to explore the way in which the student's argument has been constructed in this paragraph. The paragraph has been printed with wide margins so that you have space to annotate it. Some examples and prompts have been included for you. How does the student construct his argument and how effectively does he do this?

> The first sentence introduces the conventional view of the 'pound-of-flesh' plot and hints that the student's interpretation will be different.

> Here the student introduces his counter-argument. What do you notice about his use of conjunctions?

The suggested forfeit of a 'pound of flesh' is as notorious as Shylock himself, but Antonio does not have to be depicted as the innocent victim of a cruel plot. In his introduction to the Arden Shakespeare edition of *The Merchant of Venice*, John Russell Brown labels the bond as 'the usurer's trap', into which a 'great[ly]' generous Antonio must walk for Bassanio's sake. Brown sees Antonio as a good man, 'drawn firmly' as such by Shakespeare, whereas Shylock is 'savage and ruthless'. However, only a few lines before, Antonio clearly states his awareness of Shylock's deceptions, and he even calls him outright a 'villain with a smiling cheek' – and this is in reference to mere Bible stories. Though he seems grateful and more than willing to sign the proposed bond, his earlier, excessive caution indicates that he cannot possibly be suddenly oblivious to any perceived trap. Antonio's closing remarks of the scene suggest that he still remains conscious of their mutual enmity, with theresumption of his religious jibes: 'the gentle Jew … will turn Christian, he grows kind'.

> Here he gives an example of a critical view that is sympathetic to Antonio. Note that he gives the source of this opinion and uses short, pithy quotations, using square brackets to alter them when necessary.

> Most telling, however, is Antonio's indifference to Bassanio's deep concerns; in tandem with the fact that Antonio will continue to 'spurn' Shylock rather than forgive him, Shakespeare creates the sense that Antonio is saving face by accepting the bond. His refusal to admit even the possibility of risk in his wealth smacks of pride and the continuation of a petty rivalry, rather than what Brown believes to be 'very great' generosity.

How does this sentence contribute to the student's argument?

What do you notice about the way he concludes this paragraph?

Further examples of student writing can be found in Chapter 7. In the next chapter we explore the issue of plagiarism in detail – an issue that is clearly connected not only to students' writing but also to the ways in which they understand, assimilate and refer to the ideas they encounter in the kind of critical material we have discussed here.

Further reading

Teaching theory and criticism

There are excellent discussions of the issues explored in this chapter in *Issues in English Teaching* (Davidson and Moss 1999). Extremely valuable for teaching about theory and interpretation at this level is the English and Media Centre's resource book *Text, Reader, Critic: Introducing Contexts and Interpretations* (Ogborn *et al.* 2000). *Critical Encounters in High School English* (Appleman 2000), and articles in special 16–19 editions of the NATE journal *English Drama Media* (June 2006, October 2008 and November 2011) both outline key issues and give practical activities. *Doing English*, 3rd Edition (Eaglestone 2009), written for students about to start English at university, is also a valuable resource. Two magazines for 16–19 students, *e magazine* (English and Media Centre) and *The English Review* (Philip Allan Publishers) provide a range of accessible critical essays. *A Beginner's Guide to Critical Reading* (Jacobs 2001) offers an anthology of literary texts with accessible critical commentaries designed to illustrate a range of critical approaches, whilst *World and Time* (Barlow 2009) discusses a range of critical approaches in the context of a broader discussion of 16–19 literature teaching.

There is an extensive literature on the experience of teaching theory in universities, which is of great interest to 16–19 teachers. *Teaching Theory* (Bradford 2011) surveys a number of issues, whilst key texts in the debate include *Textual Power: Literary Theory and the Teaching of English* (Scholes 1985). *The Culture of Reading and the Teaching of English* (McCormick 1994) explores the whole range of English teaching across schools and universities.

Critical introductions to theory and criticism

There are many accessible introductions to literary theory aimed at undergraduates. The classic text is perhaps *Literary Theory: An Introduction* (Eagleton 1983). Some of the best general overviews include *English in Practice* (Barry 2003), *An Introduction to Literature, Criticism and Theory* (Bennett and Royle 2009) and *Literary Theory: A Very Short Introduction* (Culler 1997).

For introducing questions about the nature of literariness and creativity, *The Art of English: Literary Creativity* (Goodman and O'Halloran 2006) and *The Art of English: Everyday Creativity* (Maybin and Swann 2006) are valuable.

Literary terminology

Useful guides to literary terminology include *The Concise Oxford Dictionary of Literary Terms* (Baldick 2001), *The Routledge Dictionary of Literary Terms* (Childs and Fowler 2006), the *Penguin Dictionary of Literary Terms and Literary Theory* (Cuddon 1991), and the *Longman Dictionary of Literary Terms: Vocabulary for the Informed Reader* (Kennedy *et al.*, 2006).

Chapter 6

Teaching contexts

Introduction: Crossing forms, crossing time

In this chapter, we continue our discussion, begun in the previous chapter, of a number of ways of looking at literature which cross the boundaries of specific literary forms and which allow students to investigate some of the ways in which literary texts and forms can be connected, both across forms and through time.

Here, we focus on a set of specific literary contexts we have not previously discussed in detail – ideas about *narrative*, and about the *modes* of texts, the *periods* from which they come, and the *movements* they might be taken to represent. Such contexts are sometimes described as 'background' and 'given' to students in the form of notes; we argue that students can play an active role in learning about the broad literary and cultural contexts of their set texts, and that the time and energy devoted to doing this is eventually rewarded by students' enhanced understanding of why texts are as they are and ability to think about and investigate such issues with greater independence.

In approaching this chapter, we have had to recognise that, just as there is no room in this book for writing in depth about how to teach specific texts or authors, there is no room to cover *every* literary mode, period and movement, or even to discuss selected ones in depth. What follows therefore is a set of examples of approaches we have taken in introducing certain contexts to students, providing a model for this kind of literary study and indicating some of the ways in which a range of contexts might frame set-text study.

We conclude the chapter by giving advice on helping students to bring together what they know about the full range of contexts discussed in this book – linguistic, literary, cultural, historical, political – when consolidating their knowledge of set texts.

Although for convenience we have called this chapter 'Teaching contexts', we hope it is clear that in fact *the whole book* is about teaching texts in context, not just this chapter. The underpinning philosophy of this book is that text, context and interpretation are inextricably bound up with each other, and all its chapters are about all three. All text exists always and inevitably in contexts of language, literature, culture and history, and context always and inevitably informs all our reading and interpretations.

Teaching narrative

Narrative is crucially important in all the main literary forms – in drama, in prose fiction, in many forms of literary non-fiction and in poetry. (Even in poetry that does not actually tell a story, certain aspects of narrative such as voice, character and setting may be at play.) Yet it is quite possible for students to get through a 16–19 literature course without being introduced in any coherent way to the operation of narrative in literature, a topic so significant that it has its own branch of literary criticism – narratology.

Put at its simplest, narrative is the act of storytelling. Many theorists, psychologists and writers have reflected on the importance of narrative; even scientists have recently begun to focus on the evolutionary advantage that stories have given us as human beings. The US media analyst Andrew Blau has commented that:

> Human beings tell stories. It is how we learn and how we teach, how we preserve and transmit culture. It is how we understand ourselves and others. The instinct to tell stories and seek them out remains an essential part of being human.
>
> (Blau 2004: 1)

There is a form of psychotherapy – narrative therapy – that focuses on the stories people tell about themselves; the ways in which they link together sequences of events to make them meaningful. The creation and transmission of narratives permeates many aspects of our lives, from sharing gossip with friends to reading bedtime stories to children.

This simple view of narrative is, of course, only the starting point. Studying narrative – and therefore teaching it – involves making a distinction between the raw material of a story and the way it is ordered, organised and presented; between *fabula* and *sjuzet* (Todorov, in Lodge 1988: 160). It involves thinking about who is telling the story and what kind of relationship is established between the narrator and the reader. It also involves questions of representation and the values that might lie behind them. Essentially, it involves asking, 'Why is *this* story being told in *this* way?'

We deal with certain form-specific aspects of narrative in previous chapters; here, we look briefly at elements of narrative that are common across the forms. It's clear that taking a broad approach to narrative might not easily fit into syllabuses which – like many – do not allow for comparative study across literary forms or which do not specify such broad approaches to literary study. Some courses *do* require an introduction to narrative; even where this is not the case, however, an introduction to narrative can be incorporated into the study of a single set text in a single form.

It can be worthwhile taking a little time to introduce the idea of narrative to students by getting them to think about its social and cultural functions, as the activity in Panel 6.1 demonstrates.

Panel 6.1   Thinking about narrative

1   A good starting point is Todorov's theory of narrative structure (1966):

- Exposition – a situation of equilibrium at the start.
- Complication – disruption of equilibrium by agent of change.
- Climax – confrontation/conflict seeking to resolve matters.
- Resolution – return to a (transformed) equilibrium.

Try asking students to apply this structure to a variety of different types of narrative – in literature, film, song, joke, anecdote, and so on – and see whether all narratives conform to the pattern.

2   Then ask them to discuss why being able to break down narrative in this way might be useful or important:

- Does it tell us anything about *why and how* people tell stories?
- How might it help us to understand and discuss how narratives work?

3   Introduce the idea of narrative as a way of *representing* reality. Do they think *real life* is like narrative?

4   Finally, ask them to identify a number of ways in which narratives might be different in different forms, despite sharing the same basic structures. How are narratives in novels, plays, films, jokes, songs and computer games, for instance, different from each other?

One way of approaching literary narrative in more depth is to break it down into its various aspects, as one current A Level syllabus (AQA B Literature) does. In this scenario, students are asked to think about the ways in which texts deal with characterisation, voice, perspective, setting, time and sequence, and destination – a model we will use here to discuss some ways of presenting the topic. Panel 6.2 outlines some of the key questions that students might ask about the narrative of any text; clearly the division into five or six separate aspects suggests the potential for productive group work in class.

Panel 6.2   Aspects of narrative

Narrative is the way we tell stories. We construct narratives:

- setting the narrative in specific places and at specific times (setting – scenes and places);
- building characters (characterisation);
- using narrative voices to tell the story in particular ways (voice and viewpoint/ perspective);
- shaping events and making connections and links between them (structure – time and sequence);
- bringing the narrative to an end which may suggest particular meanings (destination).

Narratives are plotted across space and time, connecting characters and events that resonate with each other, perhaps suggesting patterns of relationship or cause and effect. These connections are made through the narrative voices and structures that enable the story to be told.

Narrative setting: scenes/places/locations

- When is it set? Where is it set? How many settings does it have?
- Are the settings real or imagined?

- What do the settings represent/suggest/symbolise?
- Are journeys between places important?
- What *imagery* is used to describe places?

Narrative characterisation

- Which characters are there? Which are major, which are minor?
- Who are the protagonists? The antagonists?
- To what extent are the characters stereotypes or sketched with realism?
- To what extent are the characters symbolic or metaphorical?
- How are the characters developed? Through narrative description or through dialogue/speech/action?
- To what extent does *imagery* build character?

Narrative voice and perspective

- Who is the narrator? What kind of voice does the narrator have? What do we know about the narrator? Whose perspective/point of view does the narrator represent?
- Is the narrator the same as the writer? Does the narrator identify with anyone? Who does the narrator address? What does the narrator know or divulge? How does the narrator control the narrative?
- What other voices are there? How do they contribute?
- What is the tone of the voices in the narrative? What kinds of language are characteristic of the different voices?
- Is the narrative in verse or prose, or both?

Narrative structure

- How is the narrative organised in terms of time and sequence?
- How much time elapses? Do the events happen in chronological sequence? What is the pace of the narrative?
- What is the significance of textual divisions (e.g. stanzas, chapters, scenes) in sequencing the story?
- How is narrative tension created?
- What links, patterns, echoes are there between parts?
- How are beginnings and endings significant? What transformations and turning points take place between them?
- How might Todorov's narrative progression be applied? (See Panel 6.1.)

Narrative destination

- What might the overall meanings and/or messages of the narrative be?
- What is the significance of the narrative's title?

- How much ambiguity and room for interpretation is there in the narrative?
- To what extent are the meanings highly general, philosophical, metaphorical? To what extent do they relate to a specific historical, cultural, social context?

The generic nature of these questions, which could be asked of any narrative, helps students to see the way in which narrative techniques and structures underpin any literary text. Their focus on the craft of the writer in shaping a narrative also helps them to focus attention on questions of *language, form and structure* and the constructedness of narratives. Finally, their concern with ways in which a narrative might be *interpreted* helps focus attention on the ways in which narrative techniques shape and guide readers' expectations, and open or close spaces for interpretation.

In the context of the detailed exploration of a set text, these questions can be developed to be more specific. For example, the questions in the panel below have been used to focus students on narrative technique in *Pride and Prejudice*. Similar sets of questions can, of course, be constructed for any text, whether prose fiction, drama or poetry. (Further guidance on the use of narrative techniques in poetry, the novel and drama may be found in Chapters 2, 3 and 4.)

Panel 6.3 Aspects of narrative in *Pride and Prejudice*

1. Narrative settings

- The geography of *Pride and Prejudice* is important. You need to have a clear sense of the different locations in the novel (Longbourne, Netherfield, Hunsford and Rosings, and Pemberley, as well as the scenes in London) and what they signify, as well as the social hierarchy represented by these places and the families that live in them. Pemberley in particular has important symbolic significance.
- How do the different locations represent the social structure portrayed in the novel? For instance, what are the social significances of and conventions associated with:
  — visiting and moving between the different locations?
  — the use of the space inside and around the locations?
  — the style, setting and construction of the different locations?

2. Narrative structure

- Although the narrative is chronological/linear, past events are often recounted in conversation and through letters. You need to have a clear idea of the key scenes in which such revelations occur, and the significance of these conversations and letters in driving the plot forward.
- What role does foreshadowing play in the novel? And how are parallels used in the plot?
- What are the turning points and moments of crisis in the narrative and how do these propel the narrative towards its climax?

- How is the novel divided into volumes and chapters? What logic can you see in Austen's placing of narrative breaks? To what extent are these connected with locations?

3. Narrative characterisation

- Characterisation is achieved through the presentation of what characters do, what they say, and what is said about them both by other characters and by the narrator. What is the balance between these methods, and to what extent do these different modes conflict with each other?
- How are the different characters characterised by:
  — their use of language?
  — their dress, possessions and surroundings?
  — the way they interact with others?
- To what extent do the characters display conventional behaviours of the period, and to what extent are they related to gender and class?

4. Narrative voice

- To what extent might we see the third person narrator of this novel as a character who comments on the action, and what characterises the narrative voice? (For instance, note the frequent use of an ironic/humorous voice in the endings of chapters.)
- What is the balance between narrative and dialogue in the novel? What is the role of the narrative voice in setting up and commenting on the dialogue?
- There are alternative narrative voices in the conversations and letters. Why does Austen allow the narrative to be told like this in these instances?

5. Narrative point of view

- Although this is a third-person narrative, it might be argued that the dominant point of view represented is that of Elizabeth. Why is this and how is it achieved? Can we distinguish between the narrator's and Elizabeth's viewpoints in the narration?
- How much of what we know is what Elizabeth knows, and how much do we – and perhaps other characters – know that Elizabeth does not know?
- To what extent does the narrator represent the points of view of other characters?
- Austen often uses irony to represent the different viewpoints in the novel, especially when writing about the comic characters (e.g. Mrs Bennet, Miss Bingley and Mr Collins). How do we know that her presentation here is ironic?

6. Narrative destination

- What is the significance of the title of the novel, and how does the overall sweep of the narrative support the development of the ideas contained in the title?

- How does the opening of the novel prepare for and inform our experience of the plot?
- What is the sequence of resolutions that takes place as the novel reaches its conclusion, and how satisfactory are they?
- How does Austen use the final chapter to bring the narrative to a close?

Teaching literary modes

The terms 'mode', 'genre' and 'form' are slippery customers. In various contexts, these terms might be used interchangeably. Take satire, for instance, or tragedy and comedy: are they modes, genres or forms? Any attempt to answer that question is complicated by the fact that there is sometimes no single, unequivocal answer. Tragedy, for instance, might be seen as a 'genre' within drama, or as a 'mode' that also extends to poetry and fiction.

Despite the difficulties these terms cause, it is worth trying to disentangle them. Even though the definitions are open to debate, and many texts can be categorised in different ways, there are still some patterns that can be useful in discussing literature with students. Panel 6.4 outlines the key distinctions between these terms.

Panel 6.4   Form, genre and mode

Form

A type of writing with certain clear conventions relating to the physical *layout or length* of the text.

- At a fundamental level, almost all writing takes 'verse' or 'prose' form.
- More precisely, 'poem', 'play', 'novel' and 'short story' might be identified as four key literary forms; 'graphic novel' might be identified as a form, too.
- Poetry can be subdivided into different forms – for instance, 'sonnet', 'haiku', 'free verse'; the novel can also take different forms – for instance, 'epistolary'.

Genre

A type of writing with certain clear *narrative* conventions *within a particular literary form*.

- Genres of prose fiction include 'bildungsroman', 'crime fiction', 'science fiction' and 'romantic fiction'.
- Genres of drama include 'mystery play', 'tragedy', 'comedy', 'history', 'melodrama'.
- There are subgenres within genre, such as 'farce' and 'comedy of manners' within comedy.

> ### Mode
>
> A type of writing with certain clear *representational* conventions that can occur *in different literary forms.*
>
> - Mode might refer to a certain overall style or approach – for instance, 'comic', 'tragic', 'satirical', 'realist', 'absurdist', 'stylised', 'allegorical', 'epic', 'lyric'.
> - It might also refer to a more specific mood or theme – for instance, 'pastoral', 'gothic', 'romantic'.
> - A broader use of the idea of mode (from linguistics) concerns discourse. 'Narrative' is one of a number of modes of discourse that also include 'argument', 'description' and 'exposition'.

As a means of helping students to develop critical vocabulary and to organise their textual knowledge conceptually, an activity which asks them to sort texts they have read or studied according to these various categories can be both enjoyable and illuminating.

In this section, having discussed issues of form and genre in the three chapters devoted to poetry, the novel and drama, we explore ways of teaching about modes. We take two different examples – Gothic and Pastoral, and Tragedy and Comedy – to illustrate ways of introducing modes to students.

Teaching the Pastoral and the Gothic

The Pastoral and the Gothic are generally studied as separate topics, and indeed in many respects they are quite different, not only in their concerns but also in their histories and literary manifestations. Nevertheless, there are important ways in which the two ideas are linked, which can help students to understand why these modes are so significant. Both the Pastoral and the Gothic represent different – indeed directly opposite – relationships between humanity and nature, and are indicated by a set of symbols and tropes which suggest different ways of thinking about the way we inhabit our environment and our lives within it. Thus, a good way of introducing either topic to students is to focus them on the relationship between the two.

Activity 1: Imagining the Pastoral and Gothic

A simple but effective starting point is to ask students to imagine and describe the elements of an idyllic day in the countryside, focusing on setting, characters and actions. Following that, they should imagine and describe the opposite – a nightmarish night in the countryside, again focusing on setting, characters and actions. From here, students can be shown a range of contrasting visual representations of nature. These could include classic paintings from the Renaissance and the Romantic period; photographs of contrasting natural scenes; photographs of pastoral and gothic scenes in film and theatre; and even musical representations of pastoral idylls and gothic nightmares (for instance Beethoven's 'Pastoral' Symphony and Mussorgsky's 'Night on a Bare Mountain'). By the end of this exercise, students should be able to construct a list of fundamental symbolic features of the Pastoral and the Gothic, which should look something like this:

The Pastoral emphasises the idea of nature as a haven, a retreat, a place of innocence and love. The classic images of the Pastoral include: • sunshine, light, breezes; • beauty, calm, relaxation, healing; • nymphs, shepherds, lovers, poets; • fields, gardens, verdant rolling hills, pretty lakes and rivers, rustic houses and cottages; • sheep, birds, bees; • classical imagery.	**The Gothic** emphasises the mystery and danger of nature and the presence of the supernatural. The classic images of the Gothic include: • darkness, shadow, storms; • ugliness, anxiety, terror, death; • ghosts, predators, victims, villains; • untamed nature, medieval ruins, cemeteries, dark halls, castles, churches, dungeons, labyrinths; • bats, crows, wolves; • medieval imagery.

Activity 2: The roots of Pastoral and Gothic

The next stage is to introduce students to the origins of the two modes, and explore some primary ways in which their basic symbols are used to construct a set of complex meanings. For the Pastoral, this means looking at some Renaissance poetry; for the Gothic, Romantic fiction.

The origins of the Pastoral lie, of course, in ancient Greek poetry, notably the 'Idylls' of Theocritus. For the purposes of this activity, however, poetry from the time of its revival in the Renaissance makes a good starting point. Christopher Marlowe's 'The Passionate Shepherd to His Love' and Walter Raleigh's response 'The Nymph's Reply to the Shepherd' are perfect for this purpose, straightforwardly illustrating one of the key features of the Pastoral – the tension between the innocence, beauty and joy of nature on the one hand and its tendency to become corrupt – to decay and die – on the other. Students can simply be asked to identify pastoral symbols and comment on how they are used in contrasting ways in the two poems.

One can build students' awareness of this symbolism further by introducing them to some Elizabethan madrigals: it's amusing to play good recordings of these to students (and note that there are many bad ones on YouTube, which should be avoided at all costs!) – but the words without the music will suffice. Good examples are 'Now is the Month of Maying' by Thomas Morley and 'Though Amaryllis Dance in Green' by William Byrd. Again, these two poems illustrate the contrasting moods of the Pastoral. Here, though, students are introduced to the crucial association between the Pastoral, melancholy and rejected love.

Whilst some of the symbolism characteristic of the Gothic has been used in literature since earliest times, the Gothic became a recognised literary mode in the eighteenth century, with the publication of Horace Walpole's novel *The Castle of Otranto*. Give students several short extracts from this very short novel and they will soon identify not only the symbols of the Gothic but also some of the ways these are translated into narrative – notably the plight of the heroine in the face of the male villain.

Finally, whilst the differences between the Gothic and Pastoral texts the students have seen will be obvious, it is worthwhile asking students to discuss whether they feel that they have any similarities, or similar concerns. Relationships between men and women and visions of love, death and nature are at the heart of both modes, despite their contrasting sets of symbols. Why, it might also be worth asking, have these two modes been so successful and powerful over so many centuries?

Activity 3: Researching Pastoral and Gothic

At this point, students are ready to do some research into the origins and history of the Pastoral and Gothic, working in groups to investigate a range of topics that would give their study of literary texts a more detailed historical and philosophical grounding. Topics might be assigned to different groups and might include:

- the etymology of the words 'Gothic' and 'Pastoral';
- Gothic architecture;
- Horace Walpole's Strawberry Hill and 'The Gothic Revival';
- the 'sublime' and the reaction against neo-classical rationalism;
- the Gothic novel;
- Theocritus, Virgil and the classical Pastoral;
- the rediscovery of the classical in the Renaissance;
- the ideas of Arcadia and the 'memento mori';
- the ode and the elegy.

Students could present their findings in a range of ways. These might include traditional oral presentations or posters, but could also make use of new technologies: PowerPoint, podcasting software and iPad applications such as Book Creator (which allows users to create multimodal e-books that incorporate sound and moving image clips as well as words and pictures) all give students opportunities to develop their skills as communicators and present their research imaginatively.

Activity 4: Wider reading

Finally, students can begin to explore in a little more depth a range of manifestations of the Gothic and Pastoral. Working in groups, they can use their foundational knowledge of the two modes to inform their discussion of some longer extracts, focusing on a more detailed close reading. Each group can be assigned one or two texts as appropriate, ensuring that students' ability levels are taken into account when dealing with the varied levels of challenge provided by the texts. Each group can then report back on what they have found, so that the whole class learns about all the texts. Some suggested texts are:

Pastoral poetry
'January' from The Shephearde's Calender (Edmund Spenser)
'Lycidas', lines 1–63 and 165–93 (John Milton)
'Intimations of Immortality from Recollections of Early Childhood', lines 1–77 and 173–208 (William Wordsworth)
'Fern Hill' (Dylan Thomas).

Other possibilities include a range of pastoral and anti-pastoral poetry from the Renaissance (for instance, Andrew Marvell) to modernism (for instance, Ted Hughes, Philip Larkin and Seamus Heaney), drama (*As You Like It, A Midsummer Night's Dream* etc.), and prose fiction such as *Brideshead Revisited* (Evelyn Waugh) and the novels of Thomas Hardy.

Gothic prose fiction
>   An extract from *Northanger Abbey* (Jane Austen)
>   An extract from *Frankenstein* (Mary Shelley)
>   An extract from *The Turn of the Screw* (Henry James)
>   An extract from *Dracula* (Bram Stoker).

Other possibilities include other early Gothic novels such as *The Monk* by Matthew Lewis and *The Italian* by Ann Radcliffe, and other later novels such as *The Picture of Dorian Grey* by Oscar Wilde and *Gormenghast* by Mervyn Peake. In addition, the whole realm of contemporary 'horror' fiction, e.g. the *Twilight* series, is an option.

Extension: Pastoral and Gothic in the arts

There are some very good examples of modern Pastoral in the compositions of a major group of English composers, including Ralph Vaughan Williams, Gerald Finzi and Frederick Delius. Similar musical symbolism can be explored in relation to the Gothic also. Play students 'Gargoyle' by Frank Bridge, 'Goyescas' by Granados or the 'Gothic' Symphony by Havergal Brian and ask them to explore how the melodies and harmonies of the music echo the fragmented and disrupted world of the Gothic.

A visit to almost any regional or national art gallery is also very rewarding in relation to images of the Gothic and Pastoral, and many museum education departments will be happy to devise a workshop for students along these lines. Clearly film is also an important resource, especially in relation to the Gothic.

Tragedy and comedy

Like the Pastoral and the Gothic, tragedy and comedy are clearly two sides of the same coin. The following activities, which deal with the two modes both separately and together, may be used whether studying comedy or tragedy. They are designed to help students consider the nature and significance of tragedy and comedy, and to teach them about their origins in Greek drama.

Activity 1: Notions of tragedy and comedy

Since most students will have experience of both tragedy and comedy before they start 16–19 study, a good place to start is with their existing knowledge and ideas. Ask students to discuss the following in groups or pairs:

Both 'tragedy' and 'comedy' have different meanings depending on how we use them.

1   What do we mean when we describe things in life as 'tragic' or 'a tragedy'? What do we mean when we describe a play as 'a tragedy'? How are these things similar and/or different?

2   What do we mean when we describe things in life as 'comic' or 'a farce'? What do we mean when we describe a play as 'a comedy' or 'a farce'? How are these things similar and/or different? And what is the difference between 'comedy' and 'a comedy'?

Whole-class discussion of these concepts should focus on establishing (a) the differences between literary and non-literary uses of the words 'tragedy' and 'comedy' and (b) a general overview of the differences between tragedies and comedies.

The next part of the activity focuses in more detail on the similarities and differences between tragic and comic drama.

A tragedy usually has the following characteristics:

• It involves moral dilemmas in which characters have to make decisions about how to act honourably.
• It involves social conflicts, such as the conflict between the restrictions of the family, institution or law and the needs and desires of the individual.
• It involves the workings of fate or chance, and suggests that we cannot always be in control of our lives.
• It involves tense relationships between family members – sons, daughters, mothers, fathers, uncles, aunts, brothers, sisters – and friends.
• It involves tense relationships between men and women, husbands and wives, and/or lovers.
• It involves wars, conflicts or misunderstandings between different nations, cultures, classes or other groups.
• It involves deaths, accidents and/or disasters.
• The conflicts and misunderstandings are resolved at the end of the play.

1   To what extent are these characteristics true of any tragedies you know or have studied?

2   To what extent could these characteristics also apply to comedies you know or have studied? What characteristics would you need to add, take away or change to make a list of characteristics of comedy?

Whole-class discussion should now focus on establishing a more specific view of differences and similarities between tragedy and comedy:

Finally, ask students to discuss the following questions:

1   Tragedy and comedy have traditionally been closely linked to the theatre. But they are also relevant to other cultural forms. To what extent are ideas about tragedy and comedy relevant to: novels, films, TV and radio, music? What tragic or comic culture have you encountered recently in any of these forms?
2   The first recorded tragedies and comedies were written in ancient Greece nearly 3,000 years ago. Why do you think tragedy and comedy have remained so important in literature for so long? Why do people enjoy watching them? Do you think ideas about tragedy and comedy help us to understand the world around us?

Activity 2: The roots of tragedy and comedy

In the next stage, students should be introduced to key features of tragedy and comedy, with their discussion rooted in examples from Greek drama. First, give students the information about Aristotle in Panel 6.5.

Panel 6.5   Aristotle and Greek tragedy

The Greek philosopher Aristotle first described the elements of tragedy, based on the canon of Greek tragedy, in his work *Poetics* (fourth century BCE [1996]). Some of the key elements of tragedy that Aristotle discusses are as follows:

- Six elements should work together to make the tragedy effective: plot, character, diction, thought, lyric and spectacle.
- The drama should be serious and of great magnitude, with meanings beyond the particular events of the plot, expressing ideas of universal significance.
- The plot should be carefully constructed such that the events happen 'unexpectedly but in consequence of one another', so that 'they arouse more awe than if they happened accidentally and by chance' (1996: 17).
- The central character (often referred to in modern criticism as the tragic hero) is a person of high rank or nobility who suffers a reversal of fortune ('peripeteia'), as a result of inappropriate or mistaken actions that stem from his/her 'tragic flaw', but which he/she does not yet recognise. This flaw is often a form of arrogant pride ('hubris'). Eventually, the hero recognises ('anagnorisis') the mistake(s) ('hamartia') which led to his/her decline.
- The working out of this drama – culminating in a tragic end ('catastrophe') – causes 'pity and fear' ('pathos') in the audience, and finally brings about an emotional release ('catharsis') for the audience, which is ultimately liberating or purifying.
- The fallibility of the hero, and their suffering, should help the audience to feel pity for him/her and fear for themselves. The hero must not be a wholly bad person, nor a wholly good one, for 'we feel pity for a man who does not deserve his misfortune; we fear for someone like ourselves' (1996: 21).

> • The drama should observe unities of action and time in order to make the emotional impact more concentrated. It should focus on one complete action and not contain more than one plot; and it should be confined to a 'single revolution of the sun' (1996: 9).

In groups, ask students to discuss the following questions:

1   Think of a tragedy by Shakespeare, and any modern tragic drama. To what extent do these later dramas reflect the elements Aristotle describes?
2   Do you agree that these elements are necessary to make a tragedy effective?
3   Which of these elements do you think are relevant or irrelevant to comedy? How might you rewrite or replace some of these elements to describe comedy?

During the ensuing feedback, it is useful to show students' Aristotle's comments on comedy:

> [Characters in drama] must be either admirable or inferior … or they must be better people than we are, or worse … This difference distinguishes tragedy and comedy from each other. The latter aims to imitate people worse than our contemporaries, the former better … Comedy is an imitation of inferior people – not, however, with respect to every kind of defect … The laughable is an error or disgrace that does not involve pain or destruction.
>
> (Aristotle 1996: 5, 9)

For the next stage, give students the openings of a Greek tragedy and a Greek comedy – easily available online: Aeschylus' *Agamemnon* and Aristophanes' *Lysistrata* are good examples. Ask them to discuss these openings, decide which is comic and which is tragic, and to identify the features of the writing that suggest these modes. They should readily see the differences in tone and content.

   Finally, in the light of this activity, ask students to summarise the differences and similarities between tragedy and comedy.

Activity 3: Researching Greek and Roman drama

Students are now ready to learn more about the origins of tragedy and comedy in Greek culture. Working in groups, as described in the section on 'Gothic and Pastoral', they research aspects of early drama, and present their findings. The following list covers many important areas:

- the origins of drama;
- the etymology of the words 'tragedy', 'comedy' and 'satire';
- the major Greek dramatists – Aeschylus, Sophocles, Euripides and Aristophanes;
- Greek theatres;

- how Greek drama was performed;
- the god Dionysus and the Dionysia festival in Athens;
- the ideas of carnival and festival;
- the role of fate and the gods in Greek tragedy;
- Roman drama;
- the influence of Greek and Roman drama on Shakespeare.

Activity 4: Wider reading

Finally, students can begin to explore some more complex applications of the categories of tragedy and comedy.

To demonstrate that not all tragedy and comedy are easily identifiable as such, give them pairs of extracts: first, the opening of a Shakespearean comedy (e.g. *Comedy of Errors* and *Twelfth Night* work well) and a Shakespearean tragedy (e.g. *King Lear* or *Othello*). They should decide whether these come from a tragedy or a comedy. Next, provide extracts from a Shakespearean tragedy and comedy that confound expectations by adopting a tragic or comic tone (the Gravedigger's scene from *Hamlet,* for example, and Jaques' soliloquy from *As You Like It*). Finally, they might look at examples of modern tragicomic drama or black comedy.

There are, of course, many other ways in which students can explore tragedy and comedy, either together or separately, from this point – for instance, making comparisons between extracts from a range of seventeenth-, eighteenth-, nineteenth-, twentieth- and twenty-first-century dramas, and beginning to explore the roles of heroes, villains and fools, of masks and disguises, and of various aspects of setting and symbolism in tragedy and comedy.

Extension: Tragedy and comedy in the arts

Ideas about tragedy and comedy can be explored further through the contrasts between light and dark, dance and dirge, and harmony and disharmony, which are strongly identifiable in art and music through the centuries. Such ideas can be linked with ideas about carnival, festival and ritual that should have emerged from the previous activities.

Teaching literary periods and movements

The idea of historical period is difficult. There is no universal agreement about what to call the periods of literature, and in any case period is often different in different places: thus, for instance, the Renaissance is generally regarded as having started and finished earlier in mainland Europe than in Britain. Some of the conventional ways of naming periods (often named after the reign of a monarch, e.g. Jacobean, Victorian) refer to little more than a convenient way of dividing time – even if we *can* make some broad generalisations about the characteristics of those periods.

Others indicate the broad characteristics of longer periods (e.g. medieval) or identify a period with a movement or tendency (e.g. Renaissance, Romanticism, Augustanism, Enlightenment, Modernism). Such labels are inevitably reductive, suggesting a kind of definite social, cultural and literary unity that is generally not present either across time or throughout place. One approach to the naming of periods has become widely accepted amongst academics: the division of history into three main periods – Ancient (loosely until the fall of the Roman Empire), Middle ('The Middle Ages') and Modern (loosely from the Renaissance), with subdivisions such as 'the Late Middle Ages' and 'the Early Modern period'. This approach however has not been systematically adopted in all educational contexts, and now coexists with more traditional approaches.

Despite the difficulty of establishing meaningful divisions of literary history, making connections between and within literary periods and movements can considerably enrich literary study at this level. Introducing students to something of the literary and cultural milieu of the time and place in which writers operate certainly illuminates the reading of literary texts in significant ways, whether one is approaching a single, long set text or a selection of shorter texts (e.g. an anthology of poetry by several authors). One particularly effective way of doing this is to explore texts by other writers, or other texts by the same writer, carefully chosen to highlight interesting similarities or differences: this might include reading texts from a previous and/or subsequent period as well as from the same period. Having established some of the concerns and methods of writing of the period, an introduction to some of the key cultural, political and social ideas or movements that underline those concerns might be valuable; this can be done in a number of ways – through library/internet research, teacher presentation, reading of critical extracts, or the watching of a documentary, for instance. It might also involve reading from other disciplines (e.g. history, music, religious studies, politics or economics).

A further strategy, though one which can be labour intensive, is to act on one of the central tenets of New Historicism by assembling a selection of literary *and* non-literary texts of the time relating to a particular literary idea or practice in order to illustrate the complexity of social and cultural practices and attitudes. One benefit of such an approach is to highlight the fact that the literary text is a representation which does not constitute direct truth: there is no simple correlation between the way a literary text represents society and the historical 'fact' of the period, but rather the literary text is one of a number of pieces of evidence about the period which must be weighed against other evidence. The insights of New Historicism are valuable when guiding students away from reductive or simplistic uses of background material. The British Library's website makes a range of suitable resources available via its interactive 'Timelines' facility: texts featured include handbills, political speeches, newspaper articles, diaries and letters, adding richness and variety to students' understanding of particular periods.

One of the most common manifestations of reductive approaches to context is the 'tacked-on' historical summary which sometimes introduces students' essays, apparently unrelated in any substantial way to students' literary analyses, and often making carelessly broad claims about, for instance, what 'medieval people' believed or how 'women' behaved at a particular time. If evaluation and application of context is to be valuable, it must be sensitively applied and must be carefully linked with the concerns, methods and motivations of writers. As the New Historicists suggest, it should also throw light on the ways in which the subjectivities of writers themselves are formed by the contexts in which they operate.

In this section, we suggest some of the ways in which ideas about period and movement can inform students' interpretations of text and build their literary awareness, by presenting two sets of activities designed to introduce students to Romanticism and to the writing of the First World War. We have used similar approaches to introduce students to other periods and movements, and our suggested format can be adapted accordingly.

Introducing the Romantics

This section is not intended to give an exhaustive overview of the Romantic period and its literature, it rather provides examples of how the major Romantic poets could be introduced to 16–19 students who are studying either the period as a whole or an individual writer working within the Romantic tradition. Many of the activities suggested are based on exercises that have been used successfully with 16–19 students studying William Blake and William Wordsworth.

They aim to give students an overview of:

- who the major Romantic poets were;
- when they lived;
- what they thought;
- what they wrote;
- who and what they were influenced by;
- what they were reacting to.

Nevertheless, students also need to appreciate that labelling a period of literary history like this – identifying its characteristics and drawing neat lines around it – is only the first stage in understanding it. At some point students need to recognise that such boundaries are blurred, even porous. The difficulty of defining Romanticism has exercised many critics and literary historians: indeed, Furst (1976) stated that the difficulty with Romanticism lies not just in finding one's own definition of the term, but in 'finding one's way through the maze of definitions that have already been put forward' (1976: 308). Students need to be alerted early to the fact that the poets we now think of as 'Romantic' were not, during their lifetime, part of a unified artistic movement. How might this problem of definition apply to other literary periods and movements? Introducing the basic 'facts' about such a period is relatively easy: getting students to understand the subtleties that might be involved, and steering them away from generalisations and over-simplifications, is a much more complicated process.

Activity 1: Neoclassicism v. Romanticism

My own starting point would be the notion that the poets we now think of as 'Romantic' were reacting against the orthodoxies of Neoclassicism. This would begin with a reading of the first 66 lines of Alexander Pope's mock-epic poem *The Rape of the Lock*, used to introduce students to the stylistic conventions and the experience of reading Neoclassical poetry. Students would be asked to read the extract and discuss the questions below.

This exercise would then be used as the basis for discussion. Why did the students place it where they did? Which features make it seem formal and exclusive? Who do the students think this poem was aimed at? Are they included in this target audience, or excluded? What kind of knowledge do they feel they would need to understand the poem?

Students would then repeat this exercise with a representative Romantic poem, such as William Wordsworth's 'Lines written at a small distance from my House'. How does the experience of reading this poem differ from that of reading the extract from *The Rape of the Lock*? The poems were published 86 years apart: can the differences between them be ascribed purely to their individual writers, or might other factors be involved? This latter question

---

The Rape of the Lock

Read the extract from Alexander Pope's poem. Then, in groups, consider where you would place it on each of the following scales. Mark your chosen place with an X.

Simple	_____	Complex
Informal	_____	Formal
Colloquial	_____	Educated
Free verse	_____	Highly structured
Broad appeal	_____	Narrow appeal
Accessible	_____	Exclusive
Nature	_____	Culture

---

leads, of course, to an exploration of historical events, and, in particular, of the revolutions that took place during the eighteenth century: students could be asked to research the philosophies that underpinned these events, and consider how they might influence writers.

Activity 2: Wordsworth and Romanticism

The next stage of this introduction to Romanticism involves an exploration of Wordsworth's Preface to the 1800 edition of *Lyrical Ballads*. More able students will be able to cope with reading the whole of this important Romantic text, but teachers may wish to start with some key extracts, both to support the reading of less able students and enable a close focus on core ideas. One obvious starting point is Wordsworth's statement that 'all good poetry is the spontaneous overflow of powerful feelings', which could be considered in relation to the poems by Pope and Wordsworth discussed above. Students could subsequently read and explore a more extended passage from the Preface containing Wordsworth's summary of poetic aims.

   One simple but useful exercise is to highlight the different claims Wordsworth makes for his poetry, and then summarise these claims as a list of bullet points. Students could be asked to formulate questions in response to this 'poetic manifesto'. What is the 'language really used by men'? What kinds of value-judgements does Wordsworth appear to be making? They should also consider whether 'Lines written at a small distance from my House' actually bears out Wordsworth's claims for it: in what ways does this poem embody the 'essential passions of the heart' that Wordsworth mentions? And why does Wordsworth consider such feelings to be more important than those depicted in Pope's poem?

Activity 3: Researching Romanticism

Having explored some aspects of the work of one major Romantic poet, students now work in groups, as described in the 'Gothic and Pastoral' section above. Again, students could present their findings in a range of ways. The list below is by no means exhaustive, but would nevertheless introduce most of the major aspects of Romanticism that students in the 16–19 phase would need to be familiar with:

- the etymology of the word 'Romantic';
- the opposition between Romanticism and Classicism;
- the Enlightenment;
- independence in America;
- revolution in France;
- Jean-Jacques Rousseau and his view of childhood;
- Romantic landscapes;
- the sublime.

Activity 4: Wider reading

The final stage in this brief introduction to Romanticism would involve a study of a range of poems by the five major English Romantic poets: William Blake, William Wordsworth, Samuel Taylor Coleridge, Percy Bysshe Shelley and John Keats. A suggested list is as follows:

William Blake: 'The Lamb', 'The Tyger', 'The School-Boy', 'London'.
William Wordsworth: 'Lines written in early Spring', 'Lines Written a Few Miles above Tintern Abbey', 'I wandered lonely as a Cloud'.
Samuel Taylor Coleridge: 'The Dungeon', 'Kubla Khan', 'Frost at Midnight'.
Percy Bysshe Shelley: 'Ozymandias', 'England in 1819'.
John Keats: 'Ode: To Autumn', 'Ode: To a Nightingale', 'On First Looking into Chapman's Homer'.

Students could be assigned these poems individually or in groups, with the range of poems above allowing for differentiation: they should be asked to find out about the author of the poems they have been allocated, and should try to place the poems and their authors in the context of the research on Romanticism they have carried out. The aim should be to get them to explore what their knowledge of the period, and of these key authors, can contribute to their interpretations of literary texts: the focus should be not on *how much* they can find out but on how they *use* what they find out.

Extension: Romanticism in the arts

Music is a rich source for understanding Romanticism, especially through the comparison between the 'Classical' period of Haydn and Mozart and the Romanticism of Beethoven, Mendelssohn, Brahms and so on. Play students an extract from a symphony by Haydn and one of Beethoven's later symphonies, and ask them to compare the moods and atmospheres of the pieces. Beethoven's 'Pastoral' Symphony is particularly good for illustrating the

Romantic concern with describing the moods of nature. A similar comparison between 'Classical' and Romantic modes of landscape art is also useful.

Introducing the First World War

As human beings we are natural taxonomists – we like and seek categorisation. Categories provide a measure of security and certainty. In reality, however, any attempt at taxonomy is problematic and raises as many questions as it answers. It is interesting and worthwhile to explore with 16–19 students how any form of classification in literature is simultaneously useful and problematic. The study of First World War literature provides an interesting example here. It is usually seen as fairly unproblematic; study generally focuses upon the works of a small group of well known male poets writing from the western front or writing about their front-line experiences of war – Wilfred Owen, Siegfried Sassoon, John MacRae, Rupert Brooke and occasionally Robert Graves, Ivor Gurney and Isaac Rosenberg. To limit the literature of the First World War to a mere handful of monochrome males – no disrespect intended to these great writers – is in itself a problem, however. If we are to do justice to the wider contexts of First World War literature we need to allow a much more generous exploration than this. The following is a sequence of activities or individual ideas for providing access to a range of contextual issues.

Activity 1: What do we mean by First World War literature?

It's useful in the first instance for students to challenge the idea of what constitutes First World War literature and the version of it they are studying. Introduce to students the names of the authors and/or texts they will be studying. Ask them to do some initial research into them. What characteristics do they note? Can they identify any obvious literary gaps? The following is a list of omissions they may raise:

- literature written about the war by non-combatants, including many women;
- literature about the home front;
- literature about the war by authors from other nationalities, both Allies and *Mittelmächte* (the Central Powers);
- literature about the experiences of fighting on the eastern front or in southern Europe;
- literature written during the First World War that is not specifically about the war;
- drama and fiction texts.

These questions can, of course, be fed in by the teacher should students not identify them for themselves. These can then be used as a basis for exploring why students think that poetry is the dominant literary form to emerge from the war, and why other forms are less frequently studied.

Activity 2: Historical and political issues

Once students have thought critically about why this category of literature is so particularly defined, it is interesting and important to explore some of the historical and political contexts for the war. This is not to suggest that students need to know in detail the history of the conflict, but to study the literature without at least some knowledge of who was involved, why it occurred and so on is to leave them with significant gaps in contextual understanding. The horrors so graphically presented by the poets and other writers they encounter gain poignancy and power when set against the reasons for the prosecution and continuation of the war. A range of useful information will be elicited by setting students a research task to explore the following questions:

- When did the war begin?
- What were the primary causes of the war?
- Who fought? (Students need to know it was not all white males!)
- Where was the war fought?
- Which countries formed the Allies and which the *Mittelmächte*?
- What about war on the eastern and southern fronts?
- What about the simultaneous Bolshevik Revolution occurring in Russia?

Activity 3: Other literary treatments

As has been observed above, the study of the First World War literature tends to be dominated by a clutch of great poets. This, however, does not do justice to the range of literary production about the war emanating from the war years and from subsequent periods. In order to contextualise the role and impact of the war poets, students benefit from looking into a range of the other literature of the war. In order to do this, the reading of a range of extracts in the following areas proves a very useful context:

- novels and short stories written about the First World War at various points, e.g. *His Last Bow* by Sir Arthur Conan Doyle) – a Sherlock Holmes story set in the war; *Birdsong* by Sebastian Faulks; *Mr Standfast* and *Greenmantle* by John Buchan; *The Regeneration Trilogy* and the more recent *Life Class*, which explores the work of a war artist, by Pat Barker; *The First Casualty* by Ben Elton; *Strange Meeting* by Susan Hill, and others;
- plays, e.g. *Journey's End* by R. C. Sherriff; *For Services Rendered* by Somerset Maugham; *Post Mortem* by Noel Coward;
- poetry by writers of other nationalities – information about a wealth of these writers and how their work can be accessed is available at www.scuttlebuttsmallchow.com/ wwibooks.html;
- later poetry, e.g. Larkin's 'MCMXIV', Hughes' 'Bayonet Charge', Sheers' 'Mametz Wood';
- memoirs, e.g. *Four Weeks in the Trenches* by the Austrian officer and concert violinist Fritz Kreisler; *Memoirs of an Infantry Officer* by Siegfried Sassoon; *A Testament of Youth* by Vera Brittain; *Horses Don't Fly* by Frederick Libby; *The Middle Parts of Fortune* by the Australian soldier Frederic Manning; *Storm of Steel* by the German soldier-novelist Ernst Junger; *Tommy's War*, an account of life on the Home Front by Thomas Cairns Livingstone;
- journalism and other responses, e.g. Siegfried Sassoon's famous *Finished with the War: A Soldier's Declaration*; propaganda documents; Hamilton Fyfe's reports for *The Daily Mail*; Arthur Moore's reports for *The Times*.

Interesting questions to explore in relation to these texts are how and why the war appears differently in them. What do these different genres bring to the representation of the war?

How does hindsight (sometimes, indeed from the far side of several later conflicts) lead to a different perspective? What does the journalism, produced in direct opposition – and under threat of death – to the will of Lord Kitchener, cover?

Activity 4: Non-war literature written during the war

It is also useful to discuss with students the fact that not all literary works produced during the war were directly about the war. Major writers were producing significant literary works of this sort throughout the war years (e.g. *The Shadow Line* by Joseph Conrad; *The Rainbow* by D. H. Lawrence; *The Voyage Out* by Virginia Woolf; *Dubliners, A Portrait of the Artist as a Young Man* and *Exiles* by James Joyce; *The Ivory Tower* and *The Sense of the Past* by Henry James). It is important for students to realise that the war poets formed only a part – albeit a significant one – of the literary landscape between 1914 and 1918. Useful questions to consider are:

• Why do you think some writers in the period chose to write about non-war issues?
• In what ways do non-war texts respond to the war?
• What else do these works tell us about the First World War era?

Extension: The First World War in the arts

Several interesting contexts can be explored here:

• In music there are major compositions by Benjamin Britten (*A War Requiem*); Ivor Gurney (as both poet and composer, Gurney provides a very interesting example – there is also a recent theatre piece dealing with his life, *A Soldier and a Maker*); Ralph Vaughan Williams (the 'Pastoral' Symphony is a particularly powerful example of his music inspired by the war); Sir Arthur Bliss (*Morning Heroes*).
• There is also an extensive photographic record and a surprisingly large body of moving image material. Much of this is available on the web and provides an invaluable context for what is an increasingly distant event.
• In the world of art major figures to consider are Wyndham Lewis, John Singer Sargent, C. R. W. Nevinson, Charles Masterman and Paul Nash.

Works in all of these different media provide a very interesting counterpoint to the literary texts with which students will be more familiar. Each can be used either as a stimulus to visual and/or auditory thinking, and can provide an interesting way of accessing the visual and aural worlds of the poetry and/or other First World War texts they are studying.

Bringing text and context together

In this book so far, we have set out to demonstrate ways of teaching literature that enable students to explore their set texts not only by careful close reading of the texts themselves but also by setting those texts in a variety of contexts. The last two chapters have in particular looked at ways of approaching a number of broad cultural and literary contexts that can enrich students' textual experience.

At some point in most courses, students will need to bring together the elements of their contextual learning and apply them to their final essays or presentations on their set texts. To conclude this chapter, we provide examples of two reference sheets intended to help students to consolidate what they've learnt about various contexts and revise some of the key issues they've discussed. The sheets might be used as a revision guide or as the basis for group and class discussion; most importantly, they attempt to model for students ways of bringing together abstract contextual knowledge to bear concretely on their interpretations of text. We hope they will also suggest how teachers might plan to introduce students to a range of relevant contexts and interpretations.

Panel 6.6 sets out how a range of contexts for a Shakespearean comedy (*As You Like It*) and a modern novel (*Brideshead Revisited*) may be approached.

Panel 6.6   Bringing in context

AS YOU LIKE IT

Performance context

- Performance at Wilton House, the Pembroke family's rural Arcadia.
- All-male cast produces gender/sexuality issues on stage.
- Touchstone was famous comic actor with function similar to stand-up comedy.

Literary context

- Popularity of the Pastoral – Shakespeare took the idea from Lodge's *Rosalynde*, one of many popular pastoral plays.
- Note: Shakespeare invented the characters of Jaques, Touchstone and Corin, adding them to the existing plot of *Rosalynde*.
- *As You Like It* combined Pastoral with medieval romance to make 'Pastoral Romance', combining the Classical Pastoral (Silvius, Phebe) with the quest (Orlando), and the court in exile.

Social context

- Play echoes issues about inter-familial conflict in powerful families, brother against brother, conspiracy, exile etc.
- Allusions to Robin Hood and the Greenwood link the pastoral with an English tradition of social justice/green politics. Text as early ecological politics – the usurpation of native habitats by humans (= colonialism?).
- Class politics/economics present in the relationships between pastoral characters and aristocracy; also gender politics.

BRIDESHEAD REVISITED

Literary context

- Waugh's Prologue indicates authorial thoughts about the significance of the book.
- Use of pastoral conventions deliberately echoes Classical and Renaissance Pastoral.
- Book viewed at the time as conservative and backward-looking after the Second World War.

Social context

- Decline of the aristocracy and the English country house.
- Glorification of the cult of the country house, the Classical estate etc.
- Set against a backdrop of class politics – the rise of socialism (general strike etc.), the middle classes (Hooper) and the nouveau riche (Rex).
- Arcadia as the lull between wars (First World War – Uncle Ned; Second World War – Hooper).

Biographical context

- Catholicism, public school homosexuality, aestheticism.
- Waugh's own life and attitudes.

Panel 6.7 explores how a different set of contexts relating to language, form and structure can be brought to bear.

Panel 6.7   Bringing in language, form, structure

AS YOU LIKE IT

Form

PLAY, traditional dialogue form with SONGS and an EPILOGUE; **Genre** – Pastoral comedy

Structure

- Initial *intercutting* between court and country highlights contrast and creates juxtapositions (e.g. the violence of the court next to the idyll of Arden).
- *Parallel plots* (Orlando and Oliver, Rosalind and Celia, Silvius and Phoebe) examine different angles.
- Key schematic *moments of climax* (e.g. 'And I for no woman') in which parallel plots are brought together (Rosalind's magic).

- The three parallel fools/cynics – Jaques, Touchstone, Corin – highlight the challenge to the pastoral.
- *Narrative emphasis* moves from (1) focus on court corruption to (2) focus on Pastoral to (3) focus on love and marriage, combining elements of pastoral comedy and medieval romance.

Language

- *Title* – vague comic title (like *Much Ado About Nothing* or *All's Well That Ends Well*) but it does suggest freedom from convention.
- Use of *songs* to emphasise pastoral themes and echo the music in the Classical pastoral.
- Particularly *stylised language* used in key scenes (e.g. 'And I for no woman') to create pathos, invoke magic and emphasise parallels. Also used in 'set pieces', e.g. Touchstone's rules of engagement, and in Jaques' 'All the world' speech.
- Numerous instances of *imagery, alliteration, enumeration, repetition, puns, verbal wit* etc.
- Note frequent moves between *verse and prose* – verse usually for serious, upper-class and/or public speech; prose usually for comic, lower-class and/or private speech. BUT NOTE – Shakespeare does not stick to the rules and often shifts from verse to prose to emphasise a change in action or tone (and sometimes for no apparent reason at all...).

BRIDESHEAD REVISITED

Form

NOVEL, first-person narrative; **Genre** – 'bildungsroman' – novel which focuses on the growth of a character from youth to maturity (most 'classic' novels fall into this category).

Structure

- *Linear chronology* with elements of foreshadowing and flashback, including framing epilogue and prologue.
- Divided into *three books* which characterise particular phases of the story, and loosely form the exposition, development and resolution, though each book has its own 'plot'.
- Loosely structured around *seasons* (summer, autumn, winter) and associated imagery – (sunshine, storms, avalanches).

Language

- *Title* – 'Revisited' suggests the theme of memory/nostalgia that dominates the book, as well as the cyclical nature of the narrative.
- *Symbolic subtitles* – 'Et in Arcadia Ego', 'The Twitch Upon The Thread' – both references to other literature.

- Various *tones and styles* feature – most notably the yearning, pastoral nostalgia. Also note the comic writing (which Waugh is most well known for) for characters like Charles' father and Mr Samgrass, and the wit of the Oxford aesthetes (especially Anthony Blanche).
- Use of *'rhapsody'* – highly poetic language in praise of nature, love or the past – characterised by exclamation, and other techniques such as metaphor, repetition, alliteration etc.
- Numerous instances of *metaphor*, including weather and landscape evoking and symbolising certain moods (e.g. sun, storms, avalanches). Strong *symbolism* at times, e.g. the altar lamp, the enchanted garden, the skull.

Further reading

Teaching contexts

The English and Media Centre's 'Advanced Literature Series' is a major resource for teaching texts in context. *World and Time: Teaching Literature in Context* (Barlow 2009) is an excellent introduction to the topic, and to a range of issues in the teaching of literature at this level. There is also a good website (funded by the Bible Society) dedicated to developing awareness of context in advanced literature students, www.crossref-it.info, with contextual information on a wide range of texts and authors.

Critical introductions to contexts

Cambridge University Press' 'Contexts in Literature' series is invaluable, as are the 'Cambridge Introductions', 'Oxford Companions' and 'Oxford Very Short Introductions' to various aspects of literature, and Routledge's 'New Critical Idioms' series. The major academic publishers (Routledge, Palgrave, Bloomsbury, Cambridge, Oxford) publish many introductory titles – aimed at undergraduates – which are extremely helpful, including a number of general histories of English literature; it is worth looking at their catalogues online to find out what is available.

Narrative

Studying Narrative (Bleiman and Webster 2009) and *The Forms of Narrative* (Abbs and Richardson 1990), both resources for 14–19 teaching, are invaluable. *The Cambridge Introduction to Narrative* (Porter Abbott 2008) and *The Cambridge Companion to Narrative* (Herman 2007) are also very useful undergraduate-level guides.

Gothic

Introducing the Gothic (Bleiman and Webster 2009) and *The Gothic: Frankenstein and Wuthering Heights* (Green 2003) are designed for use with 16–19 students. *The Gothic Tradition* (Stevens 2000) is a valuable guide. *The Gothic: A Very Short Introduction* (Groom 2012) and *Gothic* (Botting 1995) are excellent undergraduate-level guides.

Pastoral

Landscape and Literature (Siddall 2009) and *Pastoral* (Gifford 1999) are excellent introductions. *The Song of the Earth* (Bate 2001) and *Ecocriticism* (Garrard 2011) are introductions to broader issues about literature and the environment.

Tragedy

Tragedy: A Student Handbook (McEvoy 2009) is an excellent resource for 16–19 students. *Tragedy: A Very Short Introduction* (Poole 2005) and *The Cambridge Introduction to Tragedy* (Wallace 2007) are valuable guides. For Shakespeare, *The Cambridge Introduction to Shakespeare's Tragedies* (Dillon 2007) is excellent.

Comedy

Studying Comedy (EMC 2012) is an excellent resource for use with 16–19 students. *The Cambridge Introduction to Comedy* (Weitz 2009), *Comedy* (Stott 2005) and *Comedy: A Very Short Introduction* (Bevis 2012) are good introductions. For Shakespeare, *The Cambridge Introduction to Shakespeare's Comedies* (Gay 2008) is excellent.

Romanticism

The BBC TV series *The Romantics* (2006) is an invaluable resource. *The Cambridge Companion to British Romanticism* (Curran 2010), *Romanticism* (Day 2011) and *Romanticism: A Very Short Introduction* (Ferber 2010) are useful guides.

The First World War

The Great War in British Literature (Barlow 2000) and *The Cambridge Companion to the Literature of the First World War* (Sherry 2005) are excellent guides. There is a very useful guide to resources for 16–19 teachers at www.literaryconnections.co.uk/resources.

Chapter 7

Teaching writing

Introduction: Reading and writing, creativity and criticism

It is a fair generalisation that teachers of literature tend to see themselves as teachers of *reading, thinking and understanding* rather than of *writing*. Writing, though, is a crucial part of the study of literature 16–19. In most courses, it is the major – in many cases the only – method of assessment, meaning that it is vital for students to develop their abilities as writers. The ability to write is also of obvious importance *beyond* education as a means of communicating with audiences broader than teachers and examiners. Thus as teachers we clearly have a significant responsibility to develop students' writing skills.

Nevertheless, our interest in writing goes considerably further than this. Unlike other subjects, the thing that we actually study is *writing* – written text; it follows that writing – others' and our own – should be firmly at the centre of what we do. As literature teachers, perhaps we tend to think that we are only really concerned with teaching about the *products* of writing, rather than the writing *process* itself and the *act* of writing. In this chapter, however, we argue that reading and writing practices are closely related at this level – a principle that we hope is amply demonstrated in other parts of this book. Ideas about the circumstances of textual production and consumption – the interface between the text and the world, the craft of the writer, the role of the reader, the purpose and audience of the text, and so on – are crucial here.

A parallel issue is the relationship between creativity and criticism. It is common for English teachers to talk about 'critical' and 'creative' responses to literature as quite different things; this convenient shorthand, however, belies the complexity of the relationship between the two. Reading and writing are *both* creative *and* critical practices; to speak of a clear distinction between creativity and criticism is in many respects unhelpful. Criticism is both a creative practice and one which deploys *understanding of* creative practices; creativity often deploys understandings achieved through critical practice – a fact reflected in the growing use of creative, re-creative and transformative responses as a means of assessing students' responses to text. Thus, we seek in this chapter to suggest that the 'creative' and the 'critical' should be more equally and integrally represented in literary study, and that together they have the potential to improve learning.

Another principle that informs this chapter is the idea that 'writing floats on a sea of talk' (Britton 1970). Developing ideas about how writing should be done, and what writing should communicate, follows most effectively not only from effective reading but also from opportunities for discussion and teaching that help to shape students' thinking and understanding through structured talk and activity at an accessible level (Vygotsky 1978).

We have become used to hearing university English lecturers claim that their students 'cannot put a sentence together' and are unable to construct essays (see for instance, the Royal Literary Fund's report [RLF 2006] on writing in universities). Whilst it's clear that we need to do all we can to enable our students to become independent and effective writers, it's also clear that such claims *must* be an exaggeration. We know that even the most able students are sometimes not as sensitive to the niceties of spelling, punctuation, grammar and style as they might be (a complaint that examiners and lecturers have been making for at least a century), but that is not the same as being unable to construct intelligent sentences, paragraphs and whole essays. Indeed, recent research (for instance Hodgson and Harris 2012, 2013) suggests that poor writing in HE English is often a result not so much of students' poor writing skills as of their lack of understanding of what is being asked of them. Many produce written assignments without an adequate understanding of the ideas to be discussed or the modes of writing to be employed.

As suggested above, more emphasis on teaching students to read and write critical and creative texts, both at 16–19 *and* in HE, might help here. However, it's also crucial to employ active pedagogies (discussion, group work and so on) that help teachers to establish what students know and understand already, and enable students to share understandings, grasp new ideas, and develop confidence in talking about texts and – eventually – writing about them.

Writing for a range of purposes and in a variety of contexts lies at the heart of 16–19 literary studies. As we work to develop students both as confident readers of literature and as able producers of text, we need to provide supportive yet challenging contexts for writing. Encouraging students to explore their thinking through writing and to develop a sophisticated sense of how and why they write is fundamental to success. Developing students who are serious and disciplined about their writing, but also enjoy the creative challenges writing poses, takes time, but need not be a dull process: it can be extremely rewarding, fulfilling and even – dare we say it? – enjoyable.

Thinking, talking, reading, writing

Although different countries and different courses have different emphases, the critical essay is usually the main vehicle for the assessment of students on advanced literature courses. The equation of writing with high-stakes assessment can be problematic, however, and, under such conditions, it is not unusual to see students drilled in writing formulae or focused exclusively on writing essays under timed examination conditions. Whilst the reasons for such methods of teaching writing are understandable, they risk constricting students' thought, exploration and experimentation. Effective and exciting writers take risks with words, seeking imaginative ways to convey and explore meaning. Helping students to take such risks, and using outcomes to stimulate development, encourages them to see their writing as a vibrant and creative means of personal expression. This is, of course, not to deny the importance of students learning standard forms of writing and when these should be used; it is rather to observe that over-zealous use of formulae and an over-emphasis on one form of writing can crush individuality and limit response.

Throughout this chapter, we emphasise that the development of students' abilities and confidence as writers, as well as their understanding of what it means to be a writer, should be an integral part of the study of literature. This process of development should include opportunities for students to explore the different ways in which they use writing as part of their studies – the ways, for instance, in which they make notes, plan, draft and redraft. It should also encourage them to reflect on their own development as writers. It is important to remember that students will arrive in the 16–19 classroom with a good deal of experience of writing behind them – and with certain perceptions of themselves as writers already in place. It can be useful to explore these perceptions with students, particularly at an early stage of the course, using questions such as those in Panel 7.1 to stimulate reflection.

Panel 7.1   Thinking about writing

Jot down your responses to the following questions:

- What is writing?
- Do you write regularly?
- Do you enjoy writing?
- What kinds of writing do you do?
- Are you a meticulous planner, or do you prefer to allow writing to emerge and develop more organically? (Myhill and Watson 2011)
- What are your processes as a writer?
- Do you like or dislike redrafting your writing?
- How confident are you in your abilities as a writer?
- How does writing 16–19 differ from the writing you have done in your prior education?
- What are the features of writing you think are particularly important at 16–19 level?
- What kinds of writing would you like to do more of?
- What do you find particularly difficult as a writer?
- What skills and understanding do you wish to develop as a writer?

Students' responses to these questions can offer real insights into how they perceive themselves as writers, suggesting ways of working with them both as individuals and as a group. Teachers might find it interesting to respond to these questions themselves, and to share their responses with students, in order to understand their own identities as writers and as teachers of writing – factors that will certainly influence the experiences of writing their students will gain.

The close link between writing and assessment means that students often see writing purely in terms of 'product', rather than as a process that can assist the development of ideas. Enabling a range of forms of writing through which students can 'think aloud', exploring ideas and responses on paper, has the potential to prepare students for more successful essay writing and propagate 'creative' responses which might themselves be valuable indicators of critical thought as essays. (We use inverted commas with the word 'creative' here, as essays are also, of course, creative – a point explored by Smallwood (2002) – and 'creative' responses are by no means uncritical.) Through writing, students can both explore their own and others' responses to literature, and learn what it feels like to be a writer, making the kinds of choices made by the writers they are studying. Indeed, an increasing number of 16–19 literature courses make 'creative' written responses a feature of assessment.

Some advanced literature courses (such as IB English) make formal *oral* responses a feature of the course assessment; even where this is not the case, however, talk is a crucial means of enabling students to explore, develop and clarify ideas before, during and after reading and writing. It should be noted that effective writing skills are also crucial in preparing for formal oral and audio-visual presentations.

Supporting and developing students as writers and speakers, building on their prior experiences, looking forward to their future needs and meeting their current requirements as students of literature, is challenging. By employing a range of approaches, however – including developing an atmosphere of discussion and collaboration, and encouraging students to see writing as provisional and exploratory, not simply as final product – we can create effective and enthusiastic writing communities.

General strategies for teaching writing

Panel 7.2 presents a range of strategies that might be employed to support writers of all abilities. Teachers will need to think carefully about which methods will be most appropriate for particular groups and individuals, and at which stage of the course: the ultimate aim must always be to enable students to develop their independence as writers.

Panel 7.2 Strategies for teaching writing

Strategy	Advantages	Disadvantages
Modelling and scaffolding: shared writing; supported composition	Provides insight into how text types function; non-threatening, collaborative work.	If scaffolding is not gradually removed, students can become over-dependent on support.
Focusing on the writing process	Helps students to think 'beyond the moment', and to see that writing is a developmental, iterative process.	Can be abstract or invisible if not carefully explained.
Writing frames	Provide an essential structure for writing and insight into how different text types function.	If these are too rigid they can be limiting rather than liberating; over-dependence on frames can hinder independence.
Sentence starters, discourse markers and signposting	Provide students with ways in to writing; help students understand language constructions useful within text types and how these guide readers.	Can appear prescriptive and can limit creative, alternative approaches.
Ensuring that students understand and can use key features of text types	Helps students structure and organise their writing appropriately, and helps them develop suitable language and content.	Can become a quantitative 'checklist' (Have I used enough devices?) rather than a qualitative overview.

Strategy	Advantages	Disadvantages
Marking, feedback and target-setting	Provides insight into what students need to do to improve their work.	Can make writing seem as if it is only for assessment, stunting enjoyment and risk-taking.
In-class conferencing	Creates a varied range of contexts within which students can discuss their writing; could be drama focused (e.g. newsroom, editorial meeting) if desired.	Requires careful planning and class management; success criteria need to be made clear.
Writing/editing partners		
Providing a supportive and print-rich classroom environment, e.g. displayed texts as models for writing, word banks	Provides a range of relevant resources that students can access to support their work independently of the teacher.	Resources must be updated regularly; high levels of accuracy required; time-intensive.

(developed from Green 2012)

Talk for writing

We often see writing as a solitary activity. In reality, while elements of written composition certainly require undistracted individual work, large parts of the process provide the possibility for (and thrive upon) collaboration.

Much can be done with oral 'text' as teaching at this level tends to be discussion-based, and this is an important part of the world of words within which students function. This does not mean that all speech can (or should) be seen as writing, but there are significant areas of crossover between the spoken word and the written word, and with the array of handheld capture devices now readily available for use in the classroom, there are many ways in which students' spoken words can inform or become part of their written work. Sharing and testing of ideas, interaction of interpretations, selection of information and content, experimentation with language, exploration of style, tone and voice, and so on, can all be harnessed in talk and can feed directly into writing. Such work can be done as a whole class, or with students working in pairs or groups.

By developing appropriate forums for talking about writing, teachers can feed into students' development as writers. Helping students to internalise dialogues about what constitutes effective writing makes them more genuinely autonomous writers. Processes such as shared writing, where teachers lead collaborative development of an exemplar text, modelling the writing process (perhaps regarding vocabulary choices, use of quotation or development of argument), or the use of writing frames or scaffolds can be enormously useful with students working in the 16–19 phase. Such approaches are often seen as a means of support for use with weaker writers; the reality, however, is that writers of all ability levels benefit from structured teaching at the point of writing.

There is one important proviso. Whole-class 'modelling' and 'scaffolding' of writing processes are crucial steps in helping students to become independent writers, but they must be seen as steps towards independence, rather than as ways of continued 'spoon-feeding'. Students should learn the processes by which the models are constructed, not simply copy the model itself and must be guided to plan and construct their own essays (and other forms of writing) rather than being steered too closely towards standardised discourses. Allowing students to choose their own topics, titles or tasks – rather than working as a whole class on one common task – forces students to work independently, and might be seen as something for a class to work towards.

Whatever form they take, writing workshops are a crucial element in the teaching of writing, and teachers should set aside extended periods of time to plan and prepare writing with students, discussing choices and processes in detail, both as a whole class and through one-to-one consultation. By making writing a regular focus in the classroom we can stimulate writerly thinking rather than falling into the trap of teaching solely *post facto*, through the process of commenting on and correcting completed work. By modelling processes, structures and forms appropriate to a range of contexts for writing (including note-making, note-taking and textual annotation) we can create a rich learning environment in which students talk about their writing, create text through non-threatening collaboration, share ideas and learn to experiment and take creative risks.

Notes, blogs, wikis and journals

Contrary to popular belief (often reinforced by the media and politicians) many of the students we teach are frequent writers – texting, emailing, posting on social media sites or forums of different kinds. Such kinds of writing are often ignored or dismissed, or even blamed for perceived falling standards in the formal writing students are expected to do at school. However, to overlook this kind of writing would be an error.

Of course, we want and need our students to develop as critical, analytical and creative writers, but it is important that they do not feel alienated from this process. Only a part of the writing students do is for formal assessment, and it is both interesting and liberating to allow students to do other writing tasks (such as note-making, initial response writing, planning and annotation) in forms they feel naturally comfortable with. By acknowledging rather than demonising the types of writing students freely engage with, teachers and students can reap great benefits. Students are empowered as confident creators of text, and these energies can then be transferred into more formal written forms. To do otherwise risks undermining students at the very point where we need to be building them up.

One of the difficulties when it comes to writing is moving students away from the idea that writing is a final and conclusive process. Writing serves many purposes and only sometimes (even rarely) is writing a definitive end product. It helps students to see that much of their writing is provisional and exploratory. Note-making, free writing, textual annotation, even creative writing, might all be used as exploratory forms. It is also an excellent idea to encourage students to keep journals and/or blogs relating to their study of particular texts or more generally, using writing to record developing thoughts with regard to their studies and incorporating – where appropriate – extracts drawn from other writers. These documents will, in effect, be repositories of interesting and personal writing about a set text or about issues relating to the study of literature more generally. This encourages students to see their writing as something iterative and developmental and will move them away from the idea that writing always has a summative purpose. Both blogs and journals may, of course, contain things other than writing – such as appropriate photographs, colour schemes, paintings, stage sets, movie extracts, music clips and so on – and the potential of the blog to store multimedia texts widens the possibilities still further. You will probably wish students to keep these individually, allowing them to explore their own interests and satisfy personal curiosity. However, there may be occasions when you want this process to be more public, in which case a wiki may be more appropriate. It can also be useful for teachers to participate in discussions on wikis and similar forums, both to act as moderators who can direct the discussion and prompt debates when necessary, and to model the process of debate itself. (Students often find it interesting when teachers disagree over particular readings of a text – this can be a valuable way of demonstrating the plurality of interpretation.)

Teachers as writers

Another way to demystify the process of writing, as well as to demonstrate one's credibility as a teacher of English, is by writing *with* students. When teaching 16–19 groups we advocate undertaking timed and other writing tasks – both critical and creative – with students, for a number of reasons. First, writing with our students reminds us what it feels like to write under the conditions we impose on them. It is very easy to forget what it is like to have to produce writing in isolation, to order, and sometimes in very short time spans. Second, it is important for students to see that writing is not just something we expect them to do, but something that we also do ourselves. Our credibility as teachers depends upon their confidence that we are experts and able to do what we require of them. Finally, teachers' written work, whether produced under timed conditions or independently at home, provides good models of writing for students to read and discuss, and can form part of peer-assessment tasks, enabling students to talk to the teacher as the producer of the work, and to interrogate choices in terms of language, structure, argumentation and exemplification.

Reading as a writer, writing as a reader

Whilst reading and writing clearly relate closely to one another, the relationship between the two processes is complex. Kress (1985) describes reading and writing as functionally differentiated aspects of one process and adopts the metaphor of a coin. The obverse faces of the coin are integrally linked to one another, but face in different directions.

   In the light of this observation, it is worth reflecting on the fact that we tend, as literature teachers, to teach students to *read literary* texts and to *write critical* texts. On the whole, we don't spend much time teaching them to *read critical* texts, and even less to *write literary* texts. This doesn't seem to make much sense, especially since we know from pre-16 English teaching that one of the best ways of teaching students to *write* a particular type of text is to *read* and analyse examples of that type of text, and that one of the most effective ways of teaching students to *read* a text and understand the way it is written is to get them to *write* one themselves. Bearing in mind everything that we know about the profound relationship between reading and writing, we should perhaps ask ourselves whether we currently have a sensible balance in 16–19 English.

   Our students need to grasp and experience the mutuality of reading and writing, so we need to encourage them to read as writers and to write as readers. In general terms, we might characterise these two closely related positions as follows:

   Reading as a writer. Teaching students to use their reading as a 'window' on writing. This means looking with students at the ways in which writers working for a range of purposes achieve their effects and considering how students can incorporate these within their own writing.

Writing as a reader. Teaching students to think as they write with the mind of a reader. This means considering with students how readers are likely to respond to what they have written, how readers engage with and follow narrative and argument as it unfolds, and how writers respond to notional audiences.

It seems to us important that this strategy should be applied to the reading *and* writing of both literary *and* critical texts; thus, as suggested above, we need to ensure that students read and analyse critical texts as well as write them, and that they write literary texts as well as read them. In this way, we hope that they will achieve a more profound understanding of what it is that readers, writers and critics do, and how they can do it themselves.

Issues about reading and writing *criticism* are dealt with more fully both in Chapter 5 (Teaching theory and criticism) and in the third section of this chapter (on the critical essay). Here, we focus on what we can do to help students read and write as *literary* writers so that they can learn more about the craft of the writer, the response of the reader, the nature of textuality and the workings of the literary imagination.

Creative responses to texts

Mikhail Bakhtin, in *The Dialogic Imagination,* explores the complex relationship between readers and writers, positing a situation in which both are co-creators of meaning through dialogue with the text they share: 'Every word is directed towards an answer and cannot escape the profound influence of the answering word that it anticipates' (1981: 280). Thus, reading and the construction of meaning are essentially acts of creation or re-creation, which can be explored in students' own writing (Kress 1985; Bloom 1973; Green 2004). Creative writing engages students in creative dialogue with text, which they can transfer into their future writing and reading. The reader/writer experience represented by such activities encapsulates what Bakhtin calls a 'dialogic' relationship between the reader and the author centred on the text – a relationship in which the boundaries between author and reader are somewhat blurred. Bakhtin points out the mutual responsibility of writer and reader in constructing the meaning of text, and the profound influence the reader has upon its linguistic (re)creation. Creative and re-creative response are at the heart of reading and developing understanding of texts (Knights and Thurgar-Dawson 2006), whether of the students' own composition or by other authors. In adopting the locus of the writer, students are brought into a creative dialogue with both their writing and reading processes, and this can contribute considerably to developing understanding.

By writing creatively 'into', 'out of' and 'parallel to' texts students can gain extensive insights into the choices authors make and the positions readers and writers adopt – whether by working in the style of a writer, by intervening in the text itself, or both. By creatively adopting a writer's use of language and form or exploring aspects of narrative, detailed engagement with character, imagery, lexis and other elements of text is possible. Particularly important is the way in which creative writing forces students to engage concretely with language as the means through which ideas are communicated in literary text, and what it means to mould and craft words for specific purposes. Such creative engagements with text both emerge from and inform critical and theorised readings, especially where the act of creation is accompanied by reflective analysis.

Experimenting with texts 1: Creative rewriting/re-creative writing

Since important developments in the 1960s and 1970s, writing character diaries, screenplay adaptations of scenes from novels, alternative or predicted endings and so on, have been widely and successfully used as a means of encouraging responses to literature. There has also been a powerful movement towards such strategies in HE, for instance through the work of Rob Pope on 'textual intervention' (1995) and Ben Knights and Chris Thurgar-Dawson on 'active reading' (2006). Adoption of these strategies in 16–19 literature courses, however, has been less consistent, although syllabuses increasingly include options that allow students to offer creative exercises (sometimes referred to as 'creative rewriting', 're-creative writing' or 'textual transformation') as part of their final assessment. We would like to suggest, however, that such work can be hugely beneficial, whether or not it is part of the course assessment.

Some creative approaches may emerge directly from and in response to literary texts. Students may, for example, respond to set texts by:

- adding scenes or stanzas in the style and form of the original;
- predicting possible dramatic or narrative developments;
- imagining and constructing in writing certain key locations, settings, people, objects etc.;
- constructing events that have happened prior to or alongside events in the original;
- writing empathic responses or monologues to capture characters' responses to events;
- writing into a scene, exploring not what *is* said, but what *is not* said, and considering why this is significant;
- writing into a scene imagining what is present but not described and how this may play a significant role;
- attributing and exploring emotions, motives etc. to characters/events;
- rewriting a particular 'moment' from the point of view of a different character;
- rewriting a first-person narrative in the third person, and vice versa.

Where such experiences are carefully structured and given autonomous value, students focus not only on the literary work in question but also reflect on their own creative processes as writers. This leads to significant insights into the critical and creative dimensions of their writing.

Alternatively, students may be asked to look at the potential for portraying source texts in different literary or non-literary media, transforming the original into a different style or form. The poem below was written as an exploration of the eerie setting and central character of Susan Hill's novel *The Woman in Black*.

An Eye for an Eye

The causeway stretches, a taut vein across
the muddy face of the bay. Water sucks
beneath the pitted skin,
the ancient remembering skin. Flaccid
clouds bulge purple, pendulous with rain.
Salt tears drop,
pock-mark the surface; a gentle sigh as
water meets water, soul meets soul.

> She stands alone at
> the window, artesian eyes
> boring the muddy
> wilderness of pain,
> the torture-house of loss, craving the son
> that merciless mud will never return.
>
> The beat of hooves, the rattle of iron-rimmed
> wheels against cold stone spiral out
> of the bay. Insurgent
> noise shreds memory, beats
> a gathering tattoo on the cobbles —
> weed-green, carious.
>
> A mounting pressure rises,
> the unforgiving
> death-scream slices her raw,
> heaves her ragged, bleeds her ice-cold heart.
> Deep wells close,
> probe inward. An eye for an eye.

It is also useful to ask students to write in the style or form of the original text but with different content. 'Larkinesque' was written as an exercise to explore the way the poet constructs mood from objects.

> *Larkinesque*
>
> The future opens slowly, like an eye
> In sunny dawn-light. Curtain-filtered
> Flowers wilt on to the bed where I lie
> In all the safe delusions of unwaking, quilted
> In the pall of sleep.
>
> I stir, feel the weight of bedding
> On chest and lungs, an intimation
> Of reality, stale air spreading
> Through the body, a confirmation
> Of the imprecisions of living. Fear creeps
>
> Into focus as the eye accustoms again
> To the well-known contours of the room,
> Last night's random pile of clothes, the stained
> Unpatterned carpet, a sparse, protecting womb.
> Drops form on a glass where condensation weeps.

This type of activity benefits both reading and writing. When, for example, we speculate whether Hamlet will summon up the fortitude to kill Claudius, we mentally begin an act of writing that runs alongside and interacts with Shakespeare's. Again, when we visualise Mary Shelley's description of the creation of Frankenstein's monster we use our own abilities as writerly readers to construct what he actually looks like. And when Cordelia receives King Lear's rebukes in silence, we mentally write in all the things she does not say and store them away to help us read the events of the play as they unfold. By taking such responses and formalising them within creative writing, the benefits multiply.

Where such pieces are submitted for assessment, it is common for students to write an accompanying commentary or rationale for the piece, giving an analysis of their own writing process, and placing it in relationship with the source text. Panel 7.3 outlines how students may be prepared both for the re-creative task itself and for the writing of an accompanying commentary.

Panel 7.3　*A View from the Bridge* coursework – re-creative writing

Some ideas:

- A monologue by Catherine before Eddie's betrayal, reflecting her thoughts about Eddie's behaviour and accusations and Rodolpho's motives.
- A letter from Marco, before Eddie's betrayal, to his wife presenting his thoughts about events in the Carbone household.
- Catherine and Rodolpho have married and gone to stay with a relative in Boston for a honeymoon. Write a letter from Beatrice to Catherine.
- A monologue by Beatrice after the events of the play.
- After the events of the play, Catherine and Rodolpho OR Beatrice go to Alfieri for advice and reassurance. Write part of the scene between them.

When you write your text, you should think about how it might enable you, in your commentary, to reflect on aspects of tragedy – for instance, drawing attention to some of the ways in which Miller used the conventions of classical tragedy and the concerns of modern tragedy, e.g.

- the role of the tragic hero and/or victims;
- the narrative structure and unfolding of the tragedy;
- the roles of women in relation to the tragic hero;
- the role of jealousy and sexual tension in the tragedy;
- the role of the chorus and/or fate/prophecy;
- the use of unity of time, place and action;
- the idea of domestic tragedy – the tragedy of the common man;
- the conflict of values that leads to the tragedy.

Some key points for the re-creative piece:

- You should reflect on the actual events that took place in the play and should not focus on imagined events that did not.
- Make sure language is appropriate for the characters, and don't have them speaking in literary criticism! If their style of speaking is different from the original, comment on this in your commentary. You do not have to use American dialect.
- If you are writing a monologue or scene, use stage directions, if appropriate, in the way that Miller does.
- Include 'echoes' of the original play – references to things that happened or that people said – but not actual quotes.
- Include references to details of setting and minor characters, e.g. Vinnie Bolzano, Longshoremen, Sicily, Red Hook, Mr and Mrs Dondero etc.
- Include characters' reflections on some of the themes, e.g. gender roles (role of women, masculinity, homosexuality); pride; immigration; fate; revenge; conflict between values – but in characters' language and thoughts – keep your critical comments for the commentary.

Writing the commentary for the re-creative work

In the commentary, you have the opportunity to explain the thinking behind what you have written. Your commentary must be written well and use appropriate literary terminology, and contain some reflection on the ways:

- you (and Miller) have used language, form and structure;
- your piece highlights possible interpretations of the play;
- your piece shows awareness of contexts such as the play's setting, period, style, genre;
- the above are connected with the idea of tragedy.

You can:

- consider how the events of your piece 'fit in' to the narrative and reflect the tragic events;
- explain why you have chosen to write the particular episode you have written – and why you have chosen the form of a letter/diary/speech/scene etc.;
- explain how your piece highlights or reflects on some of the themes, issues, debates, ambiguities etc. in the original play, perhaps showing how they feed into the tragedy, e.g. revenge, fate, immigration, gender, cultural conflict etc.;
- explain how your piece conveys an interpretation or suggests alternative interpretations of the original play, and/or how it enabled you to explore certain aspects of the play;

- explain how your piece reflects some of the dramatic and linguistic elements of the original play (e.g. Miller's use of stage directions, characterisation, word choice, style, imagery) and how these might relate to the concept of tragedy. (If you have chosen a non-dramatic form like a letter or a narrative, you will nevertheless want to show how this contains some dramatic or linguistic elements similar to the original.)

As you do this, you should ensure that you show how your piece relates to the concept of tragedy and the way the tragedy is enacted in the play. For instance, you could:

- explain how your portrayal of a character highlights their role as tragic hero, victim, chorus etc; or how it emphasises the pathos of a character or situation, e.g. Eddie and Marco as protagonist and antagonist; Eddie as tragic hero – his hubris, hamartia and anagnorisis etc.; Alfieri as chorus; the tragic victims; the idea of fate; the tragic ending (catastrophe);
- reflect on the way you have echoed Miller's modern interpretation of the idea of tragedy and the tragic hero, (as he describes it in 'Tragedy and the Common Man');
- reflect on the way your piece echoes Miller's portrayal of tragic conflict and/or his adaptation of the style of ancient tragedy in a modern setting.

Panels 7.4 and 7.5 offer two examples of the kinds of work students might produce in response to such a task, along with accompanying commentaries and suggestions of how these responses relate to the differing areas of assessment. The first is an epistolary extension of *Frankenstein*.

Panel 7.4   Example of re-creative writing: *Frankenstein*

Imagine you are Walton. It is two weeks after the death of Frankenstein and you have safely returned to Archangel. After this lapse of time, what is your response to what has occurred? Write one last letter to your sister. Use Walton's style and language and the epistolary form to create an authentic tone.

Extract from answer:

To Mrs Saville, England.

Archangel, 1st October, 17—

And so my feet stand once again on solid ground, Margaret. We reached Archangel yesterday. The crew stayed no longer than to receive their pay, then broke up and drifted away from the ship just as the ice did, releasing me to make my escape. The ice has gone and the crew, but my memories are not so soon shaken. You read a letter from a different man. Day and night I am troubled – a man who was never troubled in his mind before. I feel the arrogance of certainty will never be mine again. If a creature as noble as the hapless Frankenstein could be so overthrown by too much self-possession, then that is no bad thing. I had rather live the rest of my days in doubt. Ours is an age of discovery, but my days of exploration are done, and I will make haste to return to London. How natural the familiar city will feel to me after the wilds of the frozen north.

For the day and night following the monster's departure from my ship I stood fixed to the aft rail, my eyes fixed on the horizon where the raft of ice and the monster it carried had disappeared. Who steered the ship, I know not. Who gave orders I have no recollection. I suppose it must have been me, but the crew would say never a word to me who had so nearly brought about their destruction. I looked back, expecting every moment to see the flames of his funeral pyre leaping upward, staining the sky in parody of the northern lights, but I saw nothing. Perhaps there was nothing to see. Maybe the monster had not the courage to destroy his own life, even though it had given him nothing but pain. I suppose there is something in all of us that clings fiercely to life, however cold and unendurable it may seem. I will never again be the man I was. Victor had to die, but I can live.

Student commentary

For this final letter from Walton to his sister, I have drawn on the style of the letters from the frame narrative of the novel. Walton's voice, however, has been modified to reflect the changes that he has undergone as a result of his meetings with Frankenstein and the monster. He is no longer the man he was, as he no longer has unquestioning faith in progress and science, and his arrogance is gone. I have employed some of the images from the end of the novel, such as the breaking ice and the monster's funeral pyre and have tried to apply these to Walton's own situation as he returns to the solid ground of Archangel. This solid ground is in itself intended to be symbolic. Walton is no longer on the shifting intellectual seas representing his voyage, but on something altogether more reliable. This is intended to demonstrate what he has learnt from Victor's terrible tale – the escape he refers to near the beginning. The contrast between the vocabulary of life and death is also significant, a technique that reflects Shelley's own use of contrasts in *Frankenstein*.

Assessment issues

Quality of writing

1 Vocabulary appropriate to the character of Walton, and modified to reflect circumstances.
2 Creates and sustains an appropriate tone.
3 Language picks up on and develops the language of the text.
4 Suitable metalanguage in commentary.

Form, structure and language

1   Language reflects Walton's troubled state of mind.
2   Character of Walton is clearly understood, demonstrating close knowledge of the text, and this knowledge is imaginatively applied.
3   Use of appropriate symbolic language.
4   Use of ideas from the novel, which demonstrates sophisticated understanding of the text.

Different interpretations

1   Provides Walton's interpretation after some reflection on some of the final and overarching events of the novel.

Contexts

1   References, actions and speech are appropriate to the time at which the text is set.
2   Brief but clear reference to the scientific and exploratory advances of the eighteenth and nineteenth centuries.

The second is an exercise in transformative writing based on *Wuthering Heights*.

Panel 7.5   Example of re-creative writing: *Wuthering Heights*

The supernatural is difficult to portray on screen, but *Wuthering Heights* has frequently been adapted for film and TV. Write a screen adaptation of the passage in which Lockwood is haunted by the ghost of Cathy when he is forced to spend the night at the Heights.

Extract from answer

Int: Lockwood's chamber

View of chamber, sparsely furnished with a coarse wooden chair, table and wash stand. Focus in on oak closet bed, curtains drawn. They seem to breathe in a draught of air. A low fire flickers in the grate, casting moving shadows of the furniture against the walls. From outside the howling of wind and driving snow. A fir-bough grates eerily against the window.

LOCKWOOD suddenly pulls back the curtain of the bed and sits up. Lockwood looks at the window, fear written across his face.

Lockwood: I must stop that scraping.

He pulls his nightgown around him as he crosses the room and struggles with the window. He picks up a candlestick from the table and lights it at the fire. We see the branch – or is it a small hand? – scrape across the glass. He cannot open the window. He looks more closely.

Lockwood: The catch. It is soldered tight. *(Pauses for a moment, and the branch scrapes against the pane again.)* I must stop it, nevertheless!

He looks frantically around for something to break the glass, but sees nothing and smashes the pane with his fist. As soon as he breaks the window, the howling of the wind lulls for a moment. In the unnatural silence he pushes his hand through the broken pane and grasps at the branch. Close up image of his hand as he grasps not the branch, but a stick-thin pale hand. A look of horror comes over him. He presses his face to the window, and as he does so gazes straight into the ashen face of a small girl. He leaps back, trying to let go of her, but she clasps tightly to his wrist.

Girl: Let me in – let me in!

Lockwood: Who are you? Let go! Who are you, I say?

Girl: Catherine Linton.

She pulls his arm and drags him close back to the window so they are again face to face. He screams and stares her in the face, wide-eyed with fear, then pulls back, suddenly strong and rubs her wrist against the broken glass. Blood trickles down the glass. It is black and pools on the window frame.

Student commentary

In adapting this scene for the screen I have remained faithful to the chronology of events as they occur in the novel. However, in order to achieve good visual impact, I have created a deliberately spare and empty setting. I wanted Lockwood and the ghost of the girl to be the primary foci, and so set the scene in an almost bare room. Details like the coarse wood are intended to illustrate how basic life is at the Heights – what a comfortless environment it is. The flickering fire creates an atmosphere of shadow and flickering movement that is disconcerting and threatening – this prepares us for the supernatural events to come. Unlike in the original, where Lockwood remains in the bed, here he crosses the room to the window. This allows time for us to see what he cannot – that it is a small ghostly hand, not a tree branch that is scraping at the window. The dialogue is largely drawn faithfully from the text, but two short pieces of additional dialogue have been inserted in order to carry the narrative forward. The breaking of the window pane and sudden lull in the wind that follows this event are intended to create a sudden, shocking contrast of noise and silence, followed by the shocking, unexpected appearance of the girl's face at the window. Lockwood's horrific violence – so out of character for the man – is followed by the sight of black blood is designed to create a sense of the uncanny.

Assessment issues

Quality of writing

1 Very good use of conventions of scriptwriting.
2 Details from the text are effectively modified to the needs of visual storytelling.
3 Creates and sustains an appropriate tone.
4 Language picks up on and develops the language of the text.
5 Suitable metalanguage in commentary.

Form, structure and language

1 Language reflects requirement to create supernatural effects.
2 Character of Lockwood is clearly understood, demonstrating close knowledge of the text, and this knowledge is imaginatively applied.
3 Use of appropriate symbols to create sense of fear.
4 Use of ideas from the novel, which demonstrates sophisticated understanding of the text.
5 Careful adaptation of ideas from text to suit needs of the new form.

Different interpretations

1 Provides a screen interpretation of this scene.
2 Creative use of space and props adds to interpretation.

Contexts

1 Good knowledge of the typical genre effects of the Gothic and the supernatural in text and film.
2 Setting and speech are appropriate to the time at which the text is set.

Experimenting with texts 2: Creative writing

Whereas the strategies described above relate directly to the reading of specific texts and aim primarily to increase and illuminate students' understandings of them and of the writers' methods, we deal here with a freer, more general approach to creative writing.

Creative writing is a regular part of students' experience of English pre-16, and increasingly it is a formal element of some 16–19 and HE literature courses. Newlyn and Lewis (2003,

2004) have written about the creative writing workshops they have run with undergraduates at the University of Oxford: their accounts of the methods they used, and the work that resulted, offer fascinating reading for anyone wanting to undertake similar work with their own students. Whilst many teachers will feel that there is simply no time available for this approach in 16–19 literary studies, it can be a very stimulating and enjoyable way of encouraging students to relate creatively to the literary texts they are studying and in developing their more general abilities as writers.

A range of exercises using appropriate textual, musical and visual stimulus can be employed to help students find ways into writing and into the creative space of texts they are studying. If working on Gothic, for example, you might use a combination of Havergal Brian's 'Gothic' Symphony, Granados' *Goyescas*, a selection of paintings by Goya and Caspar David Friedrich, a selection of objects, and a visit to a dark church interior to stimulate responses. Similarly, if studying *Birdsong* or *Regeneration*, you might use a combination of Benjamin Britten's *War Requiem* or Sir Arthur Bliss' *Morning Heroes*, a selection of paintings and photographs representing the First World War, a selection of artefacts, and video footage of interviews with veterans (see Chapter 6 for fuller examples). Such activities encourage creative response and enhance students' sense of the potentials of the language, structure and form of texts as well as their content. A range of creative writing exercises for use with students can be found in Chapter 4 of *A Practical Guide to Teaching English in the Secondary School* (Green 2012) and in *The Handbook of Creative Writing* (Earnshaw 2007).

The critical essay

Critical essays remains at the heart of most 16–19 literature courses, and students need to be prepared for writing them both under examination conditions and in more extended form as part of coursework. Although students will have had experience of writing critical essays in pre-16 English, they will need considerable guidance to develop their skills as academic writers as they learn to write in a more sustained way, formulate arguments, deal with increasingly complex concepts and use appropriate methods of referencing.

It is also important to distinguish between the different kinds of critical writing students undertake within their literary studies. The rules governing *different types* of course or examination essays are often quite varied. An essay written in half an hour under exam conditions will be constructed differently from an extended coursework essay; a reflective commentary on a piece of re-creative writing, or a commentary on an unseen poem, will be constructed differently from a fully fledged critical essay with a single, prepared line of argument. Certain skills required for these different assignments will be easily transferable; others will need to be taught in ways more specific to the task in hand. Teachers should therefore think carefully about how they work with students to build upon their experiences of academic writing pre-16.

Reading and analysing models of critical writing forms a vital part of this learning process. Judiciously chosen academic criticism – essays or book chapters, or extracts from these – gives students a sense of the generic qualities of critical writing (its attention to detail, the ways in which it establishes and develops argument, the way the texts cohere etc.), but must be chosen so that it is accessible to students. The formal structures and requirements of particular assignments are often best taught through exploring example student essays of the same kind, and – where available – exemplar work made available by awarding bodies. In both cases, structured opportunities for students to discuss how these texts are constructed, what they are aiming to achieve and how successful they are is invaluable. Sometimes examples requiring careful thought and development can be as instructive as good ones, allowing students to rewrite and develop material, and effectively drawing attention to the need to consider choices of phrasing and emphasis.

Teaching about sources and plagiarism

Teachers also need to look at how they introduce students to expectations surrounding academic honesty and integrity. With the plethora of material now available electronically, plagiarism has become a serious issue at all levels of education, and software for locating plagiarism is now routinely used in universities and in some schools and colleges. As they embark on 16–19 study, many students are not completely clear what plagiarism is, why it is a problem and how it might be detected. They need to be taught what constitutes fair usage of source materials in preparation for writing coursework assignments and about good ethical practice in the production of written text, and should be introduced to notions such as intellectual property. This is good preparation not only for their writing at post-16 level, but also for the world of HE and/or employment. However, the issue of technical plagiarism is only part of what is in many respects a broader issue to do with the generation of ideas and meanings in literature and literary study (also explored in Chapter 5), and needs to be discussed with students in that broader context.

Students have always been able to use study guides such as York Notes to inform their responses to literature, and whilst such aids have their place and (depending on the quality of the notes) can be useful to help students consolidate or clarify ideas, they have for many students cut short the process of personal critical response. Now, however, the majority of students have access to a vast array of websites that will immediately tell them what to think about a wide range of literary texts. Again, these can be immensely valuable when they are evaluated against personal critical response and rooted in students' careful reading of literary text. But they also amplify longstanding issues in the study of literature about how students generate and assimilate ideas about what texts mean. In other words, the issue is not only about plagiarism – the copying of other people's *words* without acknowledgement – it is also about borrowing other people's *ideas,* and the extent to which such ideas have been assimilated and acknowledged in students' thought and writing.

This is a complex area: after all, literature students get many of their ideas from their English teachers, and there is generally no requirement for them to acknowledge this in their written work. The key concept here is *assimilation*; what matters is the extent to which students show that they have been able to make others' ideas a part of their own thinking, express awareness of the process of interpretation, and acknowledge where their thinking has been strongly informed by secondary reading – whether they have directly quoted the ideas or not. Another important concept is *critical evaluation*: the extent to which they are able to make good critical judgements about the sources they read.

One way of approaching this network of issues is to discuss the concept of plagiarism directly with students. Many schools and departments have statements regarding plagiarism and collusion. The example in Panel 7.6 is used with students early in the course, and it never fails to prompt lively discussion, often revealing a layer of thinking about the mechanics of literary study, which might otherwise remain unexplored. However, as suggested above, it's also important to support technical issues about plagiarism throughout the course with a broader discourse about the nature of response to literature – for instance, by teaching students explicitly about the nature of ambiguity in literary texts; the interaction that takes place between reader, writer and text in negotiating meaning; and how to handle and write about ambiguity and uncertainty rather than 'closing down' interpretive possibilities. Meaning cannot simply be lifted from a website: it is at the heart of a complex set of reading and writing practices which good literature teaching should seek to reveal and develop.

Panel 7.6   Plagiarism and coursework

When you submit your coursework, you will have to sign a declaration that your work is all your own, and you will have to declare if you have received help other than that which is available through your teacher. You are also required to declare any sources you have used in a bibliography. It is vital that you understand what this means.

1. Coursework regulations

Coursework *must* be your own work. Your teacher will help you with planning and give you advice on ONE draft (perhaps two if the first one needs completely reworking from scratch). When you hand in your first draft, your teacher will give you **general advice** on how the essay might be improved and **point out examples** of issues that need to be addressed, but is **not** allowed to **mark** the draft, i.e. will not comprehensively mark every error or mistake in the draft. If you have made a lot of spelling or punctuation errors, your teacher will give examples of these but will not highlight them all. It is your responsibility to apply the advice you have been given.

If you receive help from friends or family, that is fine as long as it is general, informal advice or guidance. *It is not acceptable for anyone to formally mark or give you comprehensive instruction on rewriting your work.* Any changes made to the work must be done by you independently as a result of general advice rather than comprehensive instruction.

Your teacher will know the standard of work of which you are capable. If you suddenly produce work that is much better than that standard, your teacher will want to know what help you have received. If you have received any help beyond what is acceptable, you will have to declare this, and it will affect your mark.

2. Quoting, referencing and plagiarism

When you are planning and drafting, you may – indeed you *should* – read about the topic you are writing about to find out what others have said about it. Your essential ideas should already have been formed by the work you have done in class, but you may well develop them through the extra reading you do. In your bibliography, you must acknowledge the sources of any ideas that have influenced your work. This includes books, websites, films and any other medium. In particular, *you must include any works that you have quoted from directly, or from which you have directly taken ideas.*

Quotations

If you have quoted from a critical text, you must say where the quotation is taken from in the main text of the essay (e.g. put 'Eaglestone 2000' in brackets next to the quote), and then list the text, with its date, in your bibliography.

References

If you have taken an idea directly from a critical text, but not quoted from it, you should acknowledge this in the text by means of a reference. You can do this by saying something like 'Eaglestone (2000) suggests that…', and then again listing the text in your bibliography.

Good and bad sources

Acceptable texts for referencing are generally *authored texts,* i.e. texts that have the name of an author attached to them, and written by established critics or writers. Websites can pose a problem. Some websites (for instance the RSC or Shakespeare's Globe) may contain writing that is unattributed to an individual, but may be attributed to a respectable institution. Wikipedia, however, is an unauthored text and the information contained on it is not always reliable – although it can be a very useful starting point for further investigation. Nevertheless, if you do find important ideas here that you use directly, you should reference them. A greater problem is the many websites now offering student essays, many of which are unauthored. Even where they are authored, they are not generally considered good sources. We advise you strongly not to consult such websites. However, if you do, it is of course essential that you include the source in your bibliography.

Plagiarism

If you copy words from another text without acknowledging them, this is plagiarism. Of course, just one or two odd words may not matter, but if you take a sequence of words from the same sentence and paragraph, even if you change one or two of them, this could still count as plagiarism. You must *either* rewrite in your own words and give a reference *or* quote.

Assimilating ideas

However, please note that you should not be rewriting other people's ideas extensively in your essay. The ideas should be essentially yours, emerging from the classwork you have done – although it is fine to incorporate and use others' ideas where they are relevant and helpful in developing your argument. We call this the 'assimilation' of ideas – where others' ideas become an organic part of your own. This is fine, as long as you acknowledge your sources.

Alternative interpretations

One of the assessment objectives for the course involves showing awareness of different or alternative interpretations. This is an important skill in itself, but it is also a safeguard against plagiarism. Your work should show that you have considered a number of alternative ways of interpreting texts, not just taken one idea from one source and followed that.

Investigating plagiarism

The internet has made plagiarism a major problem. Students wishing to take shortcuts can succumb to temptation easily. However, it is important to remember the following:

- Teachers and examiners have as good access to internet sources as you do, and can easily check for plagiarism by simply typing groups of words into a search engine. Google, for example, has now digitised vast numbers of standard critical texts, so it is possible to search for words from books as well as websites.
- Teachers are highly experienced readers, and in particular highly experienced readers of critical writing and students' writing, who will quickly spot if there is a possibility that you have engaged in plagiarism.

If your teacher suspects there is some plagiarism, they will investigate. If anything is found, you will be penalised. At worst, your work could be disqualified. You should also note that examiners see a great deal more work than individual teachers, and are if anything MORE likely to spot and check for plagiarism.

Safeguards

As you work, make a note of all sources you have consulted, and especially any you have used directly. Also, ensure that you keep copies of the different drafts you have written, in case they are needed later for any reason. DO NOT redraft directly onto a previous Word document. Retain the original document and start a new document for your redraft.

Teaching about essay structure

Most critical essays consist of an introduction, a main body (comprised in turn of a number of paragraphs) and a conclusion. Many students will be familiar with this structure from their pre-16 work, and might have learned it through the use of familiar writing formulae and constructions such as PEE (point, evidence, explanation), the paragraph 'burger', the five paragraph essay and the assignment map ('In this essay I will...; Next, I will...; and then...; and finally...'). Some of these approaches clearly have value in the early stages of 16–19 study, but it is important that teachers spend time discussing with students how such models will need to be adapted to reflect the more complex demands of writing about literary texts at this level. This should be a shared, whole-class process.

This section draws on work carried out by students in their first year of 16–19 study, preparing essays on the character of Bertha Mason in *Jane Eyre*. In it we demonstrate how the process of writing an essay can be broken down into stages, as students learn how to plan, organise and develop their response.

The starting point for every essay is, of course, the task that has been set. Students will need to learn how to identify key terms in a question and how to use these in formulating their answer. Panel 7.7 shows how students defined the scope of their response to the question they had been set. The question was projected onto a whiteboard and the students used board markers to develop a shared annotation that they then used as the basis of their essay plan. The text in the panel reflects their initial ideas.

Panel 7.7   Responding to *Jane Eyre*: annotating an essay question

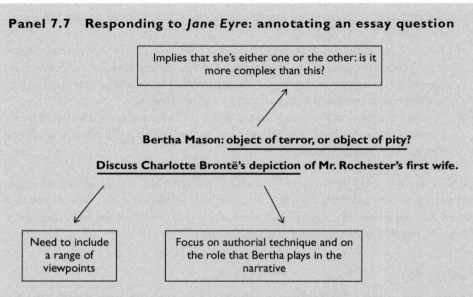

Implies that she's either one or the other: is it more complex than this?

Bertha Mason: object of terror, or object of pity?

Discuss Charlotte Brontë's depiction of Mr. Rochester's first wife.

Need to include a range of viewpoints

Focus on authorial technique and on the role that Bertha plays in the narrative

- Way Bertha is introduced before we're aware of her existence: mysterious laughter; setting Rochester's bed on fire; attack on Mason; tearing the veil; CB's use of the Gothic.
- How Bertha is described when Jane actually encounters her: animalistic imagery – 'clothed hyena'; supernatural: 'goblin' (Note: Jane is a 'sprite' – different connotations); violence; neutral pronoun 'it'.
- How Bertha functions within the narrative: obstacle to Jane and Rochester's wedding; we sympathise with Jane so logically we must want Bertha out of the way.
- Bertha described either through Jane's eyes or through Rochester's: not allowed to tell her own story.
- Madness: Victorian views v. contemporary views (although evidence that treatment of the insane was becoming more compassionate: was CB aware of this?).
- Bertha's ethnicity: stereotypes of the Creole.
- Contrasts between Jane and Bertha – is Bertha Jane's 'truest and darkest double'? (Gilbert and Gubar).

The introduction

This initial planning should then be used to formulate a line of argument – a thesis – that will, in turn, form the basis of the introduction. Students may need assistance in framing this thesis in clear, summative fashion, so that it offers an insight into the parameters and specific foci of their writing and covers essential background information, in order to acquaint the reader with the context of writing. They may also need to learn when to use their introduction to identify any significant issues they have decided to omit, explaining briefly why this is the case.

Panel 7.8 demonstrates how the students turned their initial ideas into a thesis and how one student then developed her introduction. The process of developing a thesis was scaffolded by the teacher: students were first asked to sum up their response to the question in just three sentences. Introductions were drafted in class and one student's work was projected onto the whiteboard as the basis for a shared editing exercise, an activity that can be very useful in highlighting slips in expression and getting students to suggest alternatives.

Panel 7.8   Thesis and introduction

Bertha Mason: object of terror, or object of pity?
Discuss Charlotte Brontë's depiction of Mr. Rochester's first wife.

Thesis: Bertha is initially used to create sensations of mystery and fear, intensified by Brontë's use of Gothic tropes and images. However, there are alternative ways of interpreting her character, emphasising the way Brontë's language casts her as 'other'. The contrasts and parallels between Bertha and Jane offer further potential, allowing us to see her as a representation of certain aspects of Jane's personality.

Introduction: The character of Bertha Mason in *Jane Eyre*, the mad wife locked in the attic at Thornfield Hall, evokes feelings of both fear and pity. Her role within the narrative is primarily as an obstacle in the path of Jane and Rochester's relationship. She is also the key to Mr. Rochester's secret, darker background and to the mystery that surrounds Thornfield, with Brontë's narrative drawing on elements of the Gothic and the Byronic to appeal to a contemporary audience. However, her treatment by both Mr. Rochester and the narrative itself are also troubling. It could even be argued that Bertha is not Jane's opposite, but a projection of the wilder side of her nature – an interpretation that makes Bertha more complex than she might initially seem.

The body of the essay

Cohesion is the key issue in developing the central part of an essay. Students might require assistance in developing clear and extended lines of thought and organising their ideas into logical and progressive sequences, building out of their thesis and towards their conclusions. While some students might baulk at the notion of writing detailed essay plans, there is no doubt that attention to planning will improve their work immeasurably, especially in the early stages of a course. In particular, it is useful to work with students on developing clear and effective topic sentences that can be used to introduce each paragraph and steer their argument through writing. In order to develop cohesive structures, students need to check their developing writing back against these topic sentences and against their initial thesis. This can be done by encouraging regular reference to their original ideas and to ensure these are exemplified and developed, minimising unhelpful detours and irrelevancies.

Panel 7.9 shows how the thesis for our exemplar essay on Bertha Mason might be extended into an essay plan. Topic sentences have been underlined to show how the sequence of ideas unfolds, and connecting ideas have been italicised to illustrate how each paragraph can be linked back to the question.

Panel 7.9   Bertha Mason: essay plan

Bertha Mason: object of terror, or object of pity?
Discuss Charlotte Brontë's depiction of Mr. Rochester's first wife.

Paragraph 1: Before the reader is even aware of Bertha's existence, she is surrounded by a sense of mystery. Brontë's use of Gothic tropes and imagery – strange laughter, mysterious events. Associated with acts of violence. *At this point, the reader is more inclined to associate her with fear – if not actual terror – than pity.*

Paragraph 2: When Jane is finally introduced to Bertha, the imagery used to depict her renders her even more frightening. Animalistic imagery used to dehumanise her – supernatural language creates a link with malign forces (further example of the Gothic). Depersonalised further through use of neutral pronoun 'it'. *Brontë's language is such that we see her as a creature to be afraid of rather than a human being.*

Paragraph 3: As readers, we are also aware of the role Bertha plays within the narrative. We sympathise with Jane, the first-person narrator – have been on her side through hardships of Gateshead and Lowood. Bertha is the obstacle to her newfound happiness. *The direction of the narrative means that we instinctively side with Jane rather than her antagonist.*

Paragraph 4: Nevertheless, it is significant that Jane herself shows sympathy for Bertha. Rochester's story of Bertha's past – describing her in extremely negative terms – Jane's response is 'She cannot help being mad'. Modern readers would find her treatment shocking – tempting to stereotype Victorian audiences but evidence from contemporary reports indicates that attitudes towards the mentally ill were becoming more progressive. *There is the potential, therefore, to interpret Bertha as an object of pity.*

Paragraph 5: This sense of pity – and possibly even of indignation – is heightened further when we examine a further set of images with which Bertha is surrounded, this time relating to her ethnicity. Stereotypes of the Creole to set alongside those of insanity. *In exploring the different layers of Brontë's language and its connotations, we see that interpreting Bertha is much more complex than it initially seemed.*

> **Paragraph 6:** Perhaps the most complex aspect of Brontë's depiction of Bertha lies in the parallels that can be drawn between Bertha and Jane. Initially seem to be direct opposites – height, colouring, behaviour – but similarities in terms of themes of imprisonment, savagery, passion. *Gilbert and Gubar describe Bertha not in terms of either fear or pity, but as Jane's 'truest and darkest double'.*

In the early stages of 16–19 study, it is often helpful to encourage students to distil their thoughts on a particular topic into a single paragraph. This has the virtue of encouraging concise and incisive thought and careful exposition and exemplification of it. As students become more experienced writers, they should begin to develop more complex arguments over more sustained bodies of text.

Students will also need direction in learning how to analyse, discuss and exemplify the detail of literary texts. Whilst analysis should, to some extent, be familiar to students from their study of literature pre-16, it would be a mistake to neglect this as an area for further attention, as many students' experiences of literary analysis will have been defined – and perhaps limited – by the models alluded to earlier in the chapter (PEE, the paragraph 'burger' and similar). Whilst such pre-16 models provide a useful starting point for teaching literary analysis in 16–19 courses, it is important to develop students' understanding that more sophisticated and varied versions of undertaking and presenting analysis are available. As stated earlier in this chapter, a useful way of exploring this is to read literary analysis in class. Like all genres, literary analysis has its own particular forms and features. These conventions, forms and structures are most effectively taught from models. Resources such as *e magazine* (published by the English and Media Centre) and *The English Review* (published by Philip Allan) can be used to provide excellent examples of writing written specifically for the 16–19 audience: indeed, the former frequently includes examples of students' writing. Even where articles do not address texts that the students are actually working on themselves, reading good writing about literature and understanding how it functions (e.g. how quotation can be used, how texts can be referred to without quoting, how argument can be constructed and developed) can all be absorbed.

It is particularly important that students move beyond the descriptive in their writing, looking closely at and exploring more complex issues of meaning and interpretation. Sometimes this might mean direct quotation, but it might also involve paraphrase or other allusions. Often this kind of more developed analysis will also involve drawing on ideas from critics or other readers, whose ideas may again be directly quoted or referred to. In either case, it is important that students learn how to incorporate such references and integrate them within a critical discussion of meaning. Quotations and references, therefore, should not be merely illustrative, and students should be encouraged to think carefully about how they can serve an integral function in the development of argument.

In learning to write about literary texts, students should also be taught how to handle uncertainty. As they become more sophisticated readers, they will become increasingly aware of the provisional nature of meaning and of the need – at times – to qualify their observations. Working with literary text is, after all, a game of interpretation, and it is as well to acknowledge the possibility of other ways of reading. Phrases such as 'This may suggest...'; 'This may mean that...'; 'This seems to indicate that...'; 'The author may be suggesting that...'; 'When we read ... we may feel...'; 'The word ... indicates...'; The author uses the phrase ... to convey...';

'Readers may feel that…'; 'One interpretation of this could be…'; 'Perhaps this might be seen as…'; or 'Some critics, such as Eagleton, believe…', are all very useful constructions to introduce to students. They require specific and well-targeted critical thought, but at the same time allow room for alternative views, and alert readers to the students' awareness of other possibilities, which may or may not be covered in the same essay.

The conclusion

Students may have learnt that the conclusion of an essay is simply a restatement of the initial thesis and/or a recap of the essay's major points. Such conclusions, however, are rarely satisfying, and conclusions are most effective when they look forwards rather than back. Students may be encouraged to use their conclusions to suggest the wider implications that emerge from their discussion. This may take the form of a rhetorical question or a quotation from the text or a secondary source. It is important, however, that students relate their conclusions clearly to the thesis of their essay.

Panel 7.10 shows two alternative ways of concluding the essay on Bertha Mason discussed earlier in this section. Clearly, one is more sophisticated and effective than the other – but can students explain why? Presenting students with alternatives like this, and asking them to discuss their merits and drawbacks, often results in significant developments in their own writing.

Panel 7.10   Conclusions

Ending A

In this essay, I have explored a range of ways of interpreting the character of Bertha Mason. While she initially appears frightening, she can also evoke feelings of pity, locked in an attic at Thornfield Hall and scorned by her husband. Charlotte Brontë's portrayal of her therefore allows scope for readers to make up their own minds.

Ending B

It may be, then, that the most important question to ask about Bertha Mason is not whether we pity her, but whether she is something other than simply a mad wife locked in an attic. In exploring the similarities between her and Jane, we become aware that the two characters have more in common than we initially thought. It could even be argued that far from denying Jane the possibility of happiness with Rochester, Bertha paradoxically sets her free: it is only in leaving Thornfield that Jane achieves true maturity. In exploring the role Bertha plays in the narrative of *Jane Eyre*, we move beyond questions of pity and fear and achieve a very different kind of understanding.

Teaching about essay presentation

As well as learning the difficult skills of how to structure essays, to develop coherence and to employ exemplificatory detail, students also need to be taught the conventions of essay presentation. Panel 7.11 provides an example of the kind of help they will find useful.

Panel 7.11   Essay presentation

Names

Names of characters, texts, authors, places etc. have capital letters and are written in full. In titles of texts, it's generally only the main words that are capitalised, not small words like 'of' and 'and' (unless they are at the beginning of the word), e.g. *Of Mice and Men*.

You usually call an author (say Margaret Atwood) by her full name the first time you mention her – 'Margaret Atwood' – and then by her surname only – 'Atwood'. Never call her 'Margaret'.

Titles

Titles of texts are shown in italics OR underlined, NOT in inverted commas (*Macbeth*, or <u>Macbeth</u> – not 'Macbeth'). Distinguish between Macbeth (the character) and *Macbeth* (the play).

Titles of poems or short stories are written using inverted commas, to differentiate them from the collections of poetry or stories of which they are part. (The poem 'Death of a Naturalist' is found in the book *Death of a Naturalist*. 'We Are Seven' is a poem in *Lyrical Ballads*.)

Quotations

If the quotation is a whole sentence, you can add it to the end of the sentence, incorporating it into your paragraph, but you must use a colon to introduce it:

> The opening of *Pride and Prejudice* clearly establishes the novel's obsessive relationship between marriage and wealth: 'It is a truth universally acknowledged that a single man in possession of a good fortune must be in want of a wife.' Here, Austen suggests that…

Alternatively, or if the quotation is too long to place at the end of a sentence, break the paragraph to insert the quotation by indenting and/or leaving space around it. Again, announce the quotation with a colon. Note that in this case you don't need to use quotation marks:

> The opening of *Pride and Prejudice* clearly establishes the novel's obsessive relationship between marriage and wealth:
>
> > It is a truth universally acknowledged, that a single man in possession of a good fortune must be in want of a wife. (p.1)
>
> Here, Austen suggests that…

Where the quotation is a phrase extracted from a sentence, it can form part of your sentence:

> The fact that the action of the poem is placed in 'the heart / Of the townland' demonstrates the uneasy relationship between town and country life.

(Note: in poetry, where a quotation spans a line break, a forward slash (/) is used to denote this. This isn't necessary for prose.)

If you wish to clarify an aspect of your quotation, use square brackets to demonstrate words that aren't part of the text:

> Forest on forest hung about his [Saturn's] head
> Like cloud on cloud

If you wish to omit a section of text from your quotation, use an ellipsis:

> It is a truth universally acknowledged that a single man … must be in want of a wife.

It is best to use single inverted commas for quotations, rather than double inverted commas (speech marks). If you have to quote a speech in fiction, the speech marks will appear inside the quotation marks, like this:

> '"Hello," said Martha. "How are you?"'

Bibliography

Your essay should always be followed by a bibliography — a list of books you have consulted — with some data (author, publisher, date) that will allow others to locate the texts if they want to. The following is an example of a standard way of setting out a bibliography:

McEvoy, S. (2009) *Tragedy: A Student Handbook*. London: English and Media Centre.
Shakespeare, W. (1993) *Hamlet*. Cambridge: Cambridge University Press. Web-based
    sources must also be referenced: www.norton.com/nael (accessed: 21 October 2011).

Finally...

Always include your name, the full title of the essay and a word count (if there is a word limit). If sending your essay by email, it is not enough to have your name in the document title. It must be on the essay itself.

Teaching about elements of written style

It's easy to take for granted that students commencing their advanced literature courses will already be efficient and accurate writers of English and that they have already developed appropriate forms and styles for writing about literature. As suggested previously, this may be an unwarranted assumption – and even if it were true, students at advanced level need specific guidance to develop their abilities as academic writers about literature. The reality is that students need to develop increasingly precise and controlled use of language and style so that they can effectively present their understanding of their reading, and some students at this level may still require substantial support with writing, including in terms of spelling, punctuation and grammar.

Alongside technical accuracy, issues of style will also need to be discussed. Whilst the standard academic style tends to be formal and objective, there is also an important place for students' individual voices, and it would be a mistake to remove this from their writing totally. Writing about literature draws upon and presents a range of views about texts. Many of these are critical and theoretical, and students' writing must reflect such formal properties, but subjective personal response is also central to literary study and to writing about it. As such, students need to evolve a personal style that appropriately reflects both these elements.

In developing writing, it is important that students think carefully about the needs of their readers and those responsible for assessing their work. In this situation clarity is a central focus. The use of a very informal style which largely replicates spoken English, whilst valid as a means of recording impressions on a blog or in note-taking, is not likely to serve a useful function in formal writing about literature. In academic assignments it is important to adopt more formal vocabulary choices, to avoid unsubstantiated generalisations and to employ rigorous academic sources. The watchword here is precision, as broad or vague choices are less likely to carry significant meaning and are more likely to pave the way for misunderstanding. Though stylistic choices are not strictly 'right' or 'wrong' in and of themselves, there are certain ways of expressing ideas that are best avoided in academic writing.

Finally, there is the question of the first person. In some academic subjects students are taught to avoid the first person at all costs: indeed, many readers of this book might have received similar advice during their own education. Nevertheless, given that students often explore personal views of literary texts they are studying, there will be occasions when use of the first person is appropriate. To refer to themselves as 'the reader' seems stilted and unnatural. However, this does not mean that they should use the first person repeatedly, even in personal reflective writing, as it can become anecdotal and appear uninformed. Use of the first person, therefore, needs to be carefully considered. In some elements of writing (e.g. reflective commentaries on creative, re-creative or transformative writing tasks) it is likely to occur more often than others. But even in formal academic analysis the first person has its place. Understanding how and when to use it can be an important stage in the development of a confident critical and authorial voice, and an essential part of 16–19 students' education.

Further reading

Academic writing

The available literature on teaching writing at 16–19 level is thin. Many teachers, however, will be aware of a variety of texts aimed at developing writing in the pre-16 phase, and these will provide a useful starting point when considering how to develop writing further in the 16–19 phase. *Creativity and Learning in Secondary English* (McCallum 2012) provides many excellent ideas. Additionally, *Writing About Literature* (Woolf 2005), *Studying English Literature* (Young 2008), *Starting an English Literature Degree* (Green 2009a) and *Doing English* 3rd Edition (Eaglestone 2009) all include useful sections on academic writing for students making the transition into HE – guidance that applies equally well to students in the 16–19 phase.

Creative and re-creative writing

A wealth of texts on the teaching of creative writing exists. *The Handbook of Creative Writing* (Earnshaw 2007) and *Creative Writing Guidebook* (Harper 2008) are both very good. For re-creative writing and textual intervention writing, *Textual Intervention: Critical and Creative Strategies for Literature Study* (Pope 1995) and *Active Reading: Transformative Writing in Literary Studies* (Knights and Thurgar-Dawson 2006) are seminal reading.

Afterword

Thirty years ago, Kate Flint – now Professor of English at Rutgers University, but at that time a young lecturer at Oxford University – wrote about A Level English literature from the perspective of a university teacher:

> We receive onto our courses students who believe [...] that 'Literature' is composed of unrelated Great Works – 'this week, we'll do Spenser; next week, we're doing *The Tempest*' – and hence perceive a university course as a process of ticking off texts from a shopping list of essentials. [...] The problem of encouraging students, once at university, to realise the importance of the inter-relating areas of literary, linguistic, social and economic history to the study of written texts is, of course, exacerbated by colleagues who [...] themselves were trained to believe that great literature is about conveying 'the quality of lived experience', the transmitting of 'universal feelings' which transcend historical specificity.
>
> (Flint 1982: 29)

Flint here succinctly encapsulates the tension between approaches to literary study which are focused simply on developing appreciative aesthetic responses to literary works and those which aim to enable students to set such works, and a variety of responses to them, in the context of broader knowledge about literature, language and culture.

Things have moved on since 1982, and in general schools and examining bodies function according to a different paradigm which, in seeking to develop students' responses, takes into account some of the cultural and political tensions implicit in the teaching of literature. Nevertheless, there is still often a sharp separation between the kind of critical-analytical approaches which inform university English and the more conservative approaches typical of 16–19 English, often exacerbated by the reductive demands of syllabuses and assessment systems.

We do not believe that such a gap, with the potentially limiting legacies it bequeaths students of literature, need continue to exist. In this book, we have sought to demonstrate that bridges can be built between the creative freedoms of literary study in primary and lower secondary English, the set-text focused modes of upper secondary and 16–19 English, and the broader critical modes of HE. Where personal, creative and critical approaches are seasoned by appropriate introductions to the social, political and theoretical forces at work in shaping culture at large, the study of literature takes on a new dynamic. We have sought to show how this abstract aim can be translated into classroom approaches that start with students' responses, developing their literary, cultural and linguistic awareness, so that they can, as McCormick (1994: 64) puts it, 'learn to read the *world* simultaneously with learning to read the *word*'.

Limitations of space mean that we have not been able to deal with all the aspects of literature teaching that we would have liked. In particular, we have not been able to deal explicitly with teaching 'world literature' and approaches informed by post-colonialism, such as the work of writers from ex-colonies in Africa, Asia and Australasia – or the writing of many writers in Scotland, Ireland and Wales. Such approaches can be immensely valuable. The Kenyan writer Ngũgĩ wa Thiong'o writes of the way in which Shakespeare and 'the cultural bomb' of the English language was used during colonial years to suppress Kenyan voices (1986: 3). The Scots writer James Kelman (1992) has written about the way in which English literature has excluded working-class voices, and non-standard dialects, from its pages. Such ideas do not decrease the significance of English literature or devalue its study, but they do draw attention to the cultural and political complexity of the idea of English literature – a complexity of which one UK education minister, Michael Gove, was clearly unaware when, in a typically rabble-rousing speech on educational reform in October 2010, he summed up the arguments for traditional approaches to the teaching of English literature with the simplistic claim that: 'Our literature is the best in the world.'

Gove presumably had not read the work of Robert Scholes, Professor of English at Brown University, who, in *Textual Power: Literary Theory and the Teaching of English,* writes:

> The political enters the study of English primarily through questions of representation: who is represented, who does the representing, who is object, who is subject – and how do these representations connect to the values of groups, communities, classes, tribes, sects and nations? ... Eliminating the political is the fond hope of those nostalgic for ... cultural homogeneity ... But we cannot do it now and still be responsible educators. Responsibility here must take the form of establishing a disciplinary framework strong enough to allow the political full play in the study of textuality. By being responsible in this way, we will not suppress the power and beauty of language that have always been our concern. We will simply resituate them in a more rhetorical and less literary discipline of thought and study.
>
> (Scholes 1985: 153)

In this book we suggest that we can enable students to develop their responses to literature in the 16-19 phase by helping them, as Scholes suggests, to develop their understanding of the cultural and linguistic frameworks and discourses within which they operate as readers, writers and students, and within which literary texts operate in the world. For, as Paolo Freire writes:

> Education either functions as an instrument which is used to facilitate integration of the younger generation into the logic of the present system and bring about conformity, or it becomes the practice of freedom, the means by which men and women deal critically and creatively with reality and discover how to participate in the transformation of their world.
>
> (Freire 1970: 34)

References

Abbs, P. (1990) *The Forms of Poetry: A Practical Study Guide*. Cambridge: CUP.

Abbs, P. and Richardson, J. (1990) *The Forms of Narrative*. Cambridge: CUP.

Andrews, R. (1991) *The Problem with Poetry*. Milton Keynes: Open UP.

Appleman, D. (2000) *Critical Encounters in High School English*. New York: NCTE.

Aristotle (1996) *Poetics*. M. Heath (trans.). London: Penguin.

Atherton, C. (2003) 'The New English A Level: Contexts, Criticism and the Nature of Literary Knowledge', *Use of English*, 54(2): 97–109.

Atherton, C. (2004) 'Critical Literature? Context and Criticism in A Level English Literature', *English Drama Media*, 1: 30–3.

Atherton, C. (2005) *Defining Literary Criticism*. Basingstoke: Palgrave.

Atherton, C. (2007) 'Balancing Acts: Preparing Students for University in the Mixed-Ability Classroom', *International Journal of Adolescence and Youth*, 14(1): 65–76.

Atherton, C. (2011) 'Reflections on the New English Literature A Levels', *English Drama Media*, 21: 21–6.

Ayckbourn, A. (2003) *The Crafty Art of Playmaking*. London: Faber.

Bahktin, M. (1981) *The Dialogic Imagination: Four Essays*. M. Holquist (ed.), C. Emerson and M. Holquist (trans.). Austin: Texas UP.

Bakhtin, M. (1984) *Rabelais and His World*. H. Iswolsky (trans.). Bloomington: Indiana UP.

Baldick, C. (2001) *The Concise Oxford Dictionary of Literary Terms*. Oxford: OUP.

Ball, D. L., Thames, M. H. and Phelps, G. (2008) 'Content Knowledge for Teaching: What Makes it Special?', *Journal of Teacher Education*, 59(5): 389–407. Retrieved from http://conferences.illinoisstate.edu/NSA/papers/ThamesPhelps.pdf.

Barlow, A. (2000) *The Great War in British Literature*. Cambridge: CUP.

Barlow, A. (2005) *Second Reading*. Leicester: English Association.

Barlow, A. (2009) *World and Time: Teaching Literature in Context*. Cambridge: CUP.

Barnes, D. and Barnes, D. (1984) *Versions of English*. London: Heinemann.

Barry, P. (2003) *English in Practice*. London: Arnold.

Barry, P. (2008) 'Moving On: University Expectations of Undergraduates and What Progress They Make', presentation delivered at the English Association's Autumn Conference.

Barthes, R. (1977) 'Death of the Author', in *Image, Music, Text*. New York: Hill and Wang, pp. 142–8.

Bate, J. (2001) *The Song of the Earth*. London: Picador.

Bate, J. (2008) *The Genius of Shakespeare*. London: Picador.

Bate, J. (2010) *English Literature: A Very Short Introduction*. Oxford: OUP.

Beach, R. *et al.* (2010) *Teaching Literature to Adolescents*. Abingdon: Routledge.

Beavis, C. (1995) "This Special Place': Literature in Senior Forms in the 1990's', *English in Education*, 29(1): 20–7.

Beavis, C. (1997) 'Lovely Literature: Teacher Subjectivity and Curriculum Change'. Retrieved from http://griffith.academia.edu/CatherineBeavis/Papers/744678/Lovely_Literature_Teacher_Subjectivity_and_Curriculum_Change.

Bennett, A. and Royle, N. (2009) *An Introduction to Literature, Criticism and Theory*. Harlow: Pearson.

Bentley, E. (1996) *The Life of the Drama*. London: Applause.

Bevis, M. (2012) *Comedy: A Very Short Introduction*. London: Routledge.

Bishop, S. R., Lau, M., Shapiro, S., Carlson, L., Anderson, N. D., Carmody, J., Segal, Z. V., Abbey, S., Speca, M., Velting, D. and Devins, G. (2004) 'Mindfulness: A Proposed Operational Definition'. Retrieved from www.wisebrain.org/papers/DefiningMindfulness.pdf.

Blau, A. (2004) *Deep Focus: The Future of Independent Media*. Retrieved from www.namac.org/sites/default/files/docs_upload/dfch1.pdf.

Bleiman, B. (1995) *The Poetry Pack: Exploring Poems at GCSE and A Level*. London: EMC.

Bleiman, B. and Webster, L. (2007) *Studying The World's Wife*. London: EMC.

Bleiman, B. and Webster, L. (2009) *Studying Narrative*. London: EMC.

Bleiman, B. and Webster, L. (2009) *Introducing the Gothic*. London: EMC.

Bleiman, B., Ogborn, J. and Webster, L. (2001) *The Modern Novel*. London: EMC.

Bloom, H. (1973) *The Anxiety of Influence: A Theory of Poetry*. Oxford: OUP.

Botting, F. (1995) *Gothic*. London: Routledge.

Bourdieu, P. (1990) *Reproduction in Education, Society and Culture*. London: Sage.

Bradford, R. (2010) *Poetry: The Ultimate Guide*. Basingstoke: Palgrave Macmillan.

Bradford, R. (2011) *Teaching Theory*. Basingstoke: Palgrave.

Britton, J. (1970) *Language and Learning*. Baltimore, MD: Penguin.

Brown, J. (2001) *The Oxford Illustrated History of the Theatre*. Oxford: OUP.

Brown, J. and Gifford, T. (1989) *Teaching A Level English Literature: A Student-centred Approach*. London: Routledge.

Buckingham, D. and Sefton-Green, J. (1994) *Cultural Studies Goes to School*. London: Taylor & Francis.

Burn, A. (2004) 'From The Tempest To Tomb-Raider: Computer Games In English, Media And Drama', *English Drama Media*, 2: 19–25.

CACE (1963) *The Newsom Report: Half Our Future*. London: HMSO.

Campbell, R. J. (2006) 'Hills Road Sixth Form College: A Case Study in the Personalisation of Learning', NAGTY Occasional Paper no. 16 (DFES/ University of Warwick).

Carter, R. (2004) *Language and Creativity: The Art of Common Talk*. London: Routledge.

Chambers, E. and Gregory, M. (2006) *Teaching and Learning English Literature*. London: Sage.

Childs, P. (2008) *The Essential Guide to English Studies*. London: Bloomsbury.

Childs, P. and Fowler, R. (eds) (2006) *The Routledge Dictionary of Literary Terms*. Abingdon: Routledge.

Collins, B. (1988) *The Apple That Astonished Paris*. Fayetteville: Arkansas UP.

Cox, B. (1989) *English for Ages 5 to 16*. London: HMSO.

Cox, B. (1995) *Cox on the Battle for the English Curriculum*. London: Hodder & Stoughton.

Coyle, M. (1998) *New Casebooks: The Merchant of Venice*. Basingstoke: Macmillan.

Craddock, M. (2001) 'Idealism, Theory, Practice and the New A Levels', *Use of English*, 52(2): 107–11.

Craddock, M. (2003) 'Curriculum 2000: A Teacher's Verdict', *Use of English*, 54(2): 110–19.

Cremin, T. (2011) 'Reading Teachers/Teaching Readers', *English Drama Media*, 19: 11–18.

Cuddon, J. A. (1991) *The Penguin Dictionary of Literary Terms and Literary Theory*. London: Penguin.

Culler, J. (1997) *Literary Theory: A Very Short Introduction*. Oxford: OUP.

Curran, S. (2010) *The Cambridge Companion to British Romanticism*. Cambridge: CUP.

Davidson J. and Moss, J. (1999) *Issues in English Teaching*. London: Routledge.

Daw, P. (1986) 'There is an Alternative', *English in Education*, 20(2): 62–72.

Daw, P. (1996) 'Achieving High Grades at A Level English Literature: An Investigation into Factors that Contribute to Schools' Successes', *English in Education*, 30(3): 15–27.

Day, A. (2011) *Romanticism*. London: Routledge.

Day, H. (2010) *Work-Related Learning in English Studies: A Good Practice Guide*. English Subject Centre Report 20. Retrieved from www.english.heacademy.ac.uk/explore/publications/reports.php.

Dias, P. and Hayhoe, M. (1988) *Developing Response to Poetry*. Milton Keynes: Open UP.

Dillon, J. (2007) *The Cambridge Introduction to Shakespeare's Tragedies*. Cambridge: CUP.

Dixon, J. (1967) *Growth through English*. Huddersfield: NATE.

Dymoke, S. (2002) 'The Dead Hand of the Exam: the impact of the NEAB anthology on poetry teaching at GCSE', *Changing English*, 9 (1): 85–93.

Dymoke, S. (2002) *Drafting and Assessing Poetry: A Guide for Teachers*. London: Paul Chapman.

Dymoke, S. (2009) *Teaching English Texts 11–18*. London: Bloomsbury.

Dymoke, S., Lambirth, A. and Wilson, A. (2013) *Making Poetry Matter*. London: Bloomsbury.

Eaglestone, R. (1999) 'A critical time for English', *Guardian*. Retrieved from www.guardian.co.uk/education/1999/nov/30/schools.theguardian1.

Eaglestone, R. (2000) *Doing English*. London: Routledge.

Eaglestone, R. (2001) 'Active Voice!', *English Association Newsletter*, 166: 6–7.

Eaglestone, R. (2009) *Doing English (3rd Edition)*. Abingdon: Routledge.

Eagleton, T. (1983) *Literary Theory: An Introduction*. Oxford: Blackwell.

Eagleton, T. (2006) *How To Read A Poem*. Oxford: Blackwell.

Earnshaw, S. (2007) *The Handbook of Creative Writing*. Edinburgh: Edinburgh UP.

Edgar, D. (2009) *How Plays Work*. London: Nick Hern.

Elbow, P. (1990) *What is English?* New York: MLA.

Eliot, G. (1980 [1859]) *Adam Bede*. London: Penguin.

Eliot, T. S. (1933) *The Use of Poetry and The Use of Criticism*. London: Faber.

EMC (2001) *Pre-1770 Drama: Elizabethan and Jacobean*. London: EMC.

EMC (2006) 'A Level English and Work-related Learning: Issues and Strategies'. Retrieved from www.englishandmedia.co.uk/publications/results.php.

EMC (2012) *Studying Comedy*. London: EMC.

Englund, T. (1997) 'Towards a Dynamic Analysis of the Content of Schooling: Narrow and Broad Didactics in Sweden', *Journal of Curriculum Studies*, 29(3): 267–87.

Faulks, S. (1993) *Birdsong*. London: Vintage.

Feiman-Nemser, S. and Buchman, M. (1985) *The First Year of Teacher Preparation: Transition to Pedagogical Thinking?*, Research Series no. 156. East Lansing: Michigan State University, Institute for Research on Teaching.

Fenton, J. (2003) *An Introduction to English Poetry*. London: Viking.

Ferber, M. (2010) *Romanticism: A Very Short Introduction*. Oxford: OUP.

Fielding, H. (1966 [1749]) *Tom Jones*. London: Penguin.

Fisher, R. (2007) 'Dialogic Teaching: Developing Thinking and Metacognition Through Philosophical Discussion', *Early Childhood Development and Care*, 177(6–7): 615–31.

Fisher, R. (2011) 'Dialogic Teaching', in A. Green (ed.), *Becoming a Reflective English Teacher*. Maidenhead: Open UP, pp. 90–109.

Flint, K. (1982) 'A Levels and University Teaching – The Need for Intervention', *Red Letter*, 12: 27–32.

Forster, E. M. (1990 [1927]) *Aspects of the Novel*. London: Penguin.

Freire, P. (1970) *Pedagogy of the Oppressed*. New York: Continuum.

Fry, S. (2005) *The Ode Less Travelled*. London: Arrow.

Furniss, T. and Bath, M. (2007) *Reading Poetry: An Introduction*. Harlow: Pearson Longman.

Furst, L. R. (1976) *Romanticism*. London: Methuen.

Garrard, G. (2011) *Ecocriticism*. London: Routledge.

Gay, P. (2008) *The Cambridge Introduction to Shakespeare's Comedies*. Cambridge: CUP.

Gibbons, S. (2010) 'Literature Study Post-16 Part 2'. ITE English: Readings for Discussion. Retrieved from www.ite.org.uk/ite_readings/literature_p16_II_20100303.pdf.

Gibson, R. (1998) *Teaching Shakespeare: A Handbook for Teachers*. Cambridge: CUP.

Gifford, T. (1999) *Pastoral*. London: Routledge.

Gioia, D. (2002) *Can Poetry Matter?* Minneapolis: Graywolf.

Golsby-Smith, S. (2013) 'Singing from the Same Songsheet: The Flexible Thinker and the Curriculum in the 21st Century', *English in Education*, 47(1).

Goodman, S. and O'Halloran, K. (2006) *The Art of English: Literary Creativity*. Basingstoke: Palgrave Macmillan.

Gordon, J. (2004) 'Verbal Energy: Attending to Poetry', *English in Education*, 38(1): 92–103.

Goring, P., Hawthorn, J. and Mitchell, D. (2010) *Studying Literature*. London: Bloomsbury.

Graff, G. (1987) *Professing Literature*. Chicago: Chicago UP.

Green, A. (2003) *The Gothic: Frankenstein and Wuthering Heights*. London: Philip Allen.

Green, A. (2004) 'Creative Writing', in R. Fisher and M. Williams (eds), *Unlocking Creativity*. London: David Fulton, pp. 37–54.

Green, A. (2005) *Four Perspectives on Transition: English Literature from Sixth Form to University*. London: English Subject Centre.

Green, A. (2007) 'Transition and Acculturation: Changing Expectations in the Move Between A Level and University', unpublished PhD thesis, Brunel University.

Green, A. (2009a) *Starting an English Literature Degree*. Basingstoke: Palgrave Macmillan.

Green, A. (2009b) 'Adapting Austen – an interview with Fay Weldon', *e magazine*, Vol. 45.

Green, A. (2012) 'Teaching Writing', in A. Green (ed.), *A Practical Guide to Teaching English in the Secondary School*. London: Routledge, pp. 19–29.

Greenwell, B. (1988) *Alternatives at English A Level*. Sheffield: NATE.

Groom, N. (2012) *The Gothic: A Very Short Introduction*. Oxford: OUP.

Grossman, P. L. and Shulman, L. S. (1994) 'Knowing, Believing and the Teaching of English'. Retrieved from https://secure.ncte.org/library/NCTEFiles/Resources/Books/Sample/50136chap01.pdf.

Guardian (2003) 'Nobel Laureate in Praise of Eminem', 1 July. Retrieved from www.guardian.co.uk/education/2003/jul/01/highereducation.news

Gurr, A. (2009) *The Shakespearean Stage*. Cambridge: CUP.

Haddon, J. (2009) *Teaching Reading Shakespeare*. London: Routledge.

Hardy, T. (2007 [1903]) *The Dynasts*. Gloucester: Dodo Press.

Harper, G. (2008) *Creative Writing Guidebook*. London: Continuum.

Hawthorn, J. (2010) *Studying the Novel*. Basingstoke: Palgrave.

Heathcote, D. and Bolton, G. (1995) *Drama for Learning: Dorothy Heathcote's Mantle of the Expert Approach to Education*. London: Heinemann.

Hennessy, J. and McNamara, P. (2011) 'Packaging Poetry? Pupils' Perspectives of their Learning Experience Within the Post-primary poetry Classroom', *English in Education*, 45(3): 206–23.

Henry, J. (2011) 'Teach Jane Austen, state schools to be told', *Daily Telegraph*. Retrieved from www.telegraph.co.uk/education/educationnews/8871902/Teach-Jane-Austen-state-schools-to-be-told.html.

Herman, D. (2007) *The Cambridge Companion to Narrative*. Cambridge: CUP.

HMI (1986) *A Survey of the Teaching of A Level English Literature in 20 Mixed Sixth Forms in Comprehensive Schools*. London: DES.

Hodgson, J. (2010) *The Experience of Studying English in UK Higher Education*. London: English Subject Centre.

Hodgson, J. and Harris, A. (2012) 'Improving Student Writing at HE: Putting Literacy Studies to Work', *English in Education*, 46(1): 8–21.

Hodgson, J. and Harris, A. (2013) '"It is hard to know what you are being asked to do": Deciphering codes, constructing schemas', *English in Education*, 47(1).

Hollingworth, B. (1983) 'Crisis in English Teaching', *Use of English*, 34(2): 3–8.

Holt-Reynolds, D. (2000) 'What does the teacher do? Constructivist pedagogies and prospective teachers' beliefs about the role of a teacher', *Teaching and Teacher Education*, 16: 21–32.

Hopkins, C. (2001) *Thinking about Texts*. Basingstoke: Palgrave Macmillan.

Hornbrook, D. (1998a) *Education and Dramatic Art*. London: Routledge.

Hornbrook, D. (1998b) *On the Subject of Drama*. London: Routledge.

Howard, J. E. (1984) *Shakespeare's Art of Orchestration: Stage Technique and Audience Response*. Urbana and Chicago: University of Illinois Press.

Hoyes, R. (2000) 'Richard Hoyes puts the fun back into Eng Lit', *Times Educational Supplement*. Retrieved from www.tes.co.uk/teaching-resource/Richard-Hoyes-puts-the-fun-back-into-Eng-lit-330953/.

Hughes, T. (2008 [1967]) *Poetry in the Making*. London: Faber and Faber.

Hymer, B., Whitehead, J. and Huxtable, M. (2008) *Gifts, Talents and Education: A Living Theory Approach*. London: Wiley-Blackwell.

Jacobs, R. (2001) *A Beginner's Guide to Critical Reading*. London: Routledge.

Jacobs, R. (2010) 'English Literature Post-16 Part 1'. ITE English: Readings for Discussion. Retrieved from www.ite.org.uk/ite_readings/literature_p16_I_20100303.pdf.

James, H. (2011 [1934]) *The Art of the Novel: Critical Prefaces*. Chicago: University of Chicago Press.

Jones, K., McLean, M., Amigoni, D. and Kinsman, M. (2005) 'Investigating the Production of University English in Mass Higher Education: Towards an Alternative Methodology', *Arts and Humanities in Higher Education*, 4(3): 247–64.

Kelman, J. (1992) *Some Recent Attacks*. Stirling: AK Press.

Kennedy, X. J., Gioia, D. and Bauerlein, M. (2006) *The Longman Dictionary of Literary Terms: Vocabulary for the Informed Reader*. New York: Pearson Longman.

Kermode, F. (2001) *Shakespeare's Language*. London: Penguin.

Kernan, A. (1990) *The Death of Literature*. New Haven: Yale UP.

Knights, B. (2005) 'Intelligence and Interrogation: The Identity of the English Student', *Arts and Humanities in Higher Education*, 4(1): 33–52.

Knights, B. (2008) 'Reading, Writing and "Doing English"', *English Drama Media*, 12: 17–21.

Knights, B. and Thurgar-Dawson, C. (2006) *Active Reading: Transformative Writing in Literary Studies*. London: Continuum.

Knight, P. and Yorke, M. (2004) *Learning, Curriculum and Employability in Higher Education*. London: Routledge Falmer.

Kress, G. (1985) 'Interrelations of reading and writing', in A. Wilkinson (ed.), *The Writing of Writing*. Milton Keynes: Open UP, pp. 198–214.

Kress, G. (2005) *English in Urban Classrooms*. London: Routledge.

Lakoff, G. and Johnson, M. (1981) *Metaphors We Live By*. Chicago: Chicago UP.

Leahy-Dios, C. (1996) *Literature Education as a Social Metaphor*, unpublished PhD thesis, London: Institute of Education.

Leavis, F. R. (1932) *How to Teach Reading: A Primer for Ezra Pound*. Cambridge: Minority Press.

Lennard, J. (2006) *The Poetry Handbook*. Oxford: OUP.

Lennard, J. and Luckhurst, M. (2002) *The Drama Handbook: A Guide to Reading Plays*. Oxford: OUP.

Lodge, D. (1975) *Changing Places*. London: Penguin.

Lodge, D. (1988) *Nice Work*. London: Penguin.

Lodge, D. (1994) *The Art of Fiction*. London: Penguin.

Lunzer, E. and Gardner, K. (1979) *The Effective Use of Reading*. London: Heinemann.

McCallum, A. (2012) *Creativity and Learning in Secondary English*. London: David Fulton.

McCormick, K. (1994) *The Culture of Reading and the Teaching of English*. Manchester: Manchester UP.

McEvoy, S. (1999) 'A critical time for English'. Retrieved from www.guardian.co.uk/education/1999/nov/30/schools.theguardian1?INTCMP=SRCH.

McEvoy, S. (2006) *Shakespeare: The Basics (2nd Edition)*. London: Routledge.

McEvoy, S. (2009) *Tragedy: A Student Handbook*. London: EMC.

Marland, M. (2003) 'The Transition from School to University', *Arts and Humanities in Higher Education*, 2(2): 201–11.

Matterson, S. and Jones, D. (2011) *Studying Poetry*. London: Bloomsbury.

Maybin, J. and Swann, J. (2006) *The Art of English: Everyday Creativity*. Basingstoke: Palgrave Macmillan.

Mellor, B. (1989) *Reading Hamlet*. Scarborough: Chalkface.

Millard, E. (1988) 'The Tyranny of Tastes', NATE Post-16 Committee (ed.), *English A Level in Practice*. Sheffield: NATE.

Mitchell, S. (1994) 'A Level and Beyond: A Case Study', *English in Education*, 28(2): 36–47.

Mullan, J. (2006) *How Novels Work*. Oxford: OUP.

Myhill, D. and Watson, A. (2011) 'Teaching Writing', in A. Green (ed.), *Becoming a Reflective English Teacher*. Maidenhead: McGraw Hill, pp. 58–72.

NATE Post-16 Committee (1990) *A Level English: Pressures for Change*. Sheffield: NATE.

NATE (2005) *Text: Message – The Future of A Level English*. NATE: Sheffield.

Naylor, A. and Wood, A. (2012) *Teaching Poetry*. London: Routledge.

Neelands, J. (1984) *Making Sense of Drama: A Guide to Classroom Practice*. London: Heinemann.

Neelands, J. (2000) 'Drama sets you free – or does it?', in J. Davison and J. Moss (eds), *Issues in English Teaching*. London: Routledge.

Neelands, J. and Goode, T. (1990) *Structuring Drama Work: A Handbook of Available Forms in Theatre and Drama*. Cambridge: CUP.

Newlyn, L. and Lewis, J. (2003) *Synergies: Creative Writing in Academic Practice, vol. 1: Sea Sonnets*. Oxford: Chough Publications, St Edmund Hall.

Newlyn, L. and Lewis, J. (2004) *Synergies: Creative Writing in Academic Practice, vol. 2: Breaking Moulds*. Oxford: Chough Publications, St Edmund Hall.

Noel-Tod, J. (2005) 'Further Study: Teaching Unfamiliar Texts', *Cambridge Quarterly*, 34(3): 281–5.

OCR (2012) 'English Literature, Advanced GCE A2/Advanced Subsidiary GCE AS: Report to Centres'. Retrieved from www.ocr.org.uk/images/66491-examiners-reports-june.pdf.

Ogborn, J., Webster, L. and Bleiman, B. (2000) *Text, Reader, Critic: Introducing Contexts and Interpretations*. London: EMC. The critical positions cards referred to are available online at www.english.heacademy.ac.uk/explore/resources/seminars/activities/hand outs/Critical_positions.pdf.

Palfrey, S. (2011) *Doing Shakespeare*. London: Bloomsbury.

Pennac, D. (2006) *The Rights of the Reader*. London: Walker.

Peterson, A. (1972) *The International Baccalaureate – An Experiment in International Education*. London: Harrap.

Plath, S. (1965) *Ariel*. London: Faber.

Plath, S. (1979) *Johnny Panic and the Bible of Dreams*. London: Faber.

Poole, A. (2005) *Tragedy: A Very Short Introduction*. Oxford: OUP.

Pope, R. (1995) *Textual Intervention: Critical and Creative Strategies for Literature Study*. London: Routledge.

Pope, R. (2002) *The English Studies Book*. London: Routledge.

Pope, R. (2005) *Creativity*. London: Routledge.

Porter Abbott, H. (2008) *The Cambridge Introduction to Narrative*. Cambridge: CUP.

Powell, S. (2009) 'Live Poets, Live Poetry: Poetry Live!, the anthology and poetry at GCSE', *English Drama Media*, 13: 9–13.

Protherough, R. (1986) *Teaching Literature for Examinations*. Milton Keynes: Open UP.

QCA (1999) 'Advanced Subsidiary and Advanced Level Specifications: Subject Criteria for English Literature', document 991680144. London: QCA.

QCA (2007a) *English: Programme of Study for Key Stage 3 and Attainment Targets*. London: QCA.

QCA (2007b) *English: Programme of Study for Key Stage 4 and Attainment Targets*. London: QCA.

Reid, I. (2004) *Wordsworth and the Formation of English Studies*. Farnham: Ashgate.

RLF (2006) *Writing Matters: The Royal Literary Fund Report on Student Writing in Higher Education*. London: Royal Literary Fund.

Roberts, P. (2000) *How Poetry Works*. London: Penguin.

Scholes, R. (1985) *Textual Power: Literary Theory and the Teaching of English*. New Haven: Yale UP.

Scholes, R. (1999) *The Rise and Fall of English*. New Haven: Yale UP.

Scott, P. (1989) *Reconstructing 'A' Level English*. Milton Keynes: Open UP.

Sherry, V. (2005) *The Cambridge Companion to the Literature of the First World War*. Cambridge: CUP.

Showalter, E. (2003) *Teaching Literature*. Oxford: Blackwell.

Siddall, S. (2009) *Landscape and Literature*. Cambridge: CUP.

Sinfield, A. (1985) 'Give an account of Shakespeare and Education, showing why you think they are effective and what you have appreciated about them. Support your comments with precise references', in J. Dollimore and A. Sinfield (eds), *Political Shakespeare: New Essays in Cultural Materialism*. Manchester: Manchester UP.

Singh, A. (2011) 'Helen Mirren: Schools Should Stop Making Children Read Shakespeare', *Daily Telegraph* (4 March). Retrieved from www.telegraph.co.uk/culture/culture news/8359856/Helen-Mirren-schools-should-stop-making-children-read-Shakespeare. html

Smallwood, P. (2002) 'More Creative than Creation: On the Idea of Criticism and the Student Critic', *Arts and Humanities in Higher Education*, 1(1): 59–71.

Snapper, G. (2004) 'Literature in the International Baccalaureate: An Alternative for Sixth Form English', *Use of English*, 55(3): 231–9.

Snapper, G. (2007) 'A Level Revamped: English Literature, the Universities and the Schools', *Changing English*, 14(2): 107–20.

Snapper, G. (2008) 'Voices Across Borders', *English Drama Media*, 11: 37–44.

Snapper, G. (2009) 'Beyond English Literature A Level: The Silence of the Seminar?', *English in Education*, 43(3): 193–210.

Snapper, G. (2011) 'Theory in the New A Levels', *English Drama Media*, 20: 27.

Snapper, G. (2013) 'Exploring Resistance to Poetry in Advanced English Studies', in S. Dymoke, A. Lambirth and A. Wilson (eds), *Making Poetry Matter*. London: Bloomsbury.

Sterne, L. (1991 [1759–67]) *The Life and Opinions of Tristram Shandy*. London: Everyman.

Stevens, D. (2000) *The Gothic Tradition*. Cambridge: CUP.

Stibbs, A. (2000) 'Can You (Almost) Read a Poem Backwards and View A Painting Upside Down? Restoring Aesthetics to Poetry Teaching', *Journal of Aesthetic Education*, 34 (2): 37–47.

Stott, A. (2005) *Comedy*. London: Routledge.

Todorov, T. (1966 [1988]) 'The Typology of Detective Fiction', in D. Lodge (ed.), *Modern Criticism and Theory: A Reader*. London: Longman, pp. 157–65.

Vygotsky, L. S. (1978) *Mind in Society: The Development of Higher Psychological Processes*. London: Harvard UP.

Wainwright, J. (2011) *Poetry: The Basics*. London: Routledge.

Wallace, J. (2007) *The Cambridge Introduction to Tragedy*. Cambridge: CUP.

Wallis, M. and Shepherd, S. (2010) *Studying Plays*. London: Bloomsbury.

Waters, S. (2010) *The Secret Life of Plays*. London: Nick Hern.

Wa Thiong'o, N. (1986) *Decolonising the Mind*. London: Heinemann.

Watt, I. (1957) *The Rise of the Novel*. London: Chatto and Windus.

Weitz, E. (2009) *The Cambridge Introduction to Comedy*. Cambridge: CUP.

Wickham, G. (1992) *A History of the Theatre*. London: Phaidon.

Widdowson P. (1999) *Literature*. London: Routledge.

Wilders, J. (1969) *Shakespeare: The Merchant of Venice (Casebook Series)*. London: Macmillan.

Williams, R. (2009) *The Poetry Toolkit*. London: Bloomsbury.

Winston, J. (2004) *Drama and English at the Heart of the Curriculum*. London: David Fulton.

Wolfreys, J. (2010) *The English Literature Companion*. Basingstoke: Palgrave Macmillan.

Woolf, J. (2005) *Writing About Literature*. London: Routledge.

Woolf, V. (1925) *The Common Reader*. London: Hogarth.

Wright, C. (2006) 'Tongues for the Tongueless: Developing Critical Confidence in A level English Literature', *English Drama Media*, 6: 15–20.

Young, T. (2008) *Studying English Literature*. Cambridge: CUP.

Index